PRISONS & PRISONERS
IN VICTORIAN BRITAIN

The gatehouse of HM Prison Wormwood Scrubs, *c.* 1900.

PRISONS & PRISONERS
IN VICTORIAN BRITAIN

NEIL R. STOREY

First published 2010

The History Press
The Mill, Brimscombe Port
Stroud, Gloucestershire, GL5 2QG
www.thehistorypress.co.uk

British Library Cataloguing in Publication Data.
A catalogue record for this book is available from the British Library.

ISBN 978 0 7524 5269 2

Typesetting and origination by The History Press
Printed in Great Britain

Contents

	Acknowledgements	6
	Introduction	7
I	The Victorian Prison	9
II	Prison Staff	18
III	Admitting the Prisoner	44
IV	Daily Routine	63
V	The County Prison	85
VI	The Convict Prison	90
VII	Punishments	102
VIII	Escapers	113
IX	Rogues Gallery	121
X	Some Infamous Prisoners	143
XI	Execution	188
	Select Bibliography	215
	Index	219

ACKNOWLEDGEMENTS

It has been my pleasure to encounter some most helpful curators and historians in the research and compilation of this book. I would like to mention the following in particular: Stewart P. Evans; Dr Vic Morgan; Dr Stephen Cherry; Robert Bell, assistant curator of the Wisbech and Fenland Museum; Stewart McLaughlin, serving prison officer and curator of the Wandsworth Prison Museum; Christine and David Parmenter; Jenny Phillips; Theo Fanthorpe; Ian Pycroft; Elaine Abel; Robert Green; Robert 'Bookman' Wright; the late Syd Dernley; the Galleries of Justice, Nottingham; Inverary Jail Museum; Lincoln Castle; Ely Gaol; Moyses Hall, Bury St Edmunds; Ruthin Gaol; Walsingham Bridewell; Wymondham Bridewell; Norwich Castle; Essex Police Museum; and Helen Tovey at *Family Tree Magazine*. I would also like to thank my wonderful students and lecture audiences for their comments and interest in my research. Last, but by no means least, I thank my darling Molly and son Lawrence for their love, support and interest.

Unless credited otherwise, all images in this book are from originals held in the archive of the author.

A Victorian villain and rough – caught by the long arm of the law.

INTRODUCTION

The long reign of Queen Victoria saw Great Britain ascend and acquire a global empire upon which it was said the sun never set. Britain led the world with industrial innovations and industry and those who lived in this noble country, the heart of the Empire, were left in no doubt of the expectations of them to honour Queen and Flag. Whether they were of the highest or lowest social class they were expected to uphold the law as a matter of duty – it was just one of many Victorian values. There were, however, highly robust measures to keep you on the 'straight and narrow'; woe betide you if you got caught breaking the law, for you would fall mercy to the Victorian criminal justice system, face exposure in the press and, potentially, a prison sentence.

Both the high and the low of society and all in between were, very much like today, liable to err and transgress the laws of the land, although it must be said the prison population of Victorian Britain was predominantly made up of those on the lowest incomes or with no job at all. Often the voices of these disenfranchised people are the silent majority, for they were often not literate enough to record their recollections of their time in prison. However, a dark mirror of their experiences can be assembled from the prison books maintained by the prison officials, the accounts of visitors to prisons or the experiences of prison staff – especially the prison 'ordinary' or chaplain – that were occasionally published in periodicals or books; their stories often spoke of the most harrowing cases.

The accounts of many trials were reported with zeal and, for the more horrific cases, lurid detail in the popular and local press; the more horrific the case, the greater the column inches and illustrations. Public interest would lead to follow-up stories of what the prisoner could expect in

Her Majesty Queen Victoria.

his or her prison. These stories give a fascinating insight into the working of the prisons, from uniforms and cells to the labour a prisoner or convict would be expected to undertake as part of their daily routine. Indeed, the extended accounts of prison visitors and some of the prisoners themselves have been reproduced verbatim and at length in this book.

The Victorian age was also one of enormous change and reform in the British prison system, with both good and bad results, but they were certainly far better than their gaoler ancestors at record keeping and reports, which often give a fascinating insight into the prisons of the day. Add to this the now rare, long out of print volumes and articles written by those who had experienced prison life firsthand as guardian, visitor or prisoner, as well as access to numerous unpublished manuscripts and letters, and a poignant picture may be assembled of the character, life and experience of the Victorian prison – from both sides of the bars.

Neil R. Storey, 2010

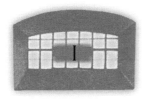

THE VICTORIAN PRISON

Between 1837 and 1901 there were more than fifteen million receptions into the prisons of Great Britain. Those serving sentences in early Victorian prisons can be divided into two main categories. Firstly, there were those who had been tried and convicted of serious crimes and were serving their sentence in convict prisons administered by the Crown, such as the King's Bench, Marshalsea and Fleet prisons (debtors prisons) and Newgate Gaol, or later in the national prisons such as Millbank or Pentonville, in Public Works prisons or by being transported (up to 1868). These men and women can truly be termed 'convicts' and their long sentences were intended to reform their character. However, by far the greatest number of those behind bars were those on short sentences of less than one calendar month for minor felonies, who were imprisoned in their county, city or borough prison or gaol that were administered locally and were not, until 1877, the responsibility or property of central government. Those serving their sentence inside these were officially termed 'prisoners'. Their experience of prison was intended to be a 'short, sharp shock' to both punish the prisoner and provide a deterrence from future acts, rather than an attempt at reform.

Despite the high-profile visits and reports by prison reformer John Howard in the 1770s, which exposed the appalling conditions suffered by British prisoners, most of Britain's prisons remained dank, unsanitary and verminous holes of misery until the 1830s, the only exceptions being the new-build prisons constructed under the Howard guidelines, such as Bury St Edmunds and Norwich City Prison.

New-build prisons that ignored Howard's recommendations were those erected for the incarceration of French prisoners of war in the later eighteenth and early nineteenth century, such as Norman Cross (Cambridgeshire), Dartmoor (1806–9) and Perth (1810–12). Norman Cross was the first of these prisons, with work commencing in 1797, and was designed to hold between 5,000 and 6,000 prisoners. The site was surrounded by a perimeter fence and ditch and then divided into four quadrants, each containing two four-storey prison blocks that house up to 500 men sleeping in hammocks. Two regiments of soldiers were stationed in the barracks to guard the prisoners. It was known for the site to house over 7,000 men. By 1801 the conditions in which the prisoners were held had become a matter of public concern; they had insufficient clothing and instances of sickness such as fever, consumption, dysentery or typhus were often rife. There were a handful of escapes and in 1804 it was discovered that the prisoners had been involved in forgery after printing plates and related implements were discovered there. With some prisoners in a state of near nakedness, the British government provided prison uniforms of sulphur yellow colour in the hope these easily identifiable uniforms would prevent further escapes. Peace with France was declared in 1814 and all prisoners had left the garrison by June. By June 1816 most of the prison buildings were finally demolished. A total of 1,770 French prisoners of war had died at Norman Cross during their years of captivity.

After such a disastrous high-profile prison debacle, the 1770s proposals for a national convict prison were revisited, and the result was Millbank Prison. Built on land purchased from the Marquis of Salisbury at Pimlico, London, Millbank Prison was designed by William Williams in 1812 in accordance with the utilitarian principles laid down by Jeremy Bentham in the 1790s and was completed in 1821. The first prisoners, all women, were admitted on 26 June 1816 and the first men arrived in January 1817. The design of the prison was, frankly, bizarre, and highly impractical. It was constructed with six pentagonal complexes of cell blocks radiating from a central hexagon; it proved difficult to patrol and with its complicated ground plan it was claimed there were instances of warders at Millbank becoming lost in their own prison. During the early years of Millbank's existence sentences of five to ten years were offered as an alternative to transportation to those considered most likely to reform. Later, it ceased to have a penitentiary function and became a holding centre for those awaiting transportation to the penal colonies.

The next significant step along the road to improved prisons should have been the 1823 Gaol Act. It had wide-ranging reforms, including: the introduction of regular inspections carried out by the Visiting Justices (magistrates) and quarterly reports despatched to the Home Secretary, the Visiting Justices became responsible for the appointment of staff, stipulations were put in place for the provision of female warders for female prisoners, and the three significant figures in the prison – the governor, chaplain and surgeon – were required to maintain journals recording their work. This all seemed like a valuable step in the direction of prison reform, but it had no teeth; there was simply no mechanism in place to enforce the directives of the Act.

Over ten years later, in 1835, matters finally began to be taken in hand with the appointment of five HM Inspectors of Prisons, followed by a Surveyor General of Prisons in 1844. The reports of the inspectors often revealed inhumane conditions

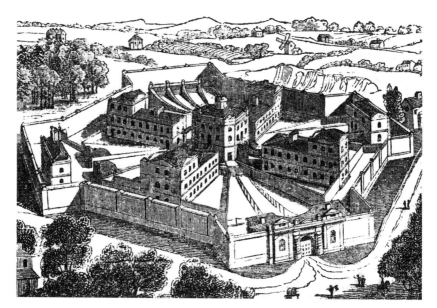

Norwich City Prison, 1827.

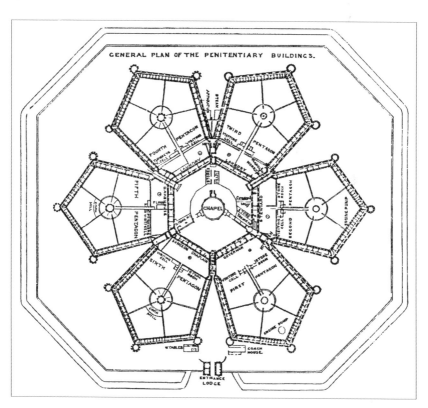

General plan of Millbank Prison showing its infamous six pentagonal complexes of cell blocks, 1862.

and deep-seated problems such as the way prisons dealt with health provision, living conditions for the prisoners and issues over discipline. In some cases the problems were extreme, as this account of the inspector's findings after his visit to Wisbech House of Correction, published in the *Report of the Prison Inspectors* (1853), reveals:

Number of Prisoners at time of Inspection: 26 Males   9 Females
No alterations have been made either in the buildings or in the discipline of the prison since the last inspection but the drainage was about to be improved. The ventilation is good. There has been one death; a prisoner who died from abscess on the side. The general health of the prisoners was represented to be good. There was one prisoner, a female, sick at the time of my visit.

There is still no regular schoolmaster; but the governor instructs the male prisoners and last year received a gratuity of £15 for this extra duty. The number of punishments for prison offences was – males 299, females 14. They were generally for talking, idleness or want of cleanliness. Some prisoners are still employed sorting oats but in addition to the making and repairing of prison clothes and shoes, sack making has been introduced. The clear profits on receipts for this kind of work was £8 15s 6d. The estimated value of work done for the prison was £27 14s 9d. All the provisions, fuel and other stores are supplied by contract. The net cost per prisoner, exclusive of any charge for repairs etc, was £26 10s 4d. I again called the attention of the visiting justices to the absence of any artificial light in the cells; the prisoners are locked up at dusk, and continue to pass much time in bed.

The practice of eating opium is indulged to a great extent in this district. One woman, who had been accustomed to take extraordinary quantities before she came to prison, felt the deprivation so keenly that she made an attempt to destroy herself. She had been some time in the prison when I saw her and expressed herself as feeling very thankful for having been broken of the habit, though she represented the deprivation as having, at first, 'almost made her mad.'

The prisoners generally are of a very low standard, both as regard morals and intellect, this in some measure attributed to the free use of this drug. I found one prisoner who had been 27 times in this gaol. He is represented to be a quite well-disposed man, until he is either drunk or under the influence of opium.

The old prisons and their long-standing problems could be tolerated no more, so in a revolutionary multi-million pound programme over ninety prisons were newly built or improved and enlarged between the years 1842 and 1877. Among them were the first Public Works prisons at Portland, Portsmouth and Chatham, built between 1848 and 1856. Here the prisoners' work was manual and hard and the hours were long; the ethos of these prisons being that criminals pay back their debt to society through hard labour. The idea proved popular with the

Victorians and further Public Works prisons followed at Borstal (1874, now HMP Rochester), Chattenden in Kent (1877) and Dover (1884).

New approaches to the reform of criminals were considered from the 1820s and '30s. One method adopted was the Silent System whereby prisoners would be locked in their cells at night and although they were allowed to mix with other prisoners for their daily employment it had to be in silence. It was believed that many convicts were habitual criminals and nothing would change them and therefore prison, although more humane than the previous century, had to put fear into the hearts of criminals to the degree they do not dare offend again. The Silent System was thought to be a vehicle whereby convicts' wills were broken by being kept in total silence and by long, pointless hard labour. Approached with new vigour in the 1860s, Assistant Director of Prisons, Sir Edmund Du Cane promised the public that prisoners would get 'Hard Labour, Hard Fare and Hard Board'.

Mrs Florence Maybrick experienced the 'evils' of serving sentence in the Silent System first-hand during her incarceration for the supposed murder of her husband, and reflected upon it in her book:

> The routine of my daily life was the same as during 'solitary confinement'. The cell door may be open, but its outer covering or gate is locked, and, although I knew there was a human creature separated from me only by a cell wall and another gate, not a whisper might I breathe. There is no rule of prison discipline so productive of trouble and disaster as the 'silent system' and the tyrannous and rigorous method with which it is enforced is the cause of two-thirds of all the misconduct and disturbance that occurs in prison. The silence rule gives supreme gratification to the tyrannous officer, for on the slightest pretext she can report a woman for talking – a turn of the head, a movement of the lips is enough of an excuse for a report. And there is heavy punishment that can be inflicted for this offence, both in the male and female prisons. An offender may be consigned to solitary confinement, put for three days on bread and water, or suffer the loss of a week's remission, which means a week added to her term of imprisonment – and all this for incautiously uttering a word.
>
> Unless it be specifically intended as a means of torture, the system of solitary confinement, even for four months, the term to which it has since been reduced, can meet only with condemnation. I am convinced that, within limits, the right of speech and the interchange of thought, at least for two hours daily, even during probation, would insure better discipline than perpetual silence, which can be enforced only by a complete suppression of nature and must result in consequent weakness of mind and ruin of temper. During the first months of her sentence a prisoner is more frequently in trouble for breach of this one rule than from all other causes. The reduction of the term of probation from nine to four months has been followed by a reduction in mental afflictions,

which is proof that nothing wholesome or good can have its growth in unnatural solitude.

The silent system has a weakening effect upon the memory. A prisoner often finds difficulty in, deciding upon the pronunciation of words which she has not heard for a considerable period. I often found myself, when desirous of using unusual words, especially in French or German, pronouncing them to myself in order to fix the pronunciation in my memory. It is well to bear in mind what a small number of words the prisoner has an opportunity of using in the monotony of prison life. The same inquiries are made day after day, and the same responses given. A vocabulary of one hundred words will include all that a prisoner habitually uses.

No defender of the silent system pretends that it wholly succeeds in preventing speech among prisoners. But be that as it may, a period of four months solitary confinement in the case of a female, and six months in the case of a male, and especially of a girl or youth, is surely a crime against civilization and humanity. Such a punishment is inexpressible torture to both mind and body. I speak from experience. The torture of continually enforced silence is known to produce insanity or nervous breakdown more than any other feature connected with prison discipline. Since the passing of the Act of 1898, mitigating this form of punishment, much good has been accomplished, as is proved by the diminution of insanity in prison life.

Mrs Maybrick's Own Story: My Lost Fifteen Years (1904)

The rival, and far more notorious method, was the American 'Separate System'. Pioneered in Philadelphia and developed at Auburn and later at Sing-Sing, this system was partly an attempt to eradicate old lags teaching young inmates the ways of crime and partly based on the belief, strongly supported by the Quaker reformers, that convicted criminals had to face up to themselves and become reformed through solitude to contemplate their wrongs, prayer, work and religious instruction. Accordingly, prisoners would be kept in their cells on their own for most of the time. When they were let out to go to chapel or for exercise, men would be required to wear cloth masks that obscured their entire face and slot blinkers for the eyes, which directed the gaze of the convict to the ground; women were required to wear veils to obtain a similar result. Prisoners were exercised in groups connected with long lengths of chain that were not allowed to touch the ground to ensure prisoners kept their distance and did not communicate. Prisoners were not allowed visitors. To accommodate this new system Pentonville Prison was constructed between 1840 and 1842 as a model prison on the Separate System. Between 1842 and 1877 nineteen radial prisons were built in England. Other extant prisons followed suit and rapidly adapted their existing buildings with such improvements as special chapels with individual box stalls for prisoners whereby they could only see the chaplain.

Exercising under the Separate System, Pentonville Prison, 1862.

By 1860 about sixty British prisons had been rebuilt or were being adapted for the Separate System, which created something in the order of 11,000 separate cells. The 'Separate System' was practiced in many prisons until the latter half of the nineteenth century.

The previous methods of imprisonment for young people were clearly unsuitable and often turned the children into even harder and skilled criminals; nineteenth-century prison reforms revised what should become of young offenders. Under the Youthful Offenders Act (1854) children who were under the age of 16 and found guilty of crimes could be sent to prison for a maximum of fourteen days then would be removed to Reformatory Schools for between two and five years. The Reformatory Schools were administered by voluntary bodies with aid from state grants. Punishment was an essential part of the strict regime, which included freezing cold baths, military style drills and hard physical labour. In 1861 a further Act was passed and different categories of children were included:

- Any child apparently under the age of 14 found begging or receiving alms.
- Any child apparently under the age of 14 found wandering and not having any home or visible means of support, or in company of reputed thieves.
- Any child apparently under the age of 12 whom, having committed an offence punishable by imprisonment or less.
- Any child under the age of 14 whose parents declare him to be beyond their control.

Interior of Newgate
Prison, *c.* 1890.

In 1866 the Industrial School Act created establishments for orphans, children of
convicted criminals and refractory children who would be subject to a strictly
instructed basic education and training in industrial and agricultural processes.
By the 1870s there were fifty industrial schools for 2,500 needy children and
sixty-five Reformatory Schools detaining about 5,000 young offenders. Despite
these best efforts, juveniles were still being sent to prison well into the 1890s. The
Borstal system of reformatory prisons for young offenders guilty of serious or
repeat offences was introduced in 1900.

   Transportation of convicts had been a key feature of judicial punishment
since the seventeenth century, when the first penal transports took convicts to
the British colony in North America. This transport ceased with the outbreak
of the American War of Independence in 1775. Thirteen years later, in 1788,
the 'First Fleet' departed from England to found the first colony in Australia
as a penal colony. In 1803, Van Diemen's Land (Tasmania) was also settled as a
penal colony followed by the Moreton Bay Settlement (Queensland) in 1824.

The other Australian colonies were non-convict 'free settlements'. However, Western Australia adopted transportation in 1851 in an attempt to fill its labour shortage. It is estimated that during the eighty years of its existence, over 160,000 convicts were transported to Australia. As early as the 1830s Australia was unhappy about being a dumping ground for Britain's convicts and began to make official moves to end penal transports to its shores. British Prison authorities could see the writing was on the wall as transportation to New South Wales terminated in 1841 followed by Van Diemen's Land in 1852. The last convict ship arrived in Western Australia in January 1868 and with the loss of the last penal colonies a new sentence of 'Penal Servitude' was introduced to replace transportation and the pressure was on for major and unprecedented reform across Britain's prisons; this came in the form of the 1877 Prison Act when, in effect, all prisons were nationalised and placed under the administration of a new central government body – the Prison Commission, with former Assistant Director of Prisons, Edmund Du Cane, the designer of Wormwood Scrubs, as its chairman.

Du Cane saw to it that by 1877 most of the worst of the local prisons had been closed down, many of them converted to new purposes, mainly domestic, many more were simply demolished and the land sold off. The 1877 Prison Act dispensed with most of the sub-standard prisons that remained and by 1878 the number of prisons in England and Wales was reduced from 113 to 69. The design of Wormwood Scrubs was mirrored in a number of the new-build local prisons of this period, including Bristol, Nottingham, Norwich and Shrewsbury.

A wide range of improvements were also enacted in the prisons as water closets and basins were removed from individual cells and replaced by ablution towers. Wire netting was fitted across open cell block corridors and raised gallery rails were both introduced as anti-suicide measures, while ancillary buildings were erected to provide new and enlarged laundries, kitchens, reception wings and hospital wards.

In 1895 the last major committee on the administration of prisons and the treatment and classification of prisoners in the nineteenth century published its findings. Chaired by Herbert Gladstone, the committee reflected the New Liberalism of the late nineteenth century and its aims and recommendations demonstrate a sincere attempt to design a prison system concentrating upon the reformation of the individual and a greater understanding of character typology and specific needs. The committee's recommendations were incorporated into the 1898 Prison Act which led to the abolition of unproductive labour in prisons and stipulated that prisoners were to work together, learn trades and have a greater access to books. The committee's findings also led to the creation of state reformatories for inebriates, young offenders (Borstal) and habitual criminals. Although some of its findings were adopted piecemeal *The Gladstone Report* remained the definitive statement on penal policy for much of the first half of the twentieth century.

PRISON STAFF

The Governor

In the early years of Victoria's reign prison governors were, as Maria Shepherd described in *Leaves from a Journal of Prison Visits* (1857), 'mere gaolers – men raised from the office of turnkey, often as ignorant and immoral as their very prisoners'; although there were exceptions, her generalisation was quite right. The award of the position had traditionally been in the gift of the local magistrates, but by the 1860s prison inspections and national regulations had pruned away much of the old guard and, as Shepherd continued, 'Men of standing in society – men of education and ability, – chiefly chosen from amongst naval and military officers' had taken their place. But, as ever with such appointments, it often did not depend upon what experience you had but who you knew.

'A Ticket of Leave Man' recalled the governor of Pentonville Prison and a particular incident which exemplified his unrelenting coldness:

> This governor was a militia or volunteer officer and so, of course, stood severely on military dignity; he insisted upon a salute from everybody, officers and prisoners, whenever he made his appearance. On this September morning my sorrowing neighbour [a prisoner who shared the same landing as our author who had been greatly disappointed at getting no news of his sick wife after bribing a warder to help him] was ushered into the awful presence of the governor. He was in a nervous state and not thinking much of military tactics, when the stern voice of the chief warder called out, – ''Ands by your side! Heyes to your front!'
>
> *Governor:* Do you know a Mrs Warner?
> *Prisoner:* Yes, sir.

Governor: Who is she? A relative?
Prisoner: She is a friend with whom my wife is staying and she kindly nurs—
Governor: That will do. There is bad news for you. Your wife is dead.
Chief Warder: Right about face! March!

The tragic widower convict was then returned to his daily routine.

Convict Life (1879)

The Rules and Regulations to be observed in the Gaol and House of Correction for the County of Huntingdon for the year 1863 were typical and stated that the governor 'ought to exercise his authority with firmness, temper and humanity, abstain from all irritating language, and not strike a Prisoner: he must enforce similar conduct on the Subordinate Officers.' His duties were to visit and inspect every ward, cell, yard and division of the prison, and see every prisoner once at least in every twenty-four hours and 'go through the Prison at an uncertain hour of the night' at least once during the week.

It fell to the governor to ensure 'every precaution necessary for preventing escape' was observed and to give specific orders for the daily examination of the cells, bars, bolts and locks along with an examination of all parcels, letters and articles, brought into the prison. He was also expected to ensure proper precautions were maintained against the danger of fire and having seen to it that thermometers were placed in different parts of the prison and that a daily record was kept of the degree of temperature. The ultimate responsibility for the prison's fabric, maintenance and all its prisoners fell to the governor; he was to acquaint himself with each one upon admission, ensure their cleanliness, monitor their visitors and ensure that the food was provided as per the dietary table.

In the smaller county prisons the governor would have far more 'hands on' responsibilities, often joined by his wife, who would take on the role of matron with responsibility for the female prisoners and all the prison clothing, bedding and linen. If required, she would assist in the purchase of any articles needed for her department and would report to the governor any deficiencies in the stock requisite for carrying on the prison work. The governor was expected to see each male prisoner once a day and each female prisoner once every seven days, accompanied by the matron, and would be known to assist the warders if necessary in the restraint of a violent prisoner.

All prison governors had to maintain the prison registers, a prison log or journal and submit regular returns and reports to the Prison Board. He would not have been permitted to be absent from the prison for a single night during his appointment without written permission from a Visiting Justice. Indeed, many governors lived with their families on site, sometimes in a separate house, sometimes in part of the prison. That was until a number of outbreaks of 'gaol fever' or other contagious diseases occurred across the country during which not only

Staff of Springfield Prison, Chelmsford, in the early twentieth century. Seated in the centre is the governor, standing behind him is his chief warder; to the governor's right is his deputy while on his left is the prison chaplain and beside him the prison surgeon.

A convict is brought before the Governor at Millbank Prison, 1873.

did numerous prisoners die but also governors and members of their families; notable is the tragic case of Captain McGorrery, the governor of Springfield Gaol, Chelmsford. He and his family were not long moved into the governor's residence inside the walls of the prison when his son William died of diphtheria, aged 7 on 2 August 1862. A week later his sister Ann contracted the same illness and died on 15 August. After the death of Ann the family moved out for a month, the house was newly whitewashed throughout and 'due precautions taken' to rid the house of any infestations and infections. A fortnight after their return their five-year-old daughter Mary Ann contracted scarlet fever and died on 1 October. The family then vacated the house permanently and moved to a residence outside the prison walls. After the nationalisation of prisons in 1877 all appointments were made by the Prison Commissioners and many of the old prisons were then improved or made redundant in favour of a brand new build – with the governor and his family living off site.

The Chaplain

A concern for the souls of prisoners can be found in some of the earliest British prisons. Chaplains would usually be present to minister to those under sentence of death but it was only in 1814 that the appointment of a prison chaplain was made compulsory. In provincial prisons a local vicar would often be called upon to take on the post and perform the chaplain duties for a stipend of around £10 a year. The larger convict prisons would have their own full-time prison chaplain appointed by the Board of Visiting Justices, but he was unable to officiate until he had obtained a license for that purpose from the bishop.

Recalling his appointment as chaplain, or, as it was known in Newgate, the 'Ordinary', for *Fraser's Magazine* in 1840, the Revd Charles Wall found the primary requirements of him, beyond his ministry to the prisoners, were for him to assay and report on the effects of public executions on those who observed them. A magistrate pointed out:

> … the office we are soliciting you to fill affords the opportunity of acquiring a great knowledge of the character of delinquents in general and of the effects all the various species of punishments have on them as individuals and a body. Formerly, the authorities in the city little heeded these matters; times are now altered and a very considerable body of gentlemen are resolved to inform themselves to the fullest on the subject; their eyes are turned to you as their principal auxiliary. Will you take the office and assist them? We will guarantee your election if you will allow yourself to be placed in nomination.

Wall agreed and he was appointed the Ordinary of Newgate.

All appointed prison chaplains were clergymen of the Church of England; if a prisoner was of another faith the governor could permit a minister of that persuasion to visit 'at proper and reasonable times'. The chaplain performed the appointed Morning and Evening Services in the prison and was expected to preach a sermon in the prison chapel on every Sunday, Christmas Day, Good Friday and on public Feast and Thanksgiving Days.

Within the separate system prison chapels had stalls rather than pews for the inmates. The prisoners looking over the tall stall fronts would only be able to see the chaplain and, if a felon condemned under sentence of death was in the gaol, he would also be seen in the pew directly in front of the pulpit. If the convict in his 'stall' looked around him he would only see the wooden wall of the stall beside and behind him and for his 'ease and comfort' was only provided with an uncomfortable 'seat' which was more like a ledge; it was a mere six inches wide and slanted downwards at a forty-five degree angle. The prison chaplain would be situated facing his congregation in a high pulpit and would look out on a congregation in what appeared to be upright coffins!

Every prisoner was seen by the chaplain on admission and discharge; most chaplains were kindly men offering hope if the prisoner repented his sins but they did not let the prisoners forget why they were there and pulled no punches when giving advice on how to best survive their time in captivity. In *Five Years Penal Servitude* (1878) the author, 'One Who has Endured It', recalled:

Divine service under the 'Separate System' in the chapel at Pentonville, 1862.

One morning the chaplain walked into my cell, and, sitting down, he entered into conversation as usual. This was the first visit I had had from him since my conviction. He watched me at work for some time.

'I see you are not used to that work,' said he. 'Let me do a little and show you an easier method.' He then took some of the strands and showed me that, by beating and rubbing them a lot together, they are softened very materially, which rendered the after work of picking them to pieces much easier. He then asked me what sentence I had received and told me there was nothing for me to do but resign myself to it. 'You must,' said he, 'just consider yourself as a slave till your time is out. Every action of your life will have to be just what your taskmasters may command you to do. Try and bear up meekly and submissively. Avoid giving offence to any of the officials and remember that though your body is condemned to slavery, your thoughts, your mind and heart are free – free to commune with God, free to pray, free to praise and free to repent.'

W.T. Stead ended up at Coldbath Fields Prison (with fellow male co-conspirator Sampson Jacques) after his high-profile expose of white slavery, published in the *Pall Mall Gazette* as 'The Maiden Tribute of Modern Babylon'. Both he and Jacques had a somewhat different experience of their prison chaplain shortly after their admission in 1886:

… in a few moments my door was unlocked, and a man with a high hat on, in appearance not unlike a 'gent with a sporting turn,' looked in. 'Well,' he said, as he scanned me from head to foot, 'don't you think you've got off very cheap?'

'To whom have I the honour of speaking?' I replied.

'I am the chaplain,' said he.

'No,' said I, 'it is the sentence I anticipated, for the three months, I am told, will be up in two months and eight days.'

'I don't know that,' said he. 'You were out on bail. Your sentence will probably count from date of conviction, not from that of the opening of the court.'

'That is hard for Jacques,' said I, 'for his punishment will be thrice as long as he expected. To me it does not matter so much.'

'Well,' he said, 'I don't suppose you will have much need of me. If you have you can send for me.' He turned on his heel and disappeared. I never saw him again save in the distance at chapel when he went through the services in a way unintelligible to me where I sat, but I was told he had a rather good voice … No doubt there was no animus, or no intention to do anything but his duty, on the part of the chaplain Stocken. Personally I make no complaint. I was, fortunately, not dependent upon that official for the ministration of sympathy. But for my fellow-prisoners, to whom he is the sole official human representative of the Divine passion of love and pity, even for the chief of sinners, I am sorry if he speaks to them in the tone and spirit in which he addressed Jacques, and me.

The chaplain would visit the infirmaries and sick daily and frequently visited every room and cell occupied by prisoners, attending those who required his spiritual advice and assistance. It was part of his remit to pay special attention to juvenile offenders. This area of pastoral care was marked well by many prison chaplains, who would not only do their best to reform the boys but would speak out if they considered their punishment too harsh. In one typical incident the Revd C.G. Lang, prison chaplain of Portsea, Hampshire spoke out against boys being made examples of simply because they were labelled 'Hooligans' during the Hooligan scare of 1901. He recognised the boys had been wayward and deserving punishment but because their petty crimes had occurred at the time of the scare they had been marked and vilified as 'Hooligans' and they had been sentenced accordingly. He wrote a moving letter to *The Times*:

I had, as Prison chaplain, seen the three boys after their first night in prison. They were a pitiable sight. They had not slept a wink. Two of them had not touched their prison breakfast; I could hear their sobs before I entered the cells. 'Please sir,' said one of them, 'a day's as long as a year in this place' … Thus, in order that these boys of 15 and 16 may be redeemed from a career of crime, they have for a foolish prank been confined to know the inside of a prison for five days and to herd with every sort of young scoundrel for three years in a reformatory.

William Cosmo Gordon 'C.G.' Lang dedicated his life to the poor, needy and unfortunate; he was elevated to Archbishop of York within eighteen years of his ordination (unprecedented in modern Church of England history) and retired as Archbishop of Canterbury in 1942.

A prison chaplain would be the head of education within the prison and would also teach the prisoners to read and write if no schoolmaster was appointed. If a schoolmaster was appointed onto prison staff he would be obliged to keep the prison chaplain informed of the prisoner's progress both verbally and with occasional written reports. Once the letters to and from prisoners had been examined by the deputy governor it would be initialled and then passed to the chaplain – both these men would censor anything they considered infringed the rules or as 'improper for a prisoner to know or communicate'. Prisoners' letters were only supposed to contain domestic and personal matters; any mention of current affairs would be struck out or the letter returned to the sender.

It was also the duty of the chaplain to supervise the distribution and preservation of books available from the prison library. He would personally inspect all books and reject 'such as he may deem improper'. Prisoners were also provided with books and tracts of religious, moral and useful instruction (prisoners of persuasions differing from the Church of England were given their religious books under the direction of the Visiting Justices). Each prisoner who could read was furnished with a Bible and Common Prayer Book during Divine Service, and a Bible and Common Prayer Book was placed in each day room, in each separate cell and in each sleeping cell (during the summer months).

The chaplain would also attend prisoners in solitary and separate confinement, in their own cells or under punishment in refractory or 'dark cells' every day. It was well known for the chaplain to take the dictation of illiterate or semi-literate prisoners and to write their letters home for them. Chaplains were also known to help lead appeals for the innocent families left in extreme poverty or even destitution by the incarceration of their breadwinner. Chaplains were particularly active in attempting to procure relief for worthy cases among debtors. The Revd Buck, chaplain to the Queen's Prison, London, was happy to lend his name to this appeal by Sir William Fraser, published in *The Times* in August 1861:

Sir, A few days ago I saw in the Queen's Bench a man who had been a prisoner for debt since the years before Waterloo [1815]. His name is W. Miller; his age 77. He is a county debtor and debarred from the enjoyments of those who support themselves. At 3 he is turned away from the sunny side of the prison into a very dismal yard on the northern side.

For 20 years he supported his mother entirely by his work in the prison as a first class cabinet maker until in 1835 he became crippled with rheumatism in his hands and is so still. W. Miller has a good character from the chaplain, he is a very intelligent and inoffensive man … The prisoner's story is and has been

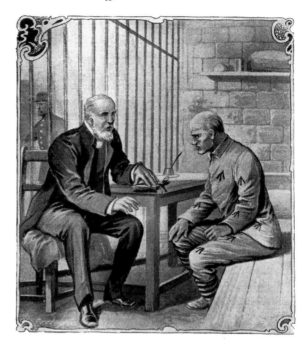

Notorious burglar and double murderer Charles Peace dictates his final condemned cell confession to the chaplain of Armley Gaol, Leeds, February 1879.

for 47 years, that his name was forged to the bond for which he was arrested by a man who had wronged his sister and that the warrant was not duly signed. He has always declined to acknowledge the legality of his arrest and to go out under the Insolvent Act. By the Act just passed all debtors are compelled to appear before the court and to leave the prison. To W. Miller, liberty is starvation or the workhouse. To ask money as charity of a friend and to put a pistol to his head with the same demand are, in my opinion, equal social offences. Perhaps some of your readers may be inclined to save a man of superior mind from dying in misery. He has not a relation in the world.

The Rev. W. Buck, chaplain, Queen's Prison London will answer all enquiries.

The prison chaplain would also attend condemned prisoners throughout their confinement and on the gallows, often writing the dictated final letters and confessions of the prisoner.

The Surgeon

There is no distinct period when prison surgeons were first appointed to the gaols of Britain, but references can be found in Quarter Sessions papers by the seventeenth century for payments being made in respect of physicians' attendance, treatment and medicine for prisoners and for the arrangement of inquests when required. During the nineteenth century, medical care for prisoners did gradually improve, along with the hygiene levels in prisons, but significant developments across our nation's prisons were only addressed after the Prison Commissioners took over in 1877.

Until the mid-nineteenth century, most cells had no heating, bad ventilation and poor sanitation and epidemics were common. In 1847 it was reported that at the Bedford New House of Correction a rare disease named as 'petticia' was prevalent within its walls. Its presence was blamed on a combination of defective ventilation and poor diet. The account went on to state 'there is no place more painfully cold in winter and distressingly hot in summer than the prison cells. They are small with only soils pots to wash in which were rinsed out with water.' In the early years of the century prisons were riddled with disease; outbreaks of cholera, typhoid and 'Gaol Fever' were well known and if not contained quickly or effectively enough would spread rapidly through the prison, infecting both prisoners and staff.

The majority of convict prisons maintained their own surgeon whereas most small prisons would use an appointed surgeon who lived near the prison. Both these appointments would have been made by the Board of Visiting Justices (Magistrates). The positions were mostly filled by surgeons already known to the justices but occasionally the position was advertised:

Borough of Portsmouth Prison: SURGEON
The Justices of the Peace for the Borough will at a Meeting to be held on Saturday, the 15th day of July instant proceed to the ELECTION of a SURGEON for the above Prison.

The Salary fixed by the Justices is £75 per Annum (which includes medicine to be supplied to the prisoners) subject to confirmation by the Town Council. Candidates must possess the necessary qualifications. Applications stating age and qualifications, with testimonials, to be sent to Samuel Greetham, Clerk.

Hampshire Telegraph and Sussex Chronicle, 8 July 1871

The authorities wishing to recruit a surgeon for a large county prison had to be more generous:

Gloucester County Prison: The Office of SURGEON to this prison will become Vacant about Christmas time. Applications and testimonials are invited to be sent to George Riddiford, Clerk of the Peace, Shirehall, Gloucester on or before the 15th day of SEPTEMBER next, stating age and other particulars. The salary is £175 per Annum. The prison is adapted for a daily average of 400 prisoners. The general duties are those of a Prison Surgeon involving visits to the Prison daily and oftener when necessary. The applicants must be duly qualified and not exceeding 40 years of age on first of January next …

Bristol Mercury, 29 August 1874

More specific rules and duties would be outlined in the rules and regulations to be observed for the gaol that appointed him, such as this selection from the *Rules and Regulations for the House of Correction for the County of Huntingdon* (1863):

> The Surgeon appointed is required to visit the Prison twice at least in every week, and oftener if necessary; and see every Prisoner confined therein … He is to report to every General or Quarter Session the condition of the Prison, and the state of health of the Prisoners.
>
> He shall examine every Prisoner brought into Prison before he is passed into the proper ward; and he shall record the Prisoner's name, age, state of health on admission, and any disease of importance to which he may have been subject. He shall record his state of health on discharge.
>
> He shall see daily such of the Prisoners as complain of illness, or appear out of health; and shall either supply such Prisoners with medicines in their wards or cells, or direct them to be removed to the Infirmary.
>
> He shall, at every Michaelmas Quarter Sessions, deliver to the Justices a report, in writing, specifying with reference to the past year, the general state of health of the Prisoners, the disorders which have been most prevalent, whether any connection may be traced between the diseases which have occurred and the locality, or state of the building, or the diet, employment or other circumstances; also the number of deaths, any case of insanity, the number of Infirmary cases, the number of Prisoners placed upon extra diet, and the proportion of sick to the whole number of Prisoners admitted during the year.

This final clause provided an important section that would form part of the report presented at the Quarter Sessions to the magistrates, who were responsible for the running of local county and borough gaols until the Prison Commissioners took over in 1877.

It would fall to the prison surgeon to ensure the prisoners were kept clean and healthy; he would frequently inspect their food and report to the governor on the quality of provisions. He would ensure prisoners were provided with soap and water and received a warm bath at least once a fortnight. He also recommend the amount of air and exercise prisoners were allowed to maintain their health. If prisoners under medical treatment required clean sheets more than once each month he would ensure that this happened or, where sheets were not in use, that the blankets be washed with the same frequency as that prescribed for the sheets. The sheets that had been used by one prisoner were not permitted to be transferred to another until they had been washed.

The surgeon would give written directions for the separation of prisoners with contagious diseases (or those suspected of having one) and give the instructions for cleansing, disinfecting and whitewashing any apartments occupied by such prisoners; and for washing, disinfecting or destroying any infected apparel.

The surgeon or medical officer would be expected to maintain relevant registers and a journal of all his work would be laid before a commissioner and inspector on their visits. The governor would occasionally check that the journal and registers were in order; failure to keep satisfactory records could result in censure and possibly dismissal for the surgeon.

Prison surgeons or medical officers also had the responsibility for assessing which inmates were fit to carry out hard labour, be it in the quarries or labouring at Public Works prisons or on the treadmill or crank. Up to the mid-nineteenth century a convict, if found healthy and able, could, if agreed by the prison surgeon, step up to the equivalent of a height of 12,000ft a day on the treadmill. Medical and scientific committees were set up in the 1860s to determine the amount of labour that could be expected from the prisoners; the experts concluded that prisoners sentenced to hard labour on the treadmill were to ascend no more than 8,640ft per day. The medical officer would also be consulted when any prisoner was to undergo punishments such as flogging and he would be in attendance when the punishment was administered and could stop the flogging at any time if he feared the prisoner might be in danger of serious injury or losing his life.

Convicts awaiting examination by the medical officer in the Reception Ward of Millbank Prison, 1873.

When the executioner had made his calculations for 'the drop' for the condemned felon he would show and explain his calculations to both the prison governor and the surgeon. The presence of the prison surgeon would be required at the execution and it fell to him to descend into the scaffold pit moments after the execution and examine the body while it was still suspended on the rope to proclaim life extinct and assess if the execution had been 'clean and efficient'.

The work of the prison surgeon or medical officer was made far more arduous by malingerers and those faking illness. 'A Ticket of Leave Man' recalled:

> The duties of a Medical Officer are not only very responsible and arduous but very difficult to perform. I recollect that during a considerable portion of last year, out of about of the 1,000 convicts, 150 applied to see the doctor every day. I speak entirely of my own knowledge and from information gained from the men themselves, when I say that certainly 100 out of 150 had nothing on earth the matter with them and had they been free men would no more have thought of going to the doctor than they would of going to church.
>
> *Convict Life* (1879)

The reasons for the convicts troubling the doctor unnecessarily were varied; some joined the queue simply out of boredom of the prison routine and would create some imaginary complaint and see how long they could deceive the medical officer, or 'Croker' as they called him, into administering a tonic or cod liver oil. Others joined the line in order to transact some covert deal with another convict such as exchanging leather or needles stolen from the cobblers shop for some illicit tobacco. There were also a large number of 'fakers', as 'A Ticket of Leave Man' continued:

> There is another large class of prisoners who systematically 'fake' themselves, as they call it; and unless the medical officer is a man of great experience, or a very shrewd fellow, he is often taken in. I knew one strong, hearty, lazy young fellow at Portland, who was able in some way to produce blood, and to deceive the medical officer with the notion that his lungs were in a bad state. I am tolerably sure that the doctor doubted the fellow, but being uncertain, gave him the benefit of the doubt. The consequence was, that he was employed at the lightest kind of labour, and at last transferred to Woking, where I have no doubt he finished his very easy lagging. This young rascal took good care to complain at all times to the medical officer; he avoided the assistant medical officer, who was too sharp for him, and for a great many more of the scamps.
>
> I knew another man, a man of some education too, and who ought to have known better, a man who, by-the-by, had been a clerk in the Convict Department. He had been sentenced to five years for some swindling in connection with it. He was a great, strong, powerful fellow, as well able to do a day's

work as any man on Portland Bill. His habit was to eat common soda, which he used to obtain from the men employed in the washhouse, and which he used to pay for with tobacco obtained from an officer. With this soda he was able to produce some effect which deceived the medical officer, and he was kept upon the lightest description of labour during his whole sentence, and was, when discharged, as fat as a porpoise.

Another deception practised to a very great extent is produced by the eating of soap. The action of the heart is very much influenced by it, and scores of men sneak into the infirmary, or evade their labour, by using it. It is also well known that quite a number of prisoners resort to more violent means to avoid labour, disabling themselves in an endless variety of ways.

Convict Life (1879)

The prison surgeon certainly had to keep his wits about him and had every right to be sceptical, but he would have to balance his views with sense and err on the side of caution because if a prisoner did fall seriously ill or died and the surgeon could not demonstrate he had undertaken all requisite steps to treat the prisoner or sustain life, then the surgeon could face disciplinary action and dismissal for neglect. Questions would also have been asked of the prison surgeon if a prisoner committed suicide.

In the days before modern understanding and treatment of mental illness, the prison doctor would often be called upon to assess a prisoner displaying signs of insanity and could be asked to give his opinion at the prisoner's trial or if a plea for commutation of death sentence had been made on grounds of the prisoner being insane. The imposture was a difficult one to pull off but if a prisoner did succeed they would be certified a 'criminal lunatic' and would be removed to Broadmoor, but, once there, to eventually obtain a release may prove very difficult. For many, mental illness and the loss of sanity in prison was all too real, but the acceptance and treatment of their illness was often slow due to the number of those who attempted to fain insanity. Prisoner Michael Davitt wrote of the impact of prison conditions on the mind of convicts:

That human reason should give way under such adverse influences is not, I think, to be wondered at; and many a still living wreck of manhood can refer to the silent system of Millbank and its pernicious surroundings as the cause of his debilitated mind.

It was here that Edward Duffy died, and where Rickard Burke and Martin Hanly Carey were for a time oblivious of their sufferings from temporary insanity, and where Daniel Reddin was paralyzed. It was here where Thomas Ahern first showed symptoms of madness, and was put in dark cells and strait-jacket for a 'test' as to the reality of these symptoms.

The Schoolmaster

From the eighteenth century ignorance was identified as one of the main factors that led to a person turning to crime and it was felt that if a convicted criminal was to be reformed then education was one of the key elements in his rehabilitation. However, the schoolmaster of Newgate, who published his opinions and thoughts of his time in *Fraser's Magazine* (1832), was in no doubt that it was not wholly ignorance but the origins and family and place in society that had led the convicts he met to a life of crime:

> The character of one is the character of the whole class; their manners and notions are all of one pattern and mould, which is accounted for by their general acquaintance with each other and their habits of association. They have a particular look of the eye, which may be known by anyone much accustomed to them and the development of their features is strongly marked with the animal propensities. So very similar are their ideas and converse that in a few minutes conversation with any one of the party, I could always distinguish them, however artfully they mislead me. They may be known almost by their very gait in the street from other persons. Some of the boys have an approximation to the face of a monkey, so striking are they distinguished by this peculiarity.

From the early nineteenth century up to the 1870s lessons would be provided for prisoners once they had finished their time on the discipline mill. In smaller prisons their schooling was often led by the turnkeys, who would teach the prisoner to read and write. By the 1860s every prison was giving over part of its weekly regime to education – religious and secular; many prisons engaged their own person, duly qualified to give elementary instruction, and in the larger prisons at least one schoolmaster and schoolmistress were appointed, and more than one where requisite. The work of the prison schoolmaster was often closely associated with that of the prison chaplain, with schoolmasters making occasional reports in writing to him regarding the conduct and progress of the prisoners. Such reports were to be filed and a minute of them made in the chaplain's journal.

The qualifications to be a prison schoolmaster appear to be little more than the ability to read and write competently; married men were often preferred as was the ability to sing, as this advertisement headed 'Devon County Prison, Schoolmaster Wanted – Salary £60 per annum' published in *Trewman's Exeter Flying Post or Plymouth and Cornish Advertiser* in March 1870, explains:

> He will be required to attend the Prison daily during such hours as may hereafter be fixed, to instruct under the direction of the chaplain, the male prisoners – to act as the Clerk of the Prison Chapel, and lead the singing – to write the letters of such of the prisoners as cannot write themselves – and to perform

such other duties as the Visiting Justices may hereafter require. He will also be employed during a portion of the day in the Office of the Clerk to the Prison.

Applications with testimonials addressed to the Visiting Justices were to be sent to the Clerk of the Prison.

Woe betide the man who did not run an efficient prison school. In a feature for the *Pall Mall Gazette* in February 1879, Mr M'Gauran, the head schoolmaster at Spike Island Convict Prison, didn't mince his words:

> If a prison school is not made efficient – thoroughly efficient – it is worse than useless; it must do harm when it does no good. Being inefficient, it becomes a farce and the prisoners are the first to perceive it. Their contempt for it urges them to turn it into ridicule, which of course, is artfully concealed but which is perfectly understood among themselves … An inefficient schoolmaster is one of the most likely objects for their amusement. They will fasten on him, in all their artful ways; cunningly worry him and seeing his distress, get into ecstasies.

There were no centralised guidelines for education in prisons before the 1870s so the amount of time the inmates spent in lessons and who taught them varied from prison to prison; in some even the warders took over as teachers, as pointed out by *The Annual Report of the Inspectors of Prisons* (1856) which recorded that turnkeys instructed the prisoners in their cells. The chief turnkey instructing the more advanced prisoners while the under turnkey attended to those who were just learning to read and write. The turnkeys received £7 10s per annum for this additional duty. Ely House of Correction records state that the schoolmaster 'imparts instruction for three and a half hours in the morning and one and a half at night, to prisoners sentenced to hard labour. The assistant matron instructs the female prisoners when required,' whereas at Chester Castle Prison the chaplain superintended the prison school, teaching for one hour a week. At Grantham Borough Gaol a schoolmaster attended twice a week whilst a schoolmaster had been engaged at the Hull House of Correction and gave instruction to prisoners for two hours, five days a week. The female prisoners were taught by the matron for two hours a day, four days a week; the report for Hull House of Correction contained the remark: 'Nearly all the females are very ignorant; they do not even know the alphabet when they first come to school.'

In the 1830s and '40s prisoners were often divided into categories for their lessons. At Coldbath Fields House of Correction in 1839 the schoolmaster instructed all boys under 16 years and above that had been recommended to him by the chaplain or governor and they were divided by the category of their crime. Thus, four groups were created and taught separately for one hour every five days. The groups were 'Felons', 'Misdemeanants' and two groups of 'Reputed Thieves' (the largest class of prisoners in the prison). The instruction consisted of reading (in the scriptures), spelling (in Mrs Trimmer's Charity School Spelling Book), writing (on slates) and learning catechism and collects by heart. The chaplain also taught arithmetic. By the 1860s and '70s the classes were focussed more on the learning needs of the student rather than their offence. Leicester Prison was typical; there were four classes: two classes were comprised of those who could read adequately and they would attend school twice a week. The other two had one class given four hours a week, the other five hours. An additional hour was also allowed for reading and writing practise in the cells, with the schoolmaster visiting individual prisoners once a week or less.

After the Prison Commissioners took over and Education Acts for all were introduced in the 1870s, most prisons dispensed with their schoolmasters but still maintained an educational programme led by the chaplain and by 'Clerk and Schoolmaster Warders' and kept the prisoners divided into ability classes for teaching purposes. Revd J.W. Horsley, Late and Last Chaplain of Her Majesty's Prison, Clerkenwell, explained his opinion upon this matter:

> But when we come to the vast majority of prisoners, and find them included in the two groups – 'of imperfect education' and 'illiterate' – what conclusions may we draw? First let me warn people to draw none of importance from the numbers in the 'imperfect' class. Stand, as I have done hundreds of times, by the recording warder in the entrance hall as he questions the prisoners who descend from the Black Maria or Queen's Bus. Amongst the questions addressed to each is 'Can you read or write?' The first says, perhaps, 'Yes, I am a doctor.' He will go down in the 'superior' class. The next says, 'Oh yes, well.' He is enrolled in the second class. The next says, as most do, simply 'Yes' and though he may be really well educated, a simple 'Yes' consigns him to the tribe of the 'imperfectly educated'. But also there is the illiterate who being an old hand, knows that it is worthwhile to have a library book in your cell for the sake of its illustrations even if you cannot read. Therefore, he says 'Yes' and is enrolled as only imperfect.
>
> *Prisons and Prisoners* (1898)

Warders selected for this post would have to demonstrate aptitude and have attended a course of instruction in clerical and school work that would have extended over a period of four months. He would have been instructed in scholastic work by the chaplain and the storekeeper for clerical work and the maintenance of books and accounts. If appointed as clerk and schoolmaster warder he would be paid an allowance of £12 per year for carrying out the special duty and would be employed exclusively in those duties from 8.45 a.m. to 5.45 p.m., with one hour for dinner. He would teach an average of twenty-five prisoners per class and would be expected to devote six hours a day to teaching, apart from Sundays, when he would be employed for three hours between 8.45 a.m. and noon. He would also be liable to be called to take his turn on Sunday duty and sleeping within the walls of the prison if required.

Warders

The Prison Commission set out clear standards for the employment of prison warders in the 1870s. Their stipulations for the type of man required and his background clearly showed that the commissioners had learned many lessons from the recruitment of men for the recently established police forces. Advertisements for prison warders often stipulated they should be over 20 years of age but under 40, some requested only married men with no children and some even specified that candidates should preferably be no less than 5ft 9in in height; all would be expected to be able to supply at least two good character references from the likes of their local vicar or 'person of respectability'.

All appointments of warders would have been made by the governor. If they passed the initial selection the probationary warders would then 'shadow' more experienced warders to 'learn the job' and recruits would be set an exam in reading, writing and arithmetic. Although men could join between the ages of 21 and 35, maturity was always a key factor in selection of recruits. Preference was given to men with a military background with a record for good conduct 'clear of misdemeanours' for at least three years immediately before leaving the colours.

Prison warder uniform was made of the same dark blue or black melton cloth or serge as police uniforms and was cut in a very similar way too. The hats were described as either kepis or shakos and were of a very similar French design to those worn by American forces in the American Civil War. Badges and insignia varied slightly from prison to prison but normally a Queen's crown would be worn as a headdress and collar badge while buttons and belt buckles would have a crown in the centre surrounded by the legend 'HM Prison' (sometimes with a location such as 'HM Prison Ely') all of which would be cast in either brass or white metal. Boots would be of the military type, with metal studs in the soles. Many officers were issued with police-style whistles on chains to raise the alarm if necessary. Their keys were affixed to their belt by a spring clip chain; the keys themselves remained attached to the chain and keyring but were carried in leather pouches worn on their leather belts and fastened with a metal stud. Some prisons issued tunics bearing numbers on the collar as well as a crown; this tended to relate to the wing the officer worked in or the prison rather than the prison officer having a 'collar number' like policemen. Senior warders were denoted by crown backed by starburst on their collar and the chief warder wore a wire badge of a crown surrounded by laurels. All prison warders were expected to be 'clean and presentable'.

During the nineteenth century it was very rare to find any mixing of male and female prisoners. Prison wardresses who guarded the female wings of prisons tended to be given a more flexible uniform, with the main stipulation that it should be midnight blue, black or dark brown in colour (one colour would be standard per prison). The skirt and bodice were separate with button fronts and mutton-chop sleeves, and the bodice was pin tucked and worn with a heavily

A group of London prison warders, *c.* 1880.

A fine study of a London prison warder in the 1880s.

Wardress Ellen Boorman,
Maidstone Prison, *c.* 1890.

boned corset underneath, all made in linen union (a cotton and linen mix).
On their head would be worn a toque style bonnet tied under the chin with a
satin ribbon. Women warders would also wear leather belts with simple, plain
buckles from which they wore their keys on chains, some had pouches similar to
the men while others simply had their keys exposed and hooked onto their belts
or left hanging like a chatelaine.

The work of the warder was described by 'Ticket of Leave Man' in *Convict Life*
(1879):

At Pentonville the warder has sole charge of what is called a 'landing' or floor,
and this includes, I think, about forty prisoners.

On this landing the warder is supreme; he distributes the food and the work
and if things go smoothly he is not interfered with or visited by the principal or
chief warder more than once in a week. He knows at what hour the governor
or Deputy-governor may be expected to 'walk his rounds' and then, of course,
everything is in apple-pie order.

In the 1870s, the hours of work for prison officers varied from prison to prison; the warders of Inveraray Prison are quite typical in that they worked from 10 p.m. to 8 p.m. the following night (during the small hours of the morning prison warders would be allowed to sleep on beds in prison quarters but would be expected to attend prisoners who rang for assistance or were troublesome). Warders were provided with two meals per day but had to work seven days a week. Pay was 14s a week; comment was made they lost many potential recruits to more lucrative labouring jobs of 'cutting wood and putting up fences', which paid between 20s and 25s a week. In the early twentieth century shift working of eight hours a day was introduced as standard unless on special duties such as escorting prisoners or condemned cell duty, when it would be difficult or considered awkward to change warders. Prison officers were often keen to volunteer for condemned cell duty as it meant more money.

As prison governors lived 'within the walls' with their families, many prisons had their warders do the same. Typically warders would be given an apartment within a block of prison warder accommodation rather than a house, but it would be provided with 'gaslight and coals'. If the warders lived 'without the walls' houses would be provided by the prison authorities which would be situated in 'approved areas' near the prison, where the neighbours were not likely to be of 'criminal type'.

Like their comrades in the police force, prison warders had to maintain high standards of discipline, along military lines. If any warder was found drunk or 'keeping bad company' he could be subject to summary dismissal. Any warder wishing to marry would have to seek permission from the prison governor and would be asked to obtain references for the good character of his wife-to-be, and they could well be invited in for an interview with the governor before final permission was granted for the marriage. To avoid fraternisation with criminal types and the frequent shuns suffered by law enforcement officers, most prisons had their own warders' clubs which staged outings and events of their own for their families. Pensions (or rather, a lack of them) were a source of grievance until the 1890 Police Act saw officers granted a half-pay pension without medical certification after twenty-five years service and a modified pension after fifteen years if an officer was discharged on medical grounds.

Times were often hard for prison warders; hours were long and often they would feel 'trapped' in a job it was difficult to leave. Occasionally their letters would be sent to and published in both local and national newspapers. One prison warder writing in 1871 under the sobriquet of 'Flagellator' pleaded the case for a reduction in hours and in doing so described much of the lot of a prison warder:

> At this time, when all classes of employees are asking for a less number of hours
> for a day's work and when nine hours are being conceded nearly everywhere,

I would ask is the condition of the convict warder never to be improved? It is one that is little thought of or cared about by the public, for we are generally regarded by the masses with a sneering kind of contempt, instead of that regard which should be bestowed on us, if they would consider the dangers and responsibilities of the duties of our office. It may not be generally known what are the hours of a convict warder. I therefore append them in Chatham Prison from March 1 to Sept 30; every other day being what is termed the early night.

He then demonstrates his hours of shift working as: Three days from 5.15 a.m. to 6.45 p.m. or three days from 5.15 a.m. to 8 p.m., Sundays from 7.15 a.m. to 8 p.m. plus Reserve Guard duty once a fortnight from 7.45 p.m. to 5.30 a.m. He averaged the total of hours worked as ninety-six hours a week. 'Flagellator' continues:

I would ask sir if we have not legitimate grounds of complaint, when we see around us nearly all classes of employees being conceded fifty-two hours for a week's work and we still required to do ninety-six hours. I am a father, living about a mile from the prison and I assure you that I often do not see my children all the week, only in their bed. They are a-bed before I get home at night and I am away in the morning long before they are astir. My life I often compare to the life of an animal. I eat, sleep and work; time for recreation or mental improvement I have none. Before I entered this service I was fond of study and used to study a good deal; but now I cannot, for if I attempt to do anything in the way of mental improvement my overstretched brain refuses to be exercised and need it be wondered as when it has been kept in a state of tension for fifteen hours already?

By clause 8 of the abstract of rules for convict prisons, I am required to bear in mind that my duties are not only to give full effect of the sentence of the prisoner, by seeing that he is industrious at all times and conforms in all respects to the prison rules but I am also required to instil into the mind of the prisoner sound moral and religious principles. Preposterous notion! How can it be expected that I can do any such thing, when no time is allowed me to cultivate morality or religious principles myself, or to instil them into my own family, much less into the convict?

Again, there is instituted in the convict service a system of fines for offences committed by officers such as being three minutes late for duty of a morning, being seen to speak to each other – yclept gossiping, etc; inadvertently turning your back on a prisoner for a moment, termed endangering the safe custody of the prisoner – which fines we are told form a fund for the relief of officers and their families but I never heard of any officer or his family being assisted from that fund, which we know must, from the amount of fines monthly imposed, be of respectable proportions and if it be so, why do we not see a balance sheet at least once a year? … By the bye, I have just heard of an officer here, who removed from one part of the prison quarters to another, was fined for leaving nail holes in the wall where he had pictures hanging …

I have heard persons, who knew not what the life was, express an opinion that the situation of a convict warder was a good one; that he had no physical labour to perform and that his salary is good. An Assistant Warder commences at £51 per annum salary, £14 per annum ration allowance and £5 4s lodging money, if not in quarters. Not a bad salary certainly but it must not be divided by the number of hours or it is spoilt at once. What would a Manchester operative say if he was required to work ninety-six hours a week on such a wage. I fancy there would be a strike among them very soon. And, moreover his labour has something to interest him but ours is a wearisome employ from its very monotony. Day after day, for a weary round of months we take out the same prisoners to labour, watching them all day with the eye of a lynx; the same spot of ground and the same employ being ours for months.

Look at what we have been doing this past year excavating one of the basins in the Chatham Dockyard Extension Works. Those of the warders who have been employed there had all the year only mud beneath their feet and around them in all directions but brick walls. Why it is as much imprisonment to us as it is to the convict. I for one must admit that whenever I get a day's leave of absence and get into the open country, I feel like a schoolboy released and oh! with what reluctance do I go to the prison at 5am next morning.

Again, if an officer falls sick he is not allowed to remain at his own home and be nursed by his wife but must come into the prison infirmary, a place with as grim a prison aspect as any part of the prison, the windows darkened by stout iron bars and again by close wires. We are allowed by the authorities ten day's leave per annum but for every day in the infirmary the warder forfeits a day's leave, so that is about the worst crime an officer can commit – to fall sick. He is punished for it by being confined in a gloomy apartment, away from the society of wife and children – but, there, I suppose the prison warder is not expected to give way to any of the tender feelings of a man and his few days leave for that year forfeited.

I firmly believe that if those who ask for appointments as warders in our convict prisons knew what the place was before they came that not one half of them would ever apply. Many are the men who come and retire in a few days, disgusted with the service, and those who remain, an enormous percentage of them waste away before they complete the minimum time for a pension – ten years. And anyone passing ten years here is totally unfitted for anything afterwards. He is worn out – an old man while yet in the prime of his age. Surely it is possible to give us fewer hours of labour and more opportunities of recreation and mental improvement and this concession would result in a superior class of officer is the firm belief of FLAGELLATOR.

Reynolds News, 17 December 1871

Some warders were reprimanded or dismissed due to misdemeanours; most common was the corrupt warder who could be bribed for privileges such as tobacco or news of the prisoner's family from outside. Occasionally, a warder would go too far and find himself in court. One such case is that of Thomas James Fowler, a warder with fifteen years service behind him at Portland Prison, who appeared at Dorchester in September 1884 charged with trafficking:

> The accused being suspected of conveying money and tobacco into prison, a test letter, containing a marked sovereign was made up and posted for one of the convicts and shortly after, on being stopped by the police on the way to the prison, the money and letter were found in his possession. Prisoner, who is a married man with ten children, thereupon decamped but he was soon after arrested under a warrant ... Prisoner, who admitted the charge, pleaded hard for mercy on behalf of his family and invalid wife.
>
> *Birmingham Daily Post*, 15 September 1884

The Bench fined Fowler £25 and he was committed for three months hard labour. Needless to say he also lost his job.

The job of the warder was also beset with dangers. Prisoners could turn nasty; one sign of weakness or an unguarded moment in front of a hardened and violent convict who wished to enact revenge for perceived (or actual) unjust treatment could lead to an attack. Some prisoners became unbalanced or simply felt they could take no more and cared not what punishments would befall him or her and so set about a warder. Minor attacks and threatening behaviour turn up fairly frequently in prison records; less so more serious attacks, but they still occurred with enough regularity to feature in the local and even national newspapers across Britain once or twice a year.

Typical of these more serious attacks was the one committed upon Warder William Hansford by convict Henry Hindle at Armley Gaol in July 1890. Hindle had been reported and put on the punishment diet a number of times previously for breaches of discipline and idleness for failing to provide the weight of oakum allotted to his labours in the day. The warder who had reported Hindle was William Hansford. The day following Hindle's latest reported transgression, Hansford was on his rounds shortly after 6.30 a.m., serving out the oakum for the day's work. While he was adjusting the card on Hindle's cell door the warder heard two steps and suddenly felt a blow on his back. His legs immediately became useless and Hansford collapsed to the floor, a knife sticking out of his back. Hansford was lucky to escape with his life. Hindle was sent to the Yorkshire Summer Assizes, where he argued that he had been subject to the 'vindictive' attentions of Warder Hansford. The jury found Hindle guilty of the attack and he was sentenced to a further twelve months with hard labour. The judge added that although no grounds could be found to support Hindle's

The *Illustrated Police News* depiction of the knife attack upon Warder William Hansford by convict Henry Hindle at Armley Gaol in July 1890.

counter allegations, it was 'arranged that he should not again be placed under the same warder'.

Attacks were not just restricted to male convicts and warders. In November 1890 Wardress Alice Davis was going about her duties at Holloway Gaol when she asked prisoner Mary Callaghan (aka Callingham) (20) where the prisoners charged with cleaning the floor were. Callaghan used bad language and said she did not know and walked on. Davis asked if there was something the matter, perhaps something had upset her? What happened next was recorded at the hearing in Westminster Police Court:

… as I [Davis] was locking the gate she slipped behind me and struck me a violent blow with something [a broken feeding bottle] behind the right ear.'
The Magistrate, Mr Lewis, asked: 'Did the blow knock you down?'
Davis: 'No, sir. She then took me by the hair of the head and dashed me to the ground. I called for help and became insensible.'
Lewis: 'Did you feel other blows?'
Davis: 'No sir, I found I had injuries afterwards but I did not feel them inflicted. When I recovered consciousness I was bleeding very much from the wounds on the face. I was taken to hospital and remained as an in-patient for a month. Since then I have been on sick leave.'

Callaghan claimed she had been spoken to by Davis in a 'nasty sort of way' and had been goaded, pushed and had a door slammed in her face by Davis and she had been driven to a 'moment of temper' and 'forgot herself.' She was charged with assault and sent back to prison to await her appearance at the next assizes. Brought before the County of London Sessions, Callaghan was sentenced to a further five years penal servitude for the assault.

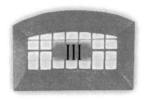

ADMITTING THE PRISONER

The procedures to be observed for the admission of prisoners were laid down in prison regulations from the early nineteenth century, standardised after the Prison Act of 1865 and incorporated in the *Rules and Standing Orders of the Prison Commissioners* from the 1870s.

When the 'Black Maria' arrived at the prison it would have been met by a senior officer and a reception officer (an experienced warder who had been selected for the supervision of the admittance of the prisoners). Their first duty was to ensure those being received were the people named on the commitment and that the convicted and unconvicted prisoners (those awaiting trial or on remand) were separated and kept apart from the moment they were received; these inmates could be identified from the other convicts because they were allowed to retain and wear their own clothes before trial.

'One Who has Endured It' recalled:

> The first thing on entering [Millbank Prison] each man was released from his handcuffs and told to seat himself on a long bench in the passage. Presently two chief warders, one a fine looking military man and the other a little man, arrived accompanied by a medical officer and a clerk. On their appearance we were told to rise and stand to 'attention', and the warders saluted their superiors in orthodox military style. The official party went into a cell, fitted up as an office [a Reception Room], and the examination and classification of the prisoners began. One of the warders walked along one line and good-humouredly at once claimed more than one of our party as old acquaintances. Asked their names, 'What name were you in last time?' was a question that called forth a laugh all round.
>
> *Five Years Penal Servitude* (1878)

A gaol delivery from the 'Black Maria', *c.* 1890.

The practice of lining up the prisoners by senior warders to see if they could recall the faces of old offenders was common. Sometimes a face might be familiar but the warder would not be able to place where they had seen the offender before. If this was the case an enquiry to that effect explaining the offence(s) upon which the prisoner was being held, often with a photograph and a description of their vital statistics and distinguishing marks, would be published in the national *Police Gazette* to see if the offender was known and possibly wanted elsewhere. Sometimes the police would think along the same lines but if the prisoner had been admitted to prison, finance would become a consideration and regulations stipulated clearly that 'Photographs supplied to the police *at their request* will be charged by the governor at cost price.'

The details from the official paperwork that had been sent with the prisoners stating their name, case, crime and sentence were entered long-hand into the Prison Record Book. As the prisoners waited, a warder would direct their attention to a large copy of the Prison Rules displayed on the wall and would read out the key rules covering the way prisoners were expected to behave, keep their cell and act towards the warders. The warder would explain that they would be expected to observe the timetable of the day, to work and attend schooling and chapel. He would also point out how good behaviour would earn a prisoner marks for privileges. The prisoners' attention would be particularly directed to the rules regarding breaches of discipline. The disciplinary offences listed on the Lincoln Castle Prison Regulations of 1866 are typical:

Weighing convicts, Millbank Prison, 1873.

The Gaoler shall have power to punish, with not more than three days close confinement, to be kept there upon bread and water for the following offences:

1. Disobedience of the regulations of the prison by any prisoner
2. Common assaults by one prisoner on another
3. Profane cursing and swearing by any prisoner
4. Indecent behaviour by any prisoner
5. Irreverent behaviour at chapel by any prisoner
6. Insulting or threatening language by any prisoner to any officer or prisoner
7. Absence from chapel without leave by any criminal prisoner
8. Idleness or negligence at work by any convicted prisoner
9. Wilful mismanagement of work by any convicted criminal prisoner

If a criminal prisoner is guilty of any other offence, or of repeated offences against prison discipline, the Visiting Justices may order the offender to be confined in a punishment cell, for, not exceeding one month; or, in the case of prisoners convicted of felony or sentenced to hard labour, by personal correction.

The prisoners would then be individually called and escorted into the Reception Room. They would be ordered to surrender all articles of personal property be they watch, wallet and money or collar and studs, even toiletries; they would all have to be handed over and a warder would enter them into the Property Book.

Next, the Prison Record Book – often simply referred to as a 'Prison Book' – would be opened with the clerk ready to transcribe the answers of the prisoner next to a series of standard questions. A prisoner would first be asked to confirm his name, age, place of birth, occupation, marital status, number of children and the religion he observed. They would then be measured and weighed in their ordinary clothes, without cap or shoes, and their weight entered in pounds in the prison record and reported to the medical officer. Prisoners would be weighed again twenty-four hours after admission and then on one of the last three days of every month by a hospital warder, who would record and report to the medical officer.

The details recorded in the Prison Book would also include descriptions of features such as complexion, hair, eyes and any distinguishing marks such as scars, birth marks, tattoos or deformities. Additional information such as further distinguishing marks about his body, and whether the man was circumcised or not, was often entered later by the clerk from the notes supplied after examination of the prisoner by the prison medical officer.

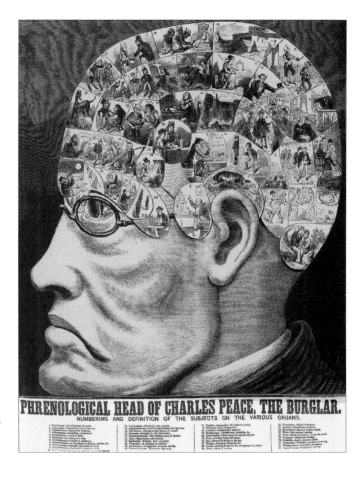

The phrenological head of Charles Peace, 1879.

Not every prisoner was compliant when it came to having his photograph taken.

From the 1870s, after the much vaunted theory of physiogmony expounded by Cesare Lombroso (appointed Professor of Forensic Medicine and Hygiene at Turin in 1878), British prisoners, particularly repeat or 'habitual' offenders, were scrutinised for physiognomic attributes or deformities, which could indicate a 'criminal type'. Lombroso also believed in the eugenics of inherited criminality. He argued that the *born criminal* could be distinguished by physical *atavistic stigmata* such as large jaws, forward-projecting jaws, low-sloping foreheads, high cheekbones, flattened or upturned noses, handle-shaped ears, hawk-like noses, fleshy lips, hard, shifty eyes, long arms and insensitivity to pain.

In 1882 French police officer and biometrics researcher Alphonse Bertillion demonstrated his criminal identification system of anthropometry. The system took measurements of the head and body, individual markings such as tattoos or scars, and considered some personality characteristics. These measurements were then made into a formula that would apply to only that person and would not change, meaning that if the convict was apprehended again in the future they could be easily identified. He used it in 1884 to identify 241 multiple offenders, and the system was rapidly adopted by both British and American police forces and special Bertillion system callipers and measures were issued to all convict prisons. The Penal Servitude Act and subsequent Prison Regulations stated the measurements to be taken included the length and breadth of the head, face and ears, the length of either foot, the fingers of either hand, the length of the cubit of the hand, span of the arms, the prisoner's height when standing and sitting and 'the size and relative position of every scar and distinctive mark upon any part of the body'.

The prisoner would then be photographed. The photographing of prisoners had been advocated by the recommendation of a House of Lords Select Committee as early as 1863 and became generally adopted by prisons across the country after the Prevention of Crime Act of 1871. Using the natural light in a prison yard, the prisoners would be taken outside and individually photographed. Sometimes these images show that a simple pale canvas background was used, others simply have a brick wall and on days when the light was proving difficult the subject would be moved to a position which may show the prison yard as a backdrop. These images show the prisoners in the clothes they were wearing at the time of their arrest and not only record the faces of prisoners but also form an invaluable archive for social historians recording the everyday working clothing worn by ordinary Victorian folk, many of them from the lowest orders – people who almost certainly would never have been able to have enough money for a studio photograph to be taken of them at the time. That said, many did not like having their photograph taken and pulled faces and even resorted to violence. Pictures of reluctant subjects sometimes show them held down by the strong hands of prison warders.

Despite being suggested from the 1880s, fingerprints were only taken and filed at Scotland Yard from 1901, thus the criminal detection service of Britain in the nineteenth century were without one of the greatest and most conclusive clues to the identity of a suspect.

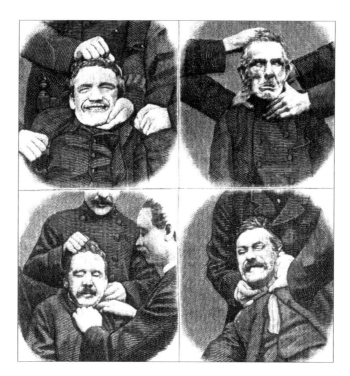

Some convicts struggled and had to be held in place for their photograph to be taken, while others attempted to hide their identity by pulling a face.

From the 1880s and up to the early years of the twentieth century convicts were mostly photographed showing both of their hands, fingers spread, raised to chest height. A chalk board stating the convict's name, prisoner number and the date the photograph was taken (usually the admission date) hung on the wall behind them. As fingerprints were not collected until 1901, the raised hands of the prisoners in the photographs would only provide clues for identification and elimination of suspects with distinctive hands, such as those that had tattoos or were deformed or had missing fingers. By the late nineteenth century most prisoner photographs were taken inside and consisted of a double portrait, one image showing the full face and the other their profile, taken on separate quarters of the same half plate-glass negative. It would then be developed as a contact print.

The Penal Servitude Act of 1891 stated that prisoners being photographed should:

> Be photographed either in the dress of the prison, or in the dress worn at the time of his arrest or trial, or in any other dress suitable to his or her ostensible position and occupation in life.

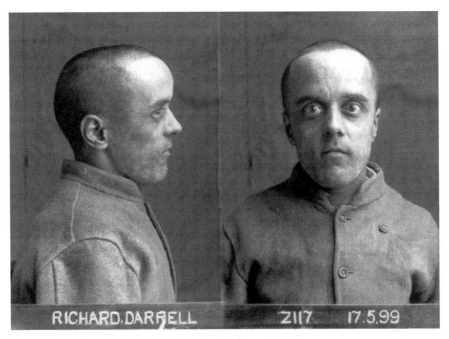

RICHARD.DARRELL   Z117   17.5.99

Convict and 'Broad Arrow Man' Richard Darrell, photographed in May 1899. By the late nineteenth century separate exposures of each half of the same photographic plate was the standard method of photographing criminals.

The name (i.e. the initials of the Christian name or names and surname) were suggested to be written on a strip of wood by the prisoner, but many convicts could not, or claimed they could not, write. Individual convicts writing their name on these boards often proved too much of an inconvenience and the photographer would simply write the name of the prisoner in printed characters, then the prisoner's number and the date on which the photograph was taken.

For many years the chairs used by the prisons for the photographing of prisoners were of the standard 'stick back' type used for seats in most prisons. From the late nineteenth century a special chair was introduced, often custom made in the prison:

> A special chair is required, the seat of which should be about 19 inches from the ground, and should measure 10 inches square, with an extra three quarter of an inch for the hollow of the back. It should have a raised edge at each side, and a triangular shaped rib fixed along the centre from before backwards. The back should rise quite vertically from the seat but may be hollowed out to the extent of three quarters of an inch and it should have a strong thick top rail, on the upper surface of which an arrow or mark should be cut from before backwards to indicate the centre, and to enable the photographer to see at a glance whether or not the seam down the centre of the back of the prisoner's coat corresponds with it and that he is sitting squarely to the camera.
>
> *Rules and Standing Orders for the Government of Local Prisons* (1902)

Once developed, the prisoner's photograph would then be affixed in the appropriate place upon his record in the Prison Record Book.

Once photographed, the prisoner is then sent to have a bath. Prison regulations were absolutely clear that all prisoners must have a bath upon admission (unless directed otherwise by the medical officer). There was a great diversity of bathing facilities from prison to prison, none gave much privacy. Some had brick-built affairs with lead linings, others a great bath with compartments above the water for perhaps four or five bathers at the same time, but then they would be followed by another four or five and then another batch depending on the number admitted in the prison delivery. Either way, you would probably end up bathing in the same water as at least four or five others, and at least one of the others probably had some verminous infestation or disease about his body; a number of old lags described such bath water as looking rather like mutton broth. Only in the late 1890s did the prison regulations state:

> The depth of the water in the bath will be at least nine inches and the temperature not less than from 95° to 97°. Carbolic soap, a small strong brush and clean towel will be issued to each prisoner … The Reception Officer will, in any case in which it appears necessary, make an examination of the prisoner after bathing, especially as to the state of his head and hair … if any prisoner is found

to have any contagious disease, or to be infested with vermin, means shall be taken effectually to eradicate and destroy the same.

'One Who has Endured It' recalled his experiences of the Millbank Prison bath house:

> I was ordered to go to the end of the passage, where the principal of the receiving ward was standing. I did not like his looks ... He ordered me to strip and go into a bath down some steps. I obeyed of course; in a very few minutes he called to me and threw me a towel, telling me to dry myself and come out. This, too, I did; and on reaching the top of the steps, leading from the bath, found my clothes has disappeared. There stood the principal however, who whisked the towel out of my hand and threw it away and told me to stand up, naked as I was. 'Turn round.' 'Lift both arms.' 'Lift the right leg.' 'Now the left.' 'Hold up the sole of the foot.' 'Now the other.' 'Now stoop.' 'Stand up.' 'Open your mouth.' 'Here take this bundle of clothes.'
>
> *Five Years Penal Servitude* (1878)

The object of the prison officer's examination was to make quite sure the prisoner had nothing hidden about himself, be it a comfort, trinket or anything liable to aid him to escape. The bundle of clothes was his prison uniform but he was told to simply wear his long shirt and carry the bundle along the corridor to another room. Here the bundle of clothes our prisoner had been wearing was shown to the prisoner and he would be asked, 'Do you identify these as your clothes?'

What happened next would vary from prison to prison. In some, if the clothes were presentable or redeemable they would be tagged and entered into the property book and, after a good wash and fumigation (clothes worn next to the skin would be treated with sulphur and oil for itch), they would be cleaned and mended accordingly and stored until the prisoner was released. If the clothes were so worn and verminous to be unsalvageable they would be destroyed and a 'liberty suit' of men's clothing 'suitable for a member of the labouring classes' would be provided at the expense of the government upon release. Because of the numbers involved, convict prisons tended not to store any prisoner's clothes but instead sold them to a dealer and the money went towards a 'liberty suit'.

The prisoner would then be ordered to proceed to the corridor of the reception ward where, dressed only in his shirt, he would wait to be summoned to the medical officer. While they waited, the prisoners remained under the supervision of the reception warders, batons in hand lest anyone 'played up' or became recalcitrant. Together with others from the prison delivery, they would stand with backs to the wall of the cold and draughty corridor awaiting their call to present themselves in the office of the medical officer (MO).

Female prisoners' own clothes store, Tothill Fields Prison, 1862.

The medical officer's main concern was that the prisoner brought in no contagious disease or infestation such as nits. He would make a note if the prisoner was on prescribed medication and if a prisoner was admitted with an abdominal belt or chest protector. It would be at the discretion of the medical officer if the prisoner was permitted to carry on wearing it. If a prisoner had been sentenced to hard labour it was up to the medical officer to ascertain if the prisoner possessed the physical fitness to undertake the task. Often the MO would ask questions of the prisoner but would not address any medical comment or diagnosis to him but instead would write it down (and, if required, make necessary arrangements) and then send the prisoner on to dress in his full prison uniform.

Prisons had a variety of colours for their convict uniforms. Some of them had jackets divided with two colours, such as chocolate brown and yellow or red and blue. One prisoner, writing under the *nom de plume* of 'Captain D-S-' in the 1880s, recalled:

Each man was dressed in a short, loose jacket and vest, and baggy knickerbockers of drab tweed with black stripes, one and a half inches broad. The lower part of their legs were encased in blue worsted stockings with bright red rings round them; low shoes and a bright grey and red worsted cap, which each man wore

Above left: The garb of a male convict serving sentence in the 'Separate System' at Pentonville (left) and a female convict from Millbank, 1862.

Above right: The veiled female convict serving sentence under the 'Separate System', Wandsworth, 1862.

in accordance to his own taste, completed the costume. One thing spoiled it. All over the whole clothing were hideous black impressions of the Broad Arrow, the 'crow's foot' denoting the articles belonged to Her Majesty.

Even the soles of the boots were studded in the shape of the broad arrow and were remarkably heavy; some boots in public works prisons could weigh as much as 14lbs (6kg). Many prisoners recalled when they first put them on they almost seemed to fasten them to the ground.

Prison uniform removed the last vestige of the prisoner's life outside the prison walls; the convict no longer had a name, just a number displayed in small metal numerals backed with calico upon the left breast of the uniform. He would, for the duration of his time within the prison walls, be addressed by that number, never by name. On his breast would be a larger round patch emblazoned with the wing, floor and cell number of the prisoner.

Prisoners were commonly referred to as 'Broad Arrow Men' from the latter half of the nineteenth century, an epithet gained from the distinctive broad arrow or 'crow's foot' stamped onto all prison uniforms. The origin of the symbol dates back to the seventeenth century, when a Master of the Ordnances in the Tower of London began marking the weaponry as Tower property with an arrow-like device from his coat of arms. Over the years this symbol has been adopted by all government departments to denote equipment as diverse as military uniforms and rifles to rulers and paperweights as Government Issue. The broad arrow was stamped onto prison garb to not only create a 'dress of shame' to be worn by convicts, but to make the clothes they wore so distinctive they would stand out as a convict if they affected an escape. Broad Arrows were discontinued on prison uniforms in 1922.

The women fared no better. Mrs Susan Willis Fletcher stated the garb of the female prisoners in Tothill Fields consisted of:

> … brown serge prison dress … with a not unbecoming white hat. The stockings are blue and red stripe, and very course. There is one flannel shirt, and a flannel under vest if the prisoner is wearing one at the time of admission; but there are no drawers (and this slight addition would prevent much suffering), a brown serge petticoat, skirt and jacket, and blue check handkerchief to wear under the jacket, and another for the pocket (very course and rough) and a white cotton cap.
>
> *Twelve Months in an English Prison* (1884)

After Mrs Florence Maybrick was sentenced to death (later commuted to life imprisonment) for poisoning her husband in September 1889, the *Illustrated Police News* gave an account of her surroundings and some of the things she would have seen when she entered the Female Convict Prison Woking, Surrey, including the various classes of female prisoner and the clothes they wore:

> Convicts doing the first nine months of their term are known as probationers and wear dark brown dresses. The next class wear dark green and those of the first class dark blue. The special class wear light-striped dresses. Convicts who have never been in prison before are also distinguished by a crimson star on the right arm. These are carefully kept apart from the habitual – one might also say hereditary – criminals, who are easily identified by their degraded, evil-looking countenances. The dejected and forlorn appearance of the better class of women is very saddening. Many of them had lived in comfortable circumstances but in an evil moment they have committed some hideous deed, at which their souls now revolt.

All prisons would divide their inmates into classes. As the Woking Prison account pointed out, there were dress codes that reflected the stage the prisoner was at in their sentence, identified repeat offenders and even helped prevent their fraternisation with the newly admitted, known as 'Star Class'. There were four stages established and regulated by which prisoners could demonstrate

Female convict attire and routine of the later nineteenth and early twentieth century are well illustrated in these depictions of the prison life of Mrs Osborne after the 'Pearl Case', where she was found guilty of both jewellery theft and perjury, 1892.

good behaviour and industry and thus earn marks to gain privileges and, of course, lose them for misconduct.

Prisoners in the First Stage would:

a) Be employed daily in strict separation on hard bodily or hard manual labour, for not more than ten hours or less than six hours, exclusive of meals
b) Sleep without a mattress for the first fourteen days
c) Earn no gratuity
d) Be allowed religious and educational books

A prisoner whose term of imprisonment was twenty-eight days or less would serve the whole time in the First Stage.

Once a prisoner had passed the First Stage they were, at the discretion of the governor, permitted to retain photographs and memorial cards from their immediate family in their cells.

Prisoners in the Second Stage would:

a) Be employed on labour of a less hard description, in association if practicable
b) Be able to earn a gratuity not exceeding 1s
c) Be allowed religious and educational books

d) Receive school instruction, if eligible under the rules made from time to time for the education of prisoners

e) Be allowed one library book each week

Prisoners in the Third Stage would:

a) Be employed on labour as in the second stage

b) Be able to earn a gratuity not exceeding 1s 6d

c) Be allowed two library books each week, besides religious and educational books

d) Receive school instruction, if eligible under the rules made from time to time for the education of prisoners

e) Be allowed to write a letter and receive a visit of twenty minutes on attaining this stage

Prisoners in the Fourth Stage would:

a) Be employed on labour as in the second stage

b) Be able to earn a gratuity not exceeding 2s in twenty-eight days and continue to earn gratuity at the same rate as long as he is in this stage, provided that the gratuity earned from the commencement of his sentence shall not exceed 10s

c) Be allowed two library books each week, besides religious and educational books

d) Receive school instruction, if eligible under the rules made from time to time for the education of prisoners

e) Be eligible for any special employment for which his services may be required

f) Be allowed to write a letter and receive a visit of thirty minutes duration

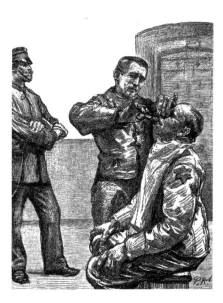

The regulation hair cut and facial hair trim at Wormwood Scrubs, 1889. Note that the convict being trimmed is a member of the 'Star Class'.

All male prisoners, regardless of infestation or not, would have their hair cropped to the scalp and whiskers and beard shaved off. In convict prisons women's hair was cut off to the nape of the neck, whereas in a number of county prisons discretion was applied and the women allowed to keep their hair unless the MO suggested otherwise. Hair would not be allowed to grow again until three months before the completion of sentence.

A baby 'at the breast' of a female prisoner could be admitted with its mother if such authority had been granted by the committing magistrate. No child could be taken from the mother until the prison MO certified it was in a fit condition for that to happen. A crib, cot or cradle was issued and the following articles of clothing provided for baby:

Binders, flannel
Boots (when necessary)
Flannels, head
Frocks, flannelette
Gowns, day, calico
Gowns, day, flannelette
Gowns, night
Hoods (when necessary)
Napkins
Petticoats, flannel
Pinafores
Shawls
Shirts, No.1
Shirts, No.2
Skirts flannelette
Socks

Babies under 6 months were fed one half to a full pint of sweetened milk daily. For those over 6 months one to four teaspoonfuls of Mellin's, Allen and Hanburys' or similar food daily and half a pint of beef tea three times a week. At 9 months the child would be assessed by the MO, who would report whether it was 'desirable or necessary' that the child be retained in prison. Only under exceptional circumstances would a child be kept in prison over the age of 12 months.

Before discharge, it was the duty of the prison governor to ascertain if there were any relative willing and able to take on the child. In the absence of a family home the child would be put into the care of the workhouse of the union in which the mother had been apprehended.

After the immediate admission procedure, the prisoner would be led along the corridors and walkways of the prison, and the sense of foreboding for the prisoner could become quite unbearable. First to hit the senses would be the smell of

Convict mothers exercise with their babies in the fresh air along the prescribed trackways of the exercise yard at Wormwood Scrubs, *c.* 1895.

the place, a strange blend of metallic aromas, natural fibre matting, carbolic soap or disinfectant and a hint of boiled meat and the sickly smell of the unwashed (the latter two are sometimes indistinguishable from each other). The sound of keys would echo in the lofty central hall and along the wing as the prisoner was walked smartly along, escorted by two warders. Each cell would be numbered above or to the side of the door. The exterior of the cell door was painted black, grey or green and was made of a frame and very solid uprights of thick wood punctuated by rivets whose edges had been made smooth and rounded by the many coats of paint received over the years.

Once the prisoner was inside and the door closed he would see that the cell side of the door was usually painted the same colour as the rest of the cell. The majority of the door was smooth, in contrast to its obverse, due to the lack of any doorknob or latch. In many instances a large metal plate covered the entire back of the door – there was to be no kicking through that metal plate. Indeed, the only features on this gaunt plain were the outline of a small trap, pulled open by the twist of a small handle that released a locking device from the outside that caused the trap to fall outwards, forming a platform towards the corridor; through this the prisoner's meals could be passed. About 2ft above the trap, in the centre of the door, was a bowl-like indentation akin to the shape of a human eye, but ten times larger. In the centre of this 'eye' was a 'pupil', plain and unseeing; it was the reverse side of a spy or peephole, which would come to life with a short

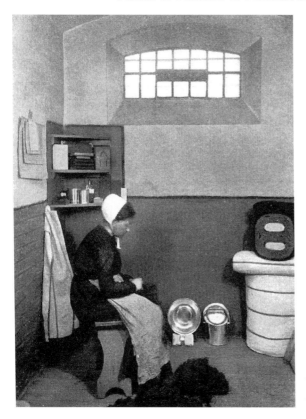

A female inmate picking
oakum in her cell at
Wormwood Scrubs, 1897.

and subtle metallic slide and the all-seeing human eye of a warder takes its place as he looks in while he patrols the corridor or takes a quick look to ensure all is well before he opens the door.

For many who had endured their first admission to prison with some stoicism and bravery, the moment of incarceration in the cell was literally the hardest step to take. Some would refuse to enter, struggling against the escorting warders crying and imploring, 'Don't put me in there.' The pleading would fall on deaf ears, as Mrs Maybrick found; 'the warder took me roughly by the shoulder, gave me a push and shut the door.' At the Female Convict Prison Woking, where she was held, the cells were described thus:

> Each cell measures about eight feet by five feet. The floor is of blue slate but in some cases, where the prisoners do not work in other rooms, the floors are of wood and the cells somewhat larger. An iron rod is attached to one end of the cell, to which are fastened the straps which at night are slung into a kind of hammock. Some of the cells have raised plank beds. There are three shelves in the corner of each cell. On one the blankets are neatly folded; on another is generally seen the Bible, prayer book and hymn book, with which each convict

is provided … In the corner next to the door of each cell is a small wooden flap, which serves as a table, from which the convict in dreamy solitude eats her meals. At night the gas penetrates through a small pane of thick glass suffusing the little chamber with a kind of 'dim religious light.'

In *Five Years of Penal Servitude*, 'One Who has Endured It' recalled his cell at Millbank:

On being locked in my cell, the first thing I did was to examine it well and its contents. Opposite to the door and on the floor was a raised wooden platform extending right across the cell. It was about 6 inches from the floor of stone flags. At one end of this platform was a step, about 4 inches higher and 12 inches deep. This platform I afterwards found was my bed-place, on which the straw mattress, now neatly rolled up, was laid and the step acted as bolster, on which I made a pillow of my clothes, no pillow being provided. On the top of the bed were very neatly rolled up … three blankets, a rug and two course linen sheets. A wooden platter and spoon, a wooden salt box, two tine pint-mugs, a bright pewter chamber utensil, an ordinary school slate, a large wooden bucket or pail, with wooden flat hoops and fitted with a close-fitting lid, a short-handled hair broom or brush, a stiff mill-board with a copy of the prison rules and regulations and a small gas-jet, without tap, protruding from the wall about 4ft from the ground … Table or stool there were none. The bucket, with its lid, performed several offices. It contained the water I washed in and which I could change twice a day. It formed my seat when at work and my table when I sat on the bed-place or platform and had my meals.

There was, however, one object that mystified our prisoner:

It was a thin lath of wood, three feet long, two and a half inches wide and a quarter of an inch thick. One half painted on both sides black and the other bright red. There were no spy or inspection holes in the door, but through the wall, alongside the door, was a loop-hole, similar to those usually seen in old castles for arrow slits and in fortified outworks for musketry firing. This slit was about two foot, six inches long and at the passage side three inches wide, extending through the thick brick wall in a radiating manner, till it formed an aperture two foot six inches wide. Anyone walking along the corridor could see at once the inmate of the cell and what he was doing and had a full view of him.

A tall, soldierly looking warder soon enters the cell:

In a racy Irish brogue he asked me if I was No. 20,001. This was the first time I had been addressed by my new numerical name and it sounded somewhat harshly to my ears. 'Now me man, see you have all the kit ye are entitled to,' said he, looking round at all my household goods. 'Bring that bucket and get some clane water.' I did so, taking the bucket to the sink and tap at the landing on top of the stairs in the round tower. 'Now bring them dirty sheets, and ye shall have clane ones.' I followed him, with the sheets of the last resident, to a cell at the centre of the ward, which he had fitted up as a store-room for the necessaries required by the men under his charge and their work. Here he gave me clean sheets, a clean towel with a piece of soap, a small horn comb and a little brush, like a nail brush, which he said was for my hair. The soap, he told me, was my allowance for a fortnight and that alternate Saturday I should have a similar piece. He also gave me rags and bath brick with which to keep my tin and pewter things bright and clean. This he told me to hang behind the door. He then came to my cell and showed me where everything was to be placed when not in use and how to roll up my bedding and fold up the blankets and sheets. He also explained the use of the mysterious red and black wand. When I wished to speak to a warder for any purpose, I was to put the red end from the inspection aperture to cause him to come to me. If a man wishes to see the governor, the doctor or the chaplain, he is to 'sport his broom', lay his little hair broom on the floor at the door directly the cell is opened in the morning. This is a signal for the warder to come to him and take down his requirements on a slate on which he makes up his morning's report.

In daylight hours the prisoner's cell would be lit by natural light from a small oblong or arched window made from many small panes of plate glass set in a sturdy frame with bars outside and situated high enough on the wall that the prisoner could not easily look out of it; he would have to stand on a stool, wooden bed or bucket to attempt to see out – but that was a punishable offence. Cell windows were seldom cleaned; when Oscar Wilde was imprisoned at Reading he found, 'Outside the day may be blue and gold but the light that creeps down through the thickly-muffled glass of the small iron-barred window beneath which one sits is grey … It is always twilight in one's cell, as it is always midnight in one's heart.'

DAILY ROUTINE

Newly admitted prisoners would need to rapidly understand the daily routine of the prison, especially the fact that specific amounts of time were allotted to specific tasks or requirements. Lateness or absences from work parties, chapel or school would result in reprimand and punishment.

In many prisons it was standard practice for prisoners to be confined to their cells for the first nine months of their sentence, only leaving it for a short period of exercise (if they were declared fit enough this would be on the treadmill, otherwise it was in the prison yard) and to attend chapel each day. Prison authorities in the mid-nineteenth century wanted to make life far from comfortable for the newly admitted; under the 1865 Prison Act prisoners were only to be provided with wooden guard beds with wooden pillows to sleep on for the first thirty days of their sentence. In *De Profundis*, Oscar Wilde draws upon his experiences as a prisoner at Reading Prison in 1897:

> With regard to the punishment of insomnia, it only exists in Chinese and in English prisons. In China it is inflicted by placing the prisoner in a small bamboo cage; in England by means of the plank bed. The object of the plank bed is to produce insomnia. There is no object in it and it invariably succeeds … It is a revolting and ignorant punishment.

In the mid-nineteenth century each day in prison would begin at 5.30 a.m., when the prison bell (hand bells rung by the warders or later a buzzer) would be sounded for the warders to assemble and the prisoners to rise (by the latter nineteenth century most prisons were rising with a 'warning bell' at 6.20 a.m. and a rising bell at 6.30 a.m.). For some, the arrival of the day was greeted with some relief; at Pentonville one prisoner recalled:

Searching a convict's cell before
he is locked up for the night at
Wormwood Scrubs, 1889.

… the horrible sensation of cold in the morning in those cheerless cells. It was
not so much the intensity of the cold, for probably the cold was not so intense,
as the abominable feeling of always waking cold and the hopeless and helpless
feeling that there was no prospect of going to sleep again, and no possible way
of getting warm till the bell rang and you were allowed to get up and put on
your clothes.

Once the prisoners were up and dressed, the cell doors would be opened and the
prisoners would do their 'slopping out' (emptying chamber pots) and attending
to their cell chores of rolling away their mattress, folding sheets and ensuring
their tinware 'brights' of chamber pot, plate and mug were properly cleaned and
burnished to a shine. All cells would be inspected to see that this had been done.

Personal hygiene was considered important in the Victorian prison, although
it does fall short of our modern standards. Prisoners were required to wash both
morning and evening and were expected to take a bath once every fortnight.
Shirts, socks and towels were washed once a week and trousers and jackets once
a month.

A typical day in a mid-nineteenth-century prison was recorded by Dr Luke
Roden, who visited Pentonville 'New Model Prison' (built 1841–2) and published a descriptive account of what he saw in the *Illuminated Magazine* in 1844:

5.30 a.m. The first bell is rung as a signal of preparation for the warders to assemble and the prisoners to rise.

6 a.m. Warders unlock and (in winter) light the gas, and deliver the prisoners their tools and utensils which had been removed for security from the prisoners when they had been locked up the previous night. At the same time two pump parties of sixteen prisoners march in file at intervals of five yards, are conducted to the pumps, where they remain an hour, one fourth of the number always resting alternately, so that the entire body only works three quarters of an hour. Other prisoners are turned out to clean the corridors distributed at intervals of ten yards, cleaning only one side of the corridors at a time, while the warders are placed in the best positions for commanding a complete inspection, and preventing communication. The cleaning is completed in an hour. During the whole of that hour the bedding, which had been unfolded and shaken at rising, is left open and exposed for the purpose of being aired.

7 a.m. All pump parties are withdrawn and the warders have breakfast. The senior warders taken charge of the prison and prepare their reports for the governor. The prisoners who had been employed cleaning the corridors, now roll hammocks, arrange their cells, and wash.

7.30 a.m. Principal warders have breakfast and the warders serve breakfast to the prisoners.

8 a.m. Pump parties turn out again. Exercise parties representing about half the prison population, moving in single file, at intervals of fifteen feet (officers were positioned along the line to prevent communication) proceed to their exercise yards for the duration of one hour.

8.05 a.m. Chapel bell rings and the other half of the inmates attend divine service in the chapel. Conducted in single file to the chapel, the prisoners are locked and bolted in separate cells, where everyone can see and be seen by the clergyman, but no prisoner can see another. The prisoners remove their caps, and hang up their brass numbers so as to be seen by the inspecting officers.

8.45 a.m. Chapel service over, the prisoners are signalled to leave their stalls by an ingenious contrivance. A large black board with two square holes in it, behind which are two discs, with letters and numbers – these being turned, present to the eyes of all, for example A, 5. The man thus designated rises, puts on his cap, draws the visor over his face, puts on his ticket, opens his door and marches out, and so in succession in each row. All prisoners are now returned to their cells and locked up.

9 a.m. All warders assemble for parade, are inspected by and present their reports to the governor or assistant governor. Immediately after this parade a new group of prisoners are set to the pumps.

10 a.m. One sixth of the inmates are returned to the chapel for school instruction. Another sixth are tutored in their cells by three assistant schoolmasters.

11 a.m. Pump and exercise parties are withdrawn and fresh ones sent out.

Noon. Prisoners at school are withdrawn, principal warders dine and the prisoners who attended schooling go for exercise.

1 p.m. Dinners for the prisoners are distributed. Warders then dine. All prisoners are returned to their cells. Governor and deputy governor make the daily
inspection, taking notes of any complaints and requisitions. Each is accompanied by a principal warder, who unlocks and afterwards proves the doors [tests
the door and lock]. After they have dined, the prisoners are at liberty to read or
write till two o'clock.

2 p.m. Warders return from their dinner and turn out the pump and exercise
parties, more lessons are given in the chapel and cells, the remainder of the
prisoners are employed in their respective trades.

3 p.m. Exercise and pump parties are exchanged.

4 p.m. All prisoners withdrawn to their cells.

4.30 p.m. Bell rings again for divine service. Those who were absent in the
morning attend this service and return to their cells at 5.15 p.m.

5.30 p.m. Suppers are delivered and warders ensure the inmates have sufficient
work to occupy them for the rest of the evening. Prisoners are counted and
cells are checked to be in proper order.

5.55 p.m. Signal is given for principal warders to make ready to go off duty.

8 p.m. Signal bell rings to cease work and sling hammocks. The ensuing hour is
spent as the prisoners please, reading or writing.

9 p.m. Lights in the cells are extinguished and open fires checked to be safe.
As the principal warder does his rounds he is followed by the warder responsible for each wing who then locks and proves all passage doors, locks and outlets,
ensuring all ladders are chained, all dangerous implements put away, and that
every portion of the prison is secure for the night.

10 p.m. Principal Warder surrenders charge of the prison to the First Warder for
the night and delivers the keys to the deputy governor and gives him a final
report of prisoners locked up and, having ensured all is right, he goes off duty.

10 p.m.–6 a.m. The night warders patrol the interior of the prison and pull the
strings of the watch-clocks every quarter of an hour.

5.30 a.m. The fourth watch rings the signal bell for warders to assemble and the
prisoners rise for another day.

In 1889 the Maybrick case saw some details of the daily routine of Woking
Women's Prison published in the *Illustrated Police News*:

First Class prisoners get better food than the others. At dinner at half past twelve
o'clock they get baked meat; those in the second class get three ounces of boiled
beef and three quarters of a pound of potatoes. At half past five First Class
prisoners get tea; the second have 'skilly' or gruel. For breakfast all have cocoa
and brown bread at half past seven and workers have a bread and cheese lunch.

At three o'clock the convicts are allowed to sit in groups of three and have a chat for an hour. One hour also is allotted to walking exercise, which in wet weather takes place under the colonnades.

There were no dining halls for prisoners; all meals, irrespective of class or gender, were taken in the cell. It was prepared and cooked in the prison kitchen and two trusted prisoners and a warder from each floor would carry up the big canteens of of food. It would be ladled out by the warder or by the 'trusties' under the close supervision of the warder into the prisoner's bowl, the prisoner would then dine alone. The dietary scale had always been a matter of concern since the first visits of prison reformer John Howard in the late eighteenth century. Up to 1815 prisoners had to pay for their keep and many had to rely upon having food brought in by relatives and friends, some prisons even had a license for the sale of beer. This example of a typical table of fees was that levied upon prisoners in Ely Gaol by direction of the Lord Bishop of Ely in 1794:

For the board of each prisoner when he diets with the Gaoler	4*s*
For room and bed furnished by the Gaoler per week:	
Straw Bedding	1*s*
Plank with bedding (otherwise you sleep on the floor)	1*s* 6*d*
For room and bed furnished by the Gaoler (an iron bed with sheets)	2*s*
Discharge fee to be paid by each Debtor	16*s* 8*d*
Gaoler's garnish to be paid by all arrivals	1*s* 4*d*

After 1815 prison food was paid for out of the local rates. This was not a popular move so magistrates had to be seen to keep the cost of the prisoner's food as low as possible actively pursue ways of saving money, and to ensure it was not better than the diet on offer to the poor on the outside. Dietaries clearly delineating what prisoners should be given at each meal were published from the 1820s, but this did not guarantee the quality of the food, nor was there much variety. Each prison worked on the standard staples of bread, cheese, gruel and suet. The Bedford County Gaol dietary scale from 1841 stated:

1. All prisoners who may be entitled by law to receive food from the County shall be provided with the following diet: Two lbs of bread, 2oz. of cheese and one onion per diem for four days in the week and 2lbs of bread, ¾ of suet puddings, three days a week.
2. For prisoners under sentence of confinement for terms not exceeding three months: Two lbs of bread, 2oz. of cheese, four days in the week, 2lbs of bread, 1 onion, three days in the week.
3. For prisoners whose term of imprisonment does not exceed six months: Two lbs. of bread, 2oz. of cheese, four days, 2lbs of bread, ¾lb of suet puddings, three days.

4. For prisoners whose term of imprisonment does not exceed twelve months: For the first six months as above, for the remaining term a pint of small beer three days in the week in addition.
5. For those prisoners who shall be for twelve months and upwards: For twelve months as above and after the twelve months an additional pint of beer per week.

After representation regarding the variable standards of prison food, legislation was passed in 1843 for a minimum standard of food in prisons across the country according to a standard dietary scale. In 1850 the scale was as follows:

CLASS 1
1st – convicted prisoners not sentenced to hard labour, whose period of confinement does not exceed seven days.

Breakfast – 1 pint of oatmeal gruel.
Dinner – 1lb of bread.
Supper – 1 pint of oatmeal gruel.

CLASS 2
1st – convicted prisoners for any term exceeding seven days and not exceeding twenty-one days.

Breakfast – 1 pint of oatmeal gruel, 6oz of bread.
Dinner – 12oz of bread.
Supper – 1 pint of oatmeal gruel, 6oz of bread.
Prisoners of this class employed at hard labour have an additional 1 pint of soup per week.

CLASS 3
1st – convicted prisoners employed at hard labour, for terms exceeding twenty-one days but not more than six weeks and convicted prisoners not employed at hard labour for terms exceeding twenty-one days but not more than four months.

2nd – convicted prisoners sentenced to hard labour but disqualified for it by natural infirmity.

3rd – convicted prisoners sentenced to hard labour, whose period of confinement exceeds fourteen days, and does not exceed six weeks.

4th – prisoners in close confinement for periods exceeding twenty-one days.

5th – Prisoners committed for trial or for further examination.

Breakfast – 1 pint of oatmeal gruel, 6oz of bread.

Dinner – four days in the week, 8oz of bread, 1lb of potatoes, or 2oz of cheese, if potatoes fail. Two days, 8oz of bread and 3oz of cooked meat (without bone). One day, 8oz of bread and 1 pint of soup.

Supper – 1 pint of oatmeal gruel, 6oz of bread.

Females to have 2oz less of bread at dinner.

CLASS 4

Convicted prisoners sentenced to hard labour, for terms exceeding six weeks, but not more than four months.

Breakfast – 1 pint of oatmeal gruel, 8oz of bread.

Dinner – three days in the week, 8oz of bread, 1lb of potatoes, or 2oz of cheese, if potatoes fail. Two days, 8oz of bread and 3 ounces of cooked meat (without bone) and half a pound of potatoes. Two days, 8oz of bread and 1 pint of soup.

Supper – 1 Pint of oatmeal gruel, 8oz of bread

Females to have 2oz less of bread at each meal.

CLASS 5

Convicted prisoners employed at hard labour for terms exceeding four calendar months.

Breakfast – 1 pint of oatmeal gruel, 10oz of bread (an option was also given for 1 pint of cocoa instead of oatmeal gruel three days a week).

Dinner – two days in the week, 11oz of bread, 1½lb of potatoes, or 3oz of cheese, when potatoes fail. Three days, 11oz of bread, 4oz of cooked meat (without bone) and ½lb of potatoes. Two days, 11oz of bread, 1 pint of soup, 1lb of potatoes.

Supper – 1 pint of oatmeal gruel, 8oz of bread.

Females had 2oz less of bread at breakfast and supper.

CLASS 6

Prisoners sentenced by court to solitary confinement.

Receive the ordinary diet of the respective class.

CLASS 7

Prisoners for examination before trial and misdemeanants of the First Division who do not maintain themselves.

Receive the same dietary as Class 4.

CLASS 8

Destitute Debtors.

Receive the same dietary as Class 4.

CLASS 9

Prisoners under punishment for prison offences for terms not exceeding three days and prisoners in close confinement for prison offences under the provision of the 42nd Section of the Gaol Act:

Breakfast – 1 pint of oatmeal gruel, 8oz of bread.
Dinner – 8oz of bread.
Supper – 1 pint of oatmeal gruel, 8oz of bread.
Females to have 2oz less of bread at each meal.

Prisoners were supposed to eat no better than the poorest outside the walls, nor better than those in the workhouse, indeed it was known for some local magistrates to appeal to reduce the quality of the diet from that recommended by the Home Office. The magistrates for Bedford County Gaol were a typical example, they appealed against the Home Office dietary scale of 1850 claiming that prisoners preferred the prison diet to that of the Union Workhouse and argued that this was no incentive to resist a life of crime.

The prison versus workhouse food disparity remained up to the twentieth century when 'incorrigibles', often of no fixed abode, would commit a minor crime to obtain a prison sentence for the winter rather than try to find work or go on the tramp, such as in the case of William Goshawk (36), who was brought before the East Suffolk Quarter Sessions in January 1907. He had been convicted at Stowmarket Magistrates for destroying a door and glass valued £5 5s – the property of the Guardians of Stow Union – and, as he had been previously convicted several times, he was sent to the Sessions to be dealt with as 'an incorrigible rogue'. When asked if he had anything to say, Goshawk replied, 'Well it's like this. To see the task of work in the union, I would rather be in prison, for the food is better there than it is in the workhouse.' The chairman said he was '… not disposed to accede to the prisoner's request and make his life too pleasant' but had no option than to hand him five calendar months imprisonment.

The Labours of the Day

In prisons across Britain some recurrent methods to employ prisoners, such as the treadwheel and oakum picking, can be found to the degree that they are almost generic to all, but a wide variety of other labours and industry also took place in prison workshops across the country.

Let us first trace some of the history of the man behind the most generic and arguably the most infamous of all the prison labour-intensive devises – the treadwheel. William Cubitt was born at Dilham in 1785. The family later moved to Southrepps, then to Bacton Wood Mill, near North Walsham, Norfolk. A self-taught but enormously skilled engineer, he patented what became the standard design for self-regulating windmill sails in 1807. He joined the principal iron-founding firm in Ipswich – Ransome & Son – in 1812; his remit was to develop their general engineering business and this he did mainly by designing and installing various iron bridges and supervising the first Ipswich gasworks.

In later years he went on to engineer canals such as the Norwich & Lowestoft Navigation and the Shropshire Union Canal and acted as consultant engineer to the South Eastern Railway. He was consultant engineer for the building of the Crystal Palace and for this work he received his knighthood. However, he will be best remembered for one of his earliest and most infamous inventions – the prison treadwheel.

The treadwheel came about from Cubitt's association with John Orridge, the forward-thinking Master of Bury Gaol. Orridge was just 24 years old when he took over the gaol in 1798, but he implemented a series of revolutionary measures which became an exemplary model for prisons across the country. Beginning with finding occupations to alleviate prisoner boredom, he did much to improve the security, general health and morals of his prisoners. When the new Bury Gaol was constructed and opened in December 1805, he argued in favour of Prison Reformer John Howard's recommendations in its design, as well as suggesting some of his own.

His most notable addition was a notional challenge he gave to Cubitt to design such a machine to occupy a number of prisoners at the same time. Installed in 1819, this devise allowed a line of prisoners to be kept occupied by treading a 'mill-wheel' of stairs which drove mill stones for grinding corn. Orridge wrote of it: 'The employment afforded by the mill has been found to produce the very best effects both on the health and morals of the prisoners, as well as inducing the habits of industry.'

Despite costing about £6,000, other prisons soon wanted their own treadwheels; some of the first to follow were at Brixton, Coldbath Fields (London), Aylesbury, Swaffham, Worcester and Liverpool. As he made more treadwheels, Cubitt refined his original design until his final model, which looked like an elongated mill wheel; each wheel contained twenty-four steps set eight inches apart, so the circumference of the cylinder was 16ft. The wheel, under the power of the convicts walking up its 'steps', revolved twice in a minute with a mechanism set to ring a bell on every thirtieth revolution to announce the spell of work was finished. Every man put to labour at the wheel worked fifteen quarter-hour sessions, climbing up to 18,000ft every day.

Some treadwheels had purposes and the motive power generated by the prisoners was used to grind corn (such as at Bedford New House of Correction) or pump water (as at Norwich Prison or Springfield Gaol, Chelmsford where there were eight treadwheels, each 5ft in diameter, of various lengths from 9½ft to 26ft). The number usually employed at this labour in the gaol was between 12 and

20 per treadwheel. There were also capstans to push around or pump for those unable to walk the treadmill. Both these devices were connected to pumps which supplied water for the use of prisoners and cleansed their sewers. However, most treadwheels drove nothing and the labour of the prisoners was to no avail.

One vivid first-hand account relates a prison visitors' view of the treadwheel in action:

> On the chocolate-coloured door are painted in white letters the two words 'Wheel-House'. As the governor's master key will open it, we will go in and see hard labour as it is.
>
> As the door opens, the dull grinding sound that we heard outside grows a little louder and clearer. The door closes behind us with the inevitable clash and click of the returning bolt. The 'house' is an apartment some thirty feet long and fifteen wide. On the left-hand side are the wheels …
>
> Each wheel is divided into compartments cutting off each prisoner from the other. The object of this is to prevent the prisoners from seeing and hearing each other, though I have heard from casual acquaintances who have 'been there' that conversation in a low voice pitched in a different key to that of 'the music of the wheel' is perfectly easy and intelligible and that newcomers who understand the trick can in a very short time send the latest news of the outside world all through the prison while climbing up the 'endless staircase'.
>
> At the farther end of the house from the door there is a gong fixed against the wall, and near this is a brass disc swung like the pendulum of a clock. Every

William Cubitt's treadwheel installed at Brixton House of Correction, 1821.

fifteen minutes this swings back and strikes the bell. Then you hear the officers in charge sing out something like this: 'A1, B1, C1, D1'.

And as each letter and number is called out a prisoner steps from the wheel on to the stilt-like steps behind his compartment, and goes thankfully to take his place on the seat, which at the same moment is vacated by another man, whose turn to take another climb has come. The regulations prescribe fifteen minutes on the wheel and five minutes off.

Not the least interesting feature of this depressing House of the Everlasting Stairs is the difference between the way in which the work is tackled by the old hands and the new ones. Just opposite to the gallery on which we were standing was a compartment occupied by a cleanly built young fellow of about 22; saving for the monotony of the exercise, the wheel apparently troubled him very little. As each step of the 'staircase' came under the edge of the wooden partition on which the handbars are fixed, his foot slipped up on to it and rested there with no apparent effort till it was time to move it up again.

On either side of him were men, pretty nearly twice his weight and a fourth as tall again, who were labouring at the same work in a style that made one's knees and thighs ache to look at them. They were making the mistake of putting their feet on too late. The result was that they were no sooner on them than they had to be off again, for the treadwheel has a way of its own with laggards. If the foot remains an instant too long on the step it moves away from under; so the foot slips off, and the next step scrapes the ankle and instep in no gentle fashion. The resulting attitude is undignified even for a felon, added to which the officer in charge generally has something pungently unpleasant to say on the subject.

The difference in the amount of labour done in the same time was very noticeable when the periods of rest came round. The young old-hand stepped down cool and calm, and looked about him with a smiling air of superiority; with the air, in short, of a man who knows his work, and can do it with the least possible effort. The new hands, possessing twice his strength, climbed bunglingly down, limped towards the seats of rest, and sat gasping and sweating, elbows on knees and head hanging forward between their hands, from which it follows that even on the treadwheel there is scope for practised skill and natural aptitude.

The problem with the treadwheel was that from its earliest deployment, it had been the subject of concern over the affect upon the bodies of the convicts put to labour upon it. John Stuart Mill penned an unsigned article described in his bibliography as 'An Article on the Atrocities of the Tread Wheel', which appeared in the *Globe & Traveller* in October 1823:

The tread-mill, the horrors of which … appear unequalled in the modern annals of legalised torture.

I inspected the men as they descended in rotation from the wheel, at the end of the quarter of an hour's task-work, and made room for fresh relays. Every one of them was perspiring – some in a dripping sweat. On asking them separately, and at a distance from each other, where was the chief stress of labour, they stated, in succession, and without the least variation, that they suffered great pain in the calf of the leg and in the ham; while most of them, though not all, complained of distress also in the instep. On examining the bottom of their shoes, it was manifest that the line of tread had not extended farther than from the extremity of the toes to about one-third of the bottom of the foot; for in several instances the shoes were new, and between this line and the heel altogether unsoiled – a fact, however, that was as obvious from the position of the foot while at work, as from the appearance of the shoe at rest. Several of the workers seemed to aim at supporting their weight by bringing the heel into action, the feet being twisted outwards; and on inquiring why this was not oftener accomplished, the reply was, that though they could gain a little in this way, it was with so painful a stress of the knees that they could only try it occasionally. The palms of their hands, in consequence of holding tight to the rail, were in every instance hardened, in many horny, in some blistered, and discharging water. The keeper, who accompanied us, admitted the truth of all these statements, and added that it was the ordinary result of the labour; and that use did not seem to render it less severe; for those who had been confined long appeared to suffer nearly or altogether as much as those who were new to the work.

Another concern about the treadwheel was the accidents that befell those operating it. Instances of prisoners falling off or getting limbs caught and horribly mutilated were common; some early accidents proved fatal. The wooden compartments to separate the convicts on the treadwheel were made in such a way that prisoners could not lean back to talk without risking observation by the warders or tumbling off the wheel so, if an exchange of words was to be attempted, it could only be done so by leaning forward towards the wheel; this was undoubtedly a very risky business, as William Burton Peeling found to his cost on 11 October 1823. He was stepping the wheel in Swaffham Gaol and began to snatch a few words with one of his neighbours but he got too involved in the conversation, forgot himself, and pushed his head too far forward and got it caught in the wheel. The rest of the prisoners had no idea what had happened and kept stepping. Peeling was drawn into the contraption and, before the alarm was raised and the wheel brought to a halt, Peeling had been crushed to death. Further concerns were raised after prisoners collapsed and died with exhaustion or succumbed to medical conditions such as heart attacks and collapsed lungs after stints on the wheel. Prison regulations were brought in for the prison medical officer to assess every prisoner to determine whether they

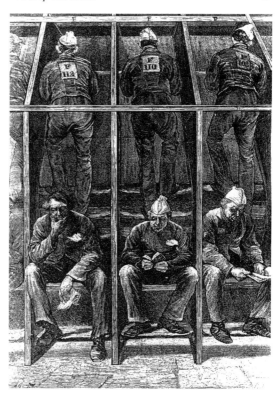

The treadwheel at Coldbath Fields, 1874.

were able to work on the treadwheel. Numerous inquests were still held after these regulations were introduced where the treadwheel was mentioned at the hearing but the death itself attributed to another reason (even though the causal factor may well have been the treadwheel). Consider, for example, the case of Arthur Simmonds, who was just 20 years old. In June 1888 he was serving a sentence of eighteen months with hard labour at Pentonville for stealing a letter. He spent three days working six hours (with the official breaks) on the treadwheel, and on the third night he complained that his feet were 'four or five times their ordinary weight' and he could hardly walk upstairs and could not eat his food. He was removed to hospital and died there a few days later. At the inquest the doctor suggested the cause of death as brain disease and the jury returned a verdict 'in accordance with the medical evidence'. Another incident involved 16-year-old Albert Trendall, who had been imprisoned at Coldbath Fields for six months in 1885 for an attempted break-in. He simply could not stand facing the wheel day after day and hanged himself from the gas bracket in his cell. A further case concerned the death of William Cooper in Norwich Prison. He had been working the treadmill when he fell ill and was sent to the medical officer; he was given medicine and sent back. Later, Cooper was observed lying on his cell floor; his condition was dismissed as a 'sulking fit' and he died there. The doctor was left with no option but to admit that 'the man's exertions caused his death'.

Although the prison authorities did not like to admit to the dangers of the treadwheel, there was growing pressure from influential reformers to eradicate them from British prisons. First to react had been the Scottish Prisons, where all such 'infernal contraptions' had been removed by the 1840s and replaced by crank labour. In 1895 there were thirty-nine treadwheels and twenty-nine cranks in use in prisons across Britain. Treadwheels used for non-productive purposes were abolished in 1899 and in 1901, when there were still thirteen treadwheels left, their use was prohibited entirely by Act of Parliament.

Shot drill was another hard labour task in both civilian and military prisons. A row of 32lb cannon shot would be laid out and evenly spaced in a line along the ground. The convicts would then form up in the rear of the shot and, upon a given signal, they stooped down and picked up the shot and then faced right or left as directed, marched three or four paces to where the next shot was and set it down again. At the next signal they took up the shot again, marched back and replaced them where they took it from. Much like the wheel, shot drill was pointless, soul-breaking and painful. Shot drill would be carried out for three hours at a time.

In *The Criminal Prisons of London* (1862) social researchers Henry Mayhew and John Binny recount their observations of shot drill at Coldbath Fields Prison:

> We first saw this drill-ground whilst making the round of the prison gardens. The ground had been strewn with cinders, which gave it the loose, black appearance of bog earth and surrounded as it was by the light-brown mould of the cabbage rows, it seemed like a patch of different material let into the soil, as though the land had been pieced and repaired like a beggar's coat. Along three sides of this square were as many rows of large cannon balls, placed at regular distances, and at the two ends were piled up pyramids of shot, those at the base being prevented from rolling out of their places by a frame of wood. It was difficult to tell whether the cannon balls so spaced out had been left after some game at bowls, or whether the spot had been cleared for action like the deck of a man-of-war, with the shot ready for the guns. We took up one of these balls to examine it, and were surprised at its weight; for, although not larger than a cocoa-nut, it required a considerable effort to lift it.
>
> The shot-drill takes place every day at a quarter-past three, and continues until half-past four. All prisoners sentenced to hard labour, and not specially excused by the surgeon, attend it; those in the prison who are exempted by the medical officer wear a yellow mark on the sleeve of their coat. Prisoners above 45 years of age are generally excused, for the exercise is of the severest nature, and none but the strongest can endure it. The number of prisoners drilled at one time is fifty-seven, and they generally consist of the young and hale.

The men are ranged so as to form three sides of a square, and stand three deep, each prisoner being three yards distant from his fellow. This equidistance gives them the appearance of chess-men set out on a board. All the faces are turned towards the warder, who occupies a stand in the centre of the open side of the square. The exercise consists in passing the shot, composing the pyramids at one end of the line, down the entire length of the ranks, one after another, until they have all been handed along the file of men, and piled up into similar pyramids at the other end of the line; and when that is done, the operation is reversed and the cannon balls passed back again. But what constitutes the chief labour of the drill is that every prisoner, at the word of command, has to bend down and carefully deposit the heavy shot in a particular place, and then, on another signal, to stoop a second time and raise it up. It is impossible to imagine anything more ingeniously useless than this form of hard labour.

The men, some with their coats and waistcoats off, and others with their sleeves tucked up to the shoulders, were hard at work when we got to the drill-ground. Before we reached the spot, we could hear the warder shouting like a serjeant to raw recruits, constantly repeating, 'One, Two—three, Four !' at the top of his voice; and each command was either followed by the tramping of many feet, or the dull, plump sound of some heavy weight falling to the ground. The men did their 'work' with the regularity of old soldiers, moving to and fro with great precision, and bending down with simultaneous suddenness.

'One!' shouted the officer on duty, and instantly all the men, stooping, took up their heavy shot. 'Two!' was scarcely uttered when the entire column advanced sideways, three yards, until each man had taken the place where his neighbour stood before. On hearing 'Three!' they every one bent down and placed the iron ball on the earth, and at 'Four!' they shifted back empty-handed to their original stations. Thus, a continual see-saw movement was kept up, the men now advancing sideways, and then returning to their former places, whilst the shot was carried from one spot to another, until it had travelled round the three sides of the square.

'Stand upright, and use both hands to put the shot down!' shouted the warder, staying for a moment his monotonous numerals. 'Pay attention to the word of command,' he added. 'Now, then, three!' and down ducked all the bodies; whereupon there came a succession of thumps from the falling shot, as if fifty paviors' rammers had descended at the same moment.

After a while the prisoners began to move more slowly, and pay less attention to the time, as if all the amusement of the performance had ceased, and it began to be irksome. One, a boy of 17, became more and more pink in the face, while his ears grew red. The warder was constantly shouting out, 'Move a little quicker, you boy, there!' The shot is about as heavy as a pail of water, and it struck us that so young a boy was no more fitted for such excessive labour than prisoners above the age of 45, who are excused.

The men grew hot, and breathed hard. Some, who at the beginning had been yellow as goose-skin, had bright spots appear, almost like dabs of rouge, on their prominent cheekbones. Now the warder had to keep on calling out either, 'Wait for the time, you men at the back,' or else, 'A little quicker, you in the second row.' Many began to drop their shot instead of putting it down carefully; but they were quickly discovered, and a reprimand of 'Stoop, and put the shot down, do you hear!' was the consequence.

When all were evidently very tired, a rest of a few seconds was allowed. Then the men pulled out their handkerchiefs and wiped their faces, others who had kept their waistcoats on, took them off, and passed their fingers round their shirt collars, as if the linen were clinging to the flesh, whilst the youth of 17 rubbed his shirt sleeve over his wet hair as a cat uses its paw when cleaning itself.

Before re-commencing, the warder harangued the troop 'Mind, men, when I say "One!" every man stoop and carry his shot to the right. Now, One! Two! Heels close together every time you take up and put down.' And the prisoners were off again, see-sawing backwards and forwards.

A warder near to us, with whom we conversed, said, 'It tries them worse taking up, because there's nothing to lay hold of, and the hands get hot and slippery with the perspiration, so that the ball is greasy like. The work makes the shoulders very stiff too.'

This exercise continues for an hour and a quarter. We counted the distance that each man walked over in the course of a minute, and found that he traversed the three yards' space fourteen times. According to this, he would have to walk altogether about one mile and three-quarters, picking up and putting down, at every alternate three yards, a weight of twenty-four pounds. It is not difficult to understand how exhausting and depressing such useless work must be.

Shot drill was finally banned in the Army prisons in April 1899 but can still be found being given as an occasional punishment into the early twentieth century, when it was stamped out after questions were asked in Parliament in 1902 after instances of shot drill were reportedly inflicted on prisoners in the military cells at Lichfield Prison, Staffordshire.

In the Public Works prisons of Chatham, Dartmoor, Portland and Portsmouth, the daily work of the prisoners was in stone quarries or on labour-intensive major construction projects such as the excavation of the 'great basins' on the Medway and the erection of new prison buildings; the stone for the New Scotland Yard building was hewn by convicts from the quarries at Portland and Dartmoor, as was the stone for Wormwood Scrubs Prison, whilst its bricks were made from clay on the site. Wormwood Scrubs was in fact built entirely by convict labour between 1875 and 1891, with carpenters, joiners and blacksmiths being found from among the prisoners at Millbank and Chatham. Over 7,000 prison-

In the quarries at Portland Prison, *c.* 1880.

ers assisted in the construction; they stayed in wooden barrack huts within the perimeter of the site, guarded by ex-soldier civilians armed with rifles. Only one prisoner escaped during the construction work.

Within the walls of both Public Works prisons and some state prisons the convicts were set to work in stone-breaking yards. They sat on stumps of wood or lumps of granite, wielding mallets and breaking iron stone into sizes suitable to mend roads with; a target of so many hundred weight would be set each day. The bodies of the convicts often became 'jarred' and stiff after a day at such labour, their shoulders painfully rounded, hands often blistered and in the cold weather they would be blighted by frostbite and chilblains. In the quarries and construction sites there were also accidents; convicts crushed by falls of granite or collapsed scaffolding, such deaths attributed, at least by the prisoners, to the ignorance of the warders appointed to superintend them.

Oakum picking was formally introduced to the working practices of convict prisons in 1840 and soon became the mainstay of convict work. It involved the prisoner being given a weighed amount of coir or, more commonly, old ships' rope or 'junk', cut into lengths which were often black with tar and deeply engrained with salt. After separating the rope into its corkscrewed coils, these would then be unrolled by sliding them back and forth on the knee with the palm of the hand until the meshes were loosened, the strands were then separated and cleaned of the salt and tar on them. The picked oakum, or 'stuff', was then sold on for use in caulking the seams in the sides and decks of wooden ships, as part of the materials to fill gaps in timber-framed buildings or for stuffing mattresses.

Mayhew and Binny described the oakum-picking shed in the Felon's Prison at Coldbath Fields Prison:

[The shed] had lately been built on so vast a plan that it has seats for nearly 500 men. This immense room is situated to the west of the main or old prison, close to the school-room. It is almost as long as one of the sheds seen at a railway terminus where spare carriages are kept, and seems to have been built after the same style of architecture, for it has a corrugated iron roof, stayed with thin rods, spanning the entire erection. We were told that the extreme length is 90 feet, but that does not convey so good a notion of distance to the mind as the fact of the wall being pierced with eight large chapel windows, and the roof with six skylights. Again, an attendant informed us that there were eleven rows of forms, but all that we could see was a closely-packed mass of heads and pink faces, moving to and fro in every variety of motion, as though the wind was blowing them about, and they were set on stalks instead of necks.

On the side fitted with windows the dark forms of the warden are seen, each perched up on a raised stool. The bright light shines on the faces of the criminals, and the officer keeps his eye rapidly moving in all directions, almost as if it went by clock-work, so as to see that no talking takes place. If a man rest over his work for a moment and raise his head, he sees, hung up on the white walls before him, placards on which texts are printed. One is to the effect that 'IT IS GOOD FOR A MAN THAT HE BEAR THE YOKE IN HIS YOUTH;' another tells the prisoners that 'GODLINESS WITH CONTENTMENT IS A GREAT GAIN;' whilst a third counsels each of them to 'GO TO THE ANT, THOU SLUGGARD, CONSIDER HER WAYS AND BE WISE' ... The quantity of *oakum* each man has to pick varies according to whether he be condemned to hard labour or not. In the former case the weight is never less than three, and sometimes as much as six, pounds; for the quantity given out depends upon the quality of the old rope or junk, i.e. according as it is more or less tightly twisted. The men not at hard labour have only two pounds' weight of junk served out to them.

Each picker has by his side his weighed quantity of old rope, cut into lengths about equal to that of a hoop-stick. Some of the pieces are white and sodden-looking as a washerwoman's hands, whilst others are hard and black with the tar upon them. The prisoner takes up a length of junk and untwists it, and when he has separated it into so many corkscrew strands, he further unrolls them by sliding them backwards and forwards on his knee with the palm of his hand, until the meshes are loosened.

The oakum shed, complete with religious notices, at Coldbath Fields, 1874.

Then the strand is further unravelled by placing it in the bend of a hook fastened to the knees, and sawing it smartly to and fro, which soon removes the tar and grates the fibres apart. In this condition, all that remains to be done is to loosen the hemp by pulling it out like cotton wool, when the process is completed.

By the rays of sun-light shining through the window, you can see that the place is full of dust; for the bright rays are sharply defined as those stream-ing through a cathedral window. The shoulders of the men, too, are covered with the brown dust almost as thickly as the shirt-front of a snuff-taker. A pris-oner with a bright tin water-can is going the round, handing up drink to the workers, who gulp it down as if choked.

'You're getting too close together on that back seat,' presently a warder shouts to some men on a form against the wall, and who instantly separate, till they are spaced out like tumblers on a shelf.

We left the building for a time, and when we returned, we found a man lying on the stone floor with a bundle of picked *oakum* supporting his head, and a warder unbuttoning his shirt and loosening his waistcoat; he was in an epileptic fit. His face had turned a bright crimson with the blood flow to the head, so that the clenched teeth between his parted lips seemed as white as a sweep's. The other prisoners went on working as though it were no business of theirs. After a few minutes a thrill ran down the limbs of the prostrate man, he began to draw in his extended arms, his tightly closed hands opened, and the eyelids quivered. 'How do you feel now, my man?' asked the warder; but the only answer was a deep-drawn breath, like that of a person going into cold water. 'We often have

Above left: A convict burnishing handcuffs in the chain room at Wormwood Scrubs, 1889.

Above right: A convict at work in his cell sewing a bag at Wormwood Scrubs, 1889.

such cases,' said the officer to us. 'After letting them lie down for half an hour they are all right again, and go back to their oakum as well as ever.'

As the day advanced, the pieces of old rope by the prisoners' sides disappeared bit by bit, and in their place the mound of treacle-brown oakum at their feet grew from the size of a scratch wig to that of a large pumpkin. At length the men had all completed their tasks, and sat each holding on his knees his immense tar-coloured ball, waiting to take his turn to go to the scales and have his pickings weighed. Then the silence of the room, which has all along been like that of a sick chamber, is suddenly broken by the warder calling out, 'The first three men!' The voice seems so loud, that it startles one like a scream in the night-time. Three gray forms rise up obediently as shepherds' dogs, and, carrying their bundles before them, advance to the weighing-machine. Now the stillness is broken by the shuffling of feet, and the pushing of forms, as prisoner after prisoner obeys the command to give in his oakum.

Two officers stand beside the weighing-machine, and a third, with a big basket before him, receives the roll as soon as it has been passed as correct. If a prisoner's oakum is found to be light, he is reported and punished; many, we were told, are wont to get rid of their junk, and so ease their labour by perhaps a pound.

'This won't do,' says the warder, pointing to the puffy hemp in the scales; 'it's half a pound short.'

'It's all I had, sir,' answers the man. 'Ask them as was next me if I haven't picked every bit.'

'Report him!' is the warder's answer; and his brother officer writes down the number of the culprit in a book.

When the men had fallen into line, and been marched off to their different yards, we inquired of one of the warders if oakum-picking was a laborious task. 'Not to the old hand,' was the answer. 'We've men here that will have done their three or four pounds a couple of hours before some of the fresh prisoners will have done a pound. They learn the knack of it, and make haste to finish, so as to be able to read; but to the new arrivals it's hard work enough; for most thieves' hands are soft, and the hard rope cuts and blisters their fingers, so that until the skin hardens, it's very painful.'

The quantity of rope picked into oakum at Coldbath Fields prison would average, says the governor, three and a half tons per week, which, at the present price of £5 the ton, would produce the sum of £17 10s.

The Criminal Prisons of London and Scenes of Prison Life (1862)

When working in the solitary cells no tools were allowed; the entire process was worked by hand. Men, women and children convicts all picked oakum. It was very hard on the fingers; rope cuts were common as were blisters, which proved very painful until the skin on the hands hardened to the work. Some prisoners managed to find a cheat to help their picking in solitary cells. 'It was a regular dodge,' declared one prisoner, 'for any man who had managed to get a nail ... to slip it between the slits of his ventilator before he leaves the prison, and the first thing an 'old hand' does when he is placed in the cell he is to occupy is to open the ventilator and push a strand of oakum through the right-hand slit of it, and twist it about until he has ascertained whether the oakum nail is there or not.' Once the secrets of successful picking had been unravelled, with or without the assistance of the nail, there was even 'a kind of pleasure to be derived from the work. When it is the right kind of junk and you give it the right kind of twist, and beat it properly on your boot sole, the fibres come apart like floss silk, and there is something fascinating about seeing the little heap growing in front of you until, by the time you have finished your task of 3lbs, it is a veritable mountain.'

Prisoners were expected to produce between 3 and 4lbs of picked oakum every two hours; shifts of oakum picking could last up to twelve hours. At Tothill Fields Prison in London the boys (all under 17) could earn up to 17s a year for their oakum pickings – literally money for old rope! Oakum picking remained a mainstay of prisoner occupation until 1895, when official recommendations were put forward to discontinue picking oakum.

Oakum picking by female convicts had begun to be phased out by the late 1880s. In 1889 the Female Convict Prison Woking, Surrey employed its inmates for the greater part of the day in twine making, a ton of twine (9,000 balls) being supplied to the General Post Office by the prison each week. Others were engaged in tailoring a great amount of uniform clothing, such as that of the Royal Naval School, Greenwich. A quantity of mosaic work was also turned out but when the demand tailed off it was phased out. The rest of the female inmates worked in the kitchens, in the garden, or washing and ironing. Female convicts in all prisons ceased to pick oakum by November 1896 but the process did linger on for men into the twentieth century, when the task was reduced from 3 to 2½ pounds every two hours, with an allowance according to the condition of the junk. Still, the prisoners did not like the task and according to figures quoted in a parliamentary debate in December 1912 there had been 11,555 punishments for idleness at oakum picking. Alternative forms of cell-work had to be found, hence sewing, stitching coal sacks, mail bags and Union Flags for the government and military, making herring nets, knitting stockings and mat-making became the predominant daily occupations of prisoners by the early twentieth century.

Once the labours of the day had been concluded the convicts were locked away and left to sleep or contemplate the walls and inky darkness and solitude of the night. Michael Davitt wrote of this time in his cell at Millbank Prison in the 1870s:

Westminster Tower clock is not far distant from the penitentiary, so that its every stroke is as distinctly heard in each cell as if it were situated in one of the prison yards. At each quarter of an hour, day and night, it chimes a bar of the 'Old Hundredth,' and those solemn tones strike on the ears of the lonely listeners like the voice of some monster singing the funeral dirge of time.

Oft in the lonely watches of the night has it reminded me of the number of strokes I was doomed to listen to and of how slowly those minutes were creeping along! The weird chant of Westminster clock will ever haunt my memory, and recall that period of my imprisonment when I first had to implore Divine Providence to preserve my reason and save me from the madness which seemed inevitable, through mental and corporal tortures combined.

The Prison Life of Michael Davitt (1886)

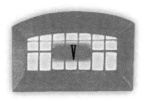

THE COUNTY PRISON

Most of Great Britain's prisoners during the age of Queen Victorian were low-grade felons; a casual glance through any county gaol book reveals such crimes as poaching, petty thefts, affray and vagrancy made the regular fare of prisoners, most of them serving sentences of one calendar month or less. In this account, G. Rayleigh Vicars relates what he saw on a visit to an English County Prison in the late nineteenth century:

Many a tramp, alone, or handcuffed to a gentleman of similar occupation, may be seen on his way to the fulfilment of his destiny in the county gaol. Day by day and week by week, file by, in motley groups, all sorts and conditions of vagrants, the itinerant vendor of notepaper, the men with combs for sale – a numerous fraternity these – the male and female couple, the lady, usually picked up on the road somewhere and dropped again to find a fresh partner if the sentences allotted to them by the judge do not coincide in length of time, and lastly, the drunken whining vagrant, who seems always starving, yet always more or less tipsy. Then there are the gentlemen of the road, too proud to be seen walking with a common policeman, who require nothing less than a spring cart to be driven in to the mansion always ready to entertain them, and provide them with creature comforts in the shape of a bath, the skill and attention of a hairdresser and the delicate enquiries of the prison surgeon with a view to the invigorating delights of the tread-wheel, or the philosophic meditations of human life generally, aroused by the picking of a few pounds of oakum.

On ringing the gate bell of the prison, a small door, with a grating, is opened and the gate porter looks at your pass, if you have one, or inquires the nature of your visit. In the gate-lodge on the left as you go in, dwells the janitor of the gate, a methodical official, who always enters the name of everyone passing through, and refers to the exact minute of the same by the aid of his clock. In front are glass-covered doors, which open into the official portion of the building and on passing through these, you will find yourself in a corridor, with various offices on either side and at the end of this passage, a pair of iron gates, leading into the prison proper. All prisons are constructed now so that to get into the cell portion of the establishment, three sets of doors or gates must be traversed.

Pass through the iron gates, and you are in the large hall, on all sides of which, above and below, you will see rows of cells, and tiers of landings. How silence reigns here! Scarcely a sound, save an occasional slamming of doors or rattle of iron gates. If it is dinner-time, there must be some hundred men or more in the cells, but without an inspection by means of the small hole in each cell door, you would scarcely believe that the cells were tenanted, so subdued and orderly everything seems. On the door of each cell are placed various cards, affording information to the prison staff as to the stage to which the prisoner belongs and his conduct, for inside gaols there are good and badly behaved men, the former largely predominating, and upon personal observance of prison rules rests, to a great extent, the individual comfort of the prisoner.

Inside a cell, the plank-bed, bed clothes, towel, and other requisites of prison life have to be kept arranged in order, or the question of dietary restrictions may be unpleasantly prominent in the meals of the prisoner. Here and there, if work is to the front, may be seen men scrubbing the floors, brushing, dusting, or making themselves generally useful, clothed in a drab suit, or sombre appearance, though not honoured with knee breeches, such as penal servitude prisoners affect.

On your right, as you enter one large room, you notice a row of wooden partitions, and behind these a structure like a huge water wheel, and, above you, a further landing also provided with partitions and a further display of wheel. The partitions are for the men working the tread-wheel; they hold on to a bar for support, and the wheel grinds the corn for the bread they eat, thus combining labour with utility. Forty men will easily turn this heavy apparatus by their individual weight; all stamping and treading done forcibly is unnecessary, the lifting of the body step by step sufficing to turn the wheel round. A certain reverend gentleman, a magistrate of the county of Lincoln, considering the wheel to be a very trifling form of labour, mounted the same, and, being unable to get off, was compelled to complete the prescribed period of revolution, from which little pleasantry he retired extremely exhausted, having emphatically refuted his own theories by a little wholesome practical illustration. Doubtless, this reverend gentleman did more than merely lift the body step by step and so experienced considerable inconvenience from this laudable enthusiasm; he could however easily have got off the wheel if he had but tried, as there is no obstacle to prevent any prisoner from so doing, beyond the inconvenience of a small difference with the warder in charge, resulting possibly in an interview with the governor next day and a reference to the nature of the dietary enjoyed by the prisoner.

In the interview or visiting room prisoners, at stated times, are allowed to see, but not to touch, or even come near their friends. There are two sets of bars, parallel and separated some ten feet or so at the far side of which stands the prisoner, the warder in the centre, the visitor at the further side, so that there is the official always between the prisoner and his guest, to prevent stray contraband articles from being handed to the prisoner: in some prisons there is also wire netting over the top of the room enclosing the bars, to prevent anything being thrown over by the visitor.

Now for the chapel, reached by ascending some stairs. One is struck by the remarkable cheerfulness of this building, with its open benches for the prisoners, and the governor's pew, which almost reminds one of the Royal Box at the Albert Hall, reared aloft to command good view of all the men.

Then, leaving the chapel, we proceed to an institution fortunately less often in use, the scaffold. Standing in the prison yard, one gets a view of the shed, which is some height from the ground and is a permanent erection, after the type of the Newgate shed; a lever (resembling a railway-signal hand-lever) projects from the floor of the scaffold; this the executioner pulls and the two boards, constituting the floor of the scaffold, separate and the culprit drops down into the space beneath the long drop. Sandbags are placed against each board, to obviate the wooden resonance of the same, as they fall away from each other ... Then there is a room in which are kept the cat-o'-nine-tails, various kinds of irons and a birch rod or two. The cat (not the prison cat with one tail, for we have seen him more than once) has nine cords attached thereto, without knots, the amount of physical pain resulting from an intimate union between the lashes and the prisoner's back varying according to the skill with which the same is handled. I remember one convict prison governor saying to me, 'I have one or two men who *can* flog,' Three dozen strokes is a very usual allowance in necessary cases; at many prisons the thirty-six lashes are divided between three warders, each taking, or rather giving, a dozen. The prisoner is flogged in nearly all cases for an assault committed in prison on a warder of fellow prisoner, or a flogging may have been imposed as part of the sentence, for instance, in cases of highway robbery with violence, garrotters and such cowardly criminals. The cat is also used when general misconduct has been of frequent occurrence – usually a penal servitude prisoner, who has become reckless, for it would not answer the purpose of a man undergoing a hard labour sentence of a two years maximum to be insubordinate for long; it would be hardly worth his while to make himself miserable, and to gain nothing but a sore back and meagre diet and perhaps leg irons for six months. The birch rod is chiefly used for boys under special sentences, but not entirely, as we find it used in convict prisons when the cat fails. Many men dread the birch more than the lash, as savouring of degradation. It may be a fine thing and something to boast of on release, that the cat had been used, but few criminals would care to parade that they had been birched like a schoolboy. The one, in the obscure light of criminal reasoning, may be heroic, the other is humiliating.

In the baking and cooking departments, one has an illustration of trade work inside a prison. In large convict prisons, many industries find representatives, but in county gaols we do not expect to get much useful labour out of men, the majority of whose sentences are very short. Bearing in mind the fact that vagrants form the staple supply of county prisons, the duration of their incarceration will not permit of much trade work. What can a man under a seven or fourteen days sentence be expected to learn? If you can make him grind the flour for his bread, keep his cell and the landings near to him clean, wash and scrub about, then you have done as much as can be expected under the circumstances.

Everything inside a prison must be done by them as a matter of economy; hence there is always plenty of work for prisoners, leaving the treadmill out of consideration. A prison is very much like a first class steamer, every part of it must be kept scrupulously clean, and if a vagrant after fourteen days hard labour does not know the meaning of the word 'cleanliness', then I do not think that he ever will.

Escapes from county gaols are very rare, the sentences scarcely justifying the risks run; it is the man under sentence of ten or fifteen years who will do anything, if desperate, to regain his freedom. In nine cases out of ten, however, the man is soon retaken and as a result, loses all his prison privileges. If a convict is suspected of harbouring designs of escape, he has to put his clothes outside his cell every night, a somewhat ingenious prevention.

It might at first sight be thought that the top of a prison was the safest place in which to lodge 'a long sentence' or desperate man. The experienced official thinks otherwise and places such men on the ground floor so that the night watchman can locate any sounds coming from a cell which might, evidently, be more accessible than if it were fifty feet above him. An ingenious escape happened at Millbank; a convict managed to get up a chimney and after thoroughly smearing himself with soot, played the part of the honest chimney sweep, marching off and sauntering past Scotland Yard quite unnoticed. He changed his clothes at the house of a friend but eventually was captured near Euston Station by an interfering detective, who happened to observe certain injuries caused by his escape and landed him safely home again.

Returning to the corridor containing the offices, we look in at the room occupied by the clerk's department of the prison and notice the book containing hundreds of photographs (the faces and hands of convicted prisoners).

This paper would be perhaps incomplete without allusion to malingering. Some prisoners will do anything, suffer almost anything, to evade labour, the great medium being illness, generally of a tragic nature, such as epileptic seizures (by chewing a piece of soap a plausible foam may be produced),

Lincoln Castle Prison, a typical nineteenth-century county prison.

bleeding from the nose, spitting blood and so on. A prisoner of whom I know something ingeniously inserted small pieces of wood in his nose, the necessary haemorrhage ensuing, which staved off the dreaded tread-wheel for a time until the acuteness of the officials concerned obtained the mastery of the secret. Anything rather than work; it was so outside the prison walls and it is so when inside the same.

In recording his thanks to those who assisted with the article, Rayleigh Vicars acknowledges the assistance of Sir Edmund Du Cane, Surveyor General of Prisons; Captain Eardley Wilmot, the governor of Lincoln Prison; and 'two gentlemen connected with the same prison, who assisted me on a special visit and to whose aid the graceful combination of birch rods, cat-o'-nine-tails and other prison comforts are due.'

THE CONVICT PRISON

Our nation's convict prisons held those found guilty of serious offences that carried sentences of six calendar months or more. Rather than the short, sharp, shock treatment meted out in the county prisons, the emphasis of the convict prison was more towards the reform of the prisoner – to break his criminal will and to look to himself in shame and regret of his crime. The most infamous of the convict prisons outside London was Dartmoor and in this chapter we are fortunate to have two accounts of this desolate and windswept place so often surrounded by leaden skies. The latter relates a convict's first-hand experiences of life behind bars at Dartmoor, but we begin with an account by one who was at liberty to leave of his own free will. Written by an un-named author, the following recounts 'A Visit to Dartmoor Prison' published in the *Leisure Hour*, March 1855:

> This great government receptacle for prisoners under sentence of transportation stands, with its neighbourhood of barracks and small houses by the same name of 'Prince-town,' amidst the wild heath scenery which is peculiar to many parts of the great waste called Dartmoor, in the county of Devonshire. A ride from Plymouth, of some sixteen miles in length, in the right direction, concerning which sundry guide posts are very eloquent and explicit, will bring the visitor to the dismal and dreary spot in which the prison, with an evident eye to the advantages of association, is suitably situated … With the exception of the inhabited and cultivated ground immediately around the prison, a hilly wilderness presents itself to the eye of the observer in every direction. A succession of the sterile, granite-strewn heights, yielding at best but very scanty herbage for a few straggling flocks of melancholy and unsociable looking sheep, stretch away in undulating lines on all sides, until the horizon bounds and completes the view. No tree or hedgerow diversifies, no human habitation enlivens the scene; unless, indeed we accept an occasional moor-man's hut, which adds, if

possible, to the wretchedness of the locality by the meanness and misery of its
appearance. All is gloomy and forbidding enough on fine days, which in this
elevated, cloud invested, boggy spot are indeed 'few and far between'; but on a
dull and rainy day, such as it was on the occasion of our visit, the place seemed
the chosen abode of dreariness and desolation. As we gazed that morning on
the lowering sky and the dismal landscape, and thought how well adapted the
situation was for punitory purposes, the official who accompanied us said, as if
a thing to be proud of, 'We never see a sparrow here sir!' and our admiration
of the sagacity and good sense of the knowing little bird referred to rose and
increased exceedingly.

The prison, which was originally erected for the reception of prisoners of
war, consists of a series of large buildings, built of great blocks of stone and radiating from a common centre. A stone wall about twenty feet high encircles the
whole establishment and encloses, as may be supposed, a considerable area. Four
of the great buildings to which we have averted are occupied by prisoners and
are called 'Nos. 1, 2, 3 and 4 prisons.' The others are used for various industrial
and useful purposes.

On entering the outer gate of the prison – over which is engraven a Latin
inscription, bespeaking mercy and compassion for the fallen – plain looking
houses, the residences of the governor, the deputy- governor, the steward and
other officials, stand to the right and left and a stone-paved roadway leads down
to the central building, which is divided and subdivided into offices, mess-
rooms and dormitories for the warders. This edifice, on the whole plain and
unpretending, has its gate, its porters lodge, its clock and its bell tower sur-
mounted by a weather cock, made apparently of gilded tin, and twisted in the
form of a crown, which certainly swings and turns and creaks as if it felt proud
of holding a government situation and none of the lowest either.

'We will first go to No.1 prison,' said, or rather soliloquised, our conductor
– a fine, elderly prison warder, with a stick in his hand and a gold-laced cap on
his head; smart, erect and evidently an old soldier; so forthwith, we turned to
the right through a gateway and crossed the parade ground, a well kept piece
of gravelled ground, about 450 yards long and 50 feet wide, as it appeared to
us; then turning to the right again and going through a smaller gateway, kept
carefully locked, we ascended a pathway, flanked to the left by a piece of garden
ground, where, from the nature of soil and situation, we suppose, we beheld
an inspiring exhibition of vegetables growing 'under difficulties'. Another turn
to the right brought us to 'No.1'. This prison has a ground floor and an upper
floor, both of which are sectioned into 'wards' or; large rooms, called respec-
tively A ward, B ward, C ward etc. We went first, in due alphabetical order, into
A ward where we found about fifty prisoners busily engaged in making and
repairing shoes. As soon as the officer in charge of the 'shoemaker's shop' saw
us and our guide approaching, he shouted in a military style 'Attention!' The

Warders at the gate of Dartmoor Convict Prison in the early twentieth century.

rattle of the hammers and lapstones immediately subsided and perfect silence ensued. On our suggestion, however, the work resumed. The warder in charge, who was very properly a shoemaker by trade, took evident pleasure in answering our inquiries and in exhibiting specimens of the prisoners' work. The best samples of workmanship, he said, were from the hands of 'real tradesmen' or men apprenticed to the 'gentle craft' of whom there were but few; and he then, at our request, showed us some rough but strong and creditable work, done by prisoners who had learnt all they knew of shoemaking since they came into prison.

The men seemed to labour with as much willingness as might be reasonably expected under the circumstances of their position – were decently clad in light brown dress – had badges and red stripes on their arms to denote their length of sentence, and the number of months during which they have been 'very good' or otherwise – seemed healthy – and were permitted to converse but not noisily, during the hours of labour. We learned, on inquiry, that these men slept and took their meals in this workshop and we observed a corroboration of the statement in the hammocks and bedding of the men rolled up very tastefully and placed in a very orderly manner upon shelves or racks above their heads. But we could not avoid feeling, nor forbear feeling, that it seemed to us a ground of regret that the men were not provided with another room for a dormitory, as this working ward, in spite of the utmost attention to cleanliness and ventilation, had about it a sickly, earthy, close odour, which was anything but agreeable to us and when the place is shut up during the night must be anything but healthful for the men.

We found 'B ward' full of tailors, menders and stocking darners. A few of these prisoners were *bona fide* tailors, worked in company and were making clothes for the officers and various authorities of the establishment. The others were busily engaged in making and repairing clothing for their fellow prisoners. They seemed to be chiefly invalids and cripples, who had obtained indoor work on account of their physical inability to perform the heavier tasks required of the outdoor labourers. On our remarking that they appeared to be a body of docile and well-behaved men, we were informed by an experienced official that although there were amongst them, as in all large bodies of convicts, a good proportion of tractable and properly conducted prisoners, yet as a general rule, the invalids were the most sly, deceptive and unmanageable convicts in the place. Assuredly, the furtive glances and forbidding looks of many of these men fully attested the truth and accuracy of the statement made by the officer.

We were, by this time, glad to leave the room, for its atmosphere was very close and oppressive. We were informed that the occupants of the ward worked, slept, and lived in this place day and night for years, or the greater part of every year of their detention, with the exception of an hour's exercise daily in the adjoining yard, when the state of the weather permitted it. We came to the conclusion – it might be an erroneous one, but we came to it – that if these men were healthy on the whole, as we were told they were, they were healthy rather in spite of this arrangement than on account of it.

We now went upstairs to the floor which is fitted up and used as an infirmary. We found about fifty prisoners here, in various stages of debility and disease, from a slight cold to a rapid consumption. Only a few were in extreme and immediate danger. The state of things considering that there are, ordinarily, about 1,200 men in the prison and that nearly every man is invalided hither from other stations is eminently indicative of the salubrity of the locality and highly creditable to the care and skill of the medical officers who have charge of the injured and afflicted in this extensive establishment.

The infirmary has an efficient staff of warders and assistant warders acquainted with the peculiar duties required and assiduously attentive to the comfort and welfare of the patients, as far as the rules and discipline of a prison will allow. The nurses are prisoners of good character, who have been appointed, at their own request, to the post they occupy and have been found to possess patience, steadiness, industry and other indispensable qualifications.

There appear to be much less 'malingering' or pretended disease among the convicts since the abolition of transportation as it was and the adoption of 'penal servitude' at home in lieu of expatriation to the colonies. Under the old system, as soon as any tidings of the sailings of a 'convict ship' were heard amongst the men on 'public works' such hosts of prisoners besieged the surgeon every morning with complaints of pains in the side; there was much spitting of blood, such palpitation of the heart, there were fits and such sores on the legs of many of the convicts that any one not versed in prison matters would have thought that the Angel of Death had breathed in the faces of the men and filled the prison with expiring sufferers. But the 'old hands' on the medical staff were quite aware of the fact that all these aliments, and many others, might be and often were, simulated or caused by sundry means with which they were well acquainted. The attacks used to continue, in many cases, with great violence until the 'doctor' had rejected the afflicted ones and the 'convict ship' had sailed.

The recent changes in the law as to secondary punishments has led to pretended invalids to find that they have been, to use their own phrase, 'playing a losing game'. Formerly a convict might manage to mislead the medical officer, get 'invalided' and sent to a 'hulk' or any other station where he might have extra diet and a life of almost entire idleness and be liberated as soon or even sooner than a well-conducted able bodied man. But according to the rules brought recently into operation, these inducements have ceased to exist and the advantage is on the side of the hardworking, uncomplaining prisoner, who gains his liberty, other things being equal, at an earlier period than the useless and invalided man. But we must now go to 'No. 2 prison'.

This large rectangular edifice opened in front upon the parade ground and is occupied by artisans and able bodied labourers. On entering one of the halls, which you step into on crossing the threshold, a singular and somewhat striking sight presents itself to the eye of the visitor. He sees before him the fronts of more than 160 cells, in four tiers and about forty in each. They are constructed of corrugated iron and being painted white, contrast very pleasantly with the wood-work, which is grained like old oak, and the light wire railings, which is of a dark green colour. A flight of stairs at each end of the hall conducts to the three upper landings which are paved with slate and kept, as everything else is, beautifully clean. Each cell is about seven feet high, seven feet in length and nearly four feet in breadth. This seems but scant space but as the men are in their cells at night only and at meal hours during the day and as cell furniture is very compactly arranged and ventilation is well provided for the room is said to be found quite sufficient.

In this prison, and in 'No. 4 prison', strict silence is enforced whilst the men are in their cells and all conversational communication is forbidden. This rule has been found necessary from the noise and confusion which prevailed when the prisoners went at their pleasure from cell to cell and conversed without any hindrance on the part of their officers. The plan, at present in successful operation, preserves quietude and proves a great privilege to those who wish to read without interruption after they have returned from labour. This class of men is, we were glad to find, by no means inconsiderable.

'No. 3' is a large building resembling 'No. 2' in size, form and materials of construction. It is, however, fitted up very differently. It has three floors and each storey is a large open ward in which the prisoners dwell together in open and allowed association.

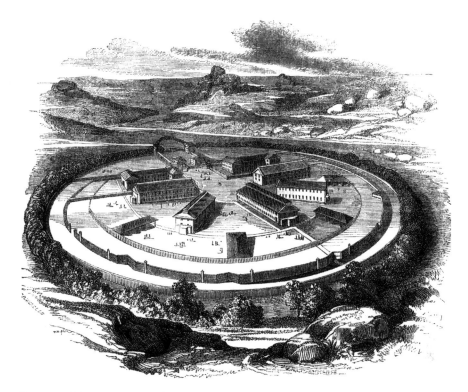

Dartmoor Prison, an original illustration that accompanied *A Visit to Dartmoor Prison* published in the *Leisure Hour*, March 1855.

On being ushered into the chapel, a plain, commodious edifice, made out of an old prison, we found it in use during the day as a schoolroom. At the time of our visit there were about 100 prisoners in attendance, under the charge of two officers to preserve order and three schoolmasters to impart instruction. Excellent discipline was kept and generally speaking attention was paid to the useful and suitable lessons given by the masters. These gentlemen seemed to labour very earnestly in their vocation and yet appeared, we thought, in speaking of their arduous and interesting work, to toil under some degree of discouragement. They have, it must be owned, a very hard and uphill task to perform. They have not to cast the imperishable seeds of truth into the opening and susceptible mind of youth; they have on the contrary to deal, for the most part, with fierce, keen, obdurate, sin hardened men, who come to school, not willingly nor kindly but perforce and angrily, more bent on imparting to each other the evil they have learned than to receive good at the hands of their instructors. But, let all who struggle on in such trying spheres of Christian toil remember, for their encouragement, that the fiercer the contest the more glorious the victory and that the Christian labourer works for Him who looks rather at the spirit in which his work is done than at the issues and results that his toiling servants see. We observed two prisoners seated at a table, busily employed in issuing and exchanging library books for their fellow prisoners. There is, it appears, a love of reading amongst the greater part of these men. If the reading be, as we believe it is here, of a profitable and improving kind this habit may, under the divine blessing, be the means of installing with dew-like quietude and efficacy, good and wholesome principles into the minds of these outcasts of society. We need scarcely say that we were gratified on observing that the monthly volumes of the Religious Tract Society were very prominent amongst the books in general circulation and on learning that the *Leisure Hour* was so attractive as to be in very general request among the prisoners.

It is time, however, to draw our description to a close and in order, therefore, to give our readers a concise but clear view of the work done by the convicts at Dartmoor Prison, the discipline to which they are subjected and the dietary to which they are restricted, we will endeavour to describe very briefly the avocations of an ordinary day.

Clang! Clang! Clang! The first bell is ringing. It is almost five o'clock in the morning and the prisoners awake, knowing that in a few minutes they must 'turn out'. As the clock strikes five the bell rings again, the prison doors fly open for the admission of the day officers and they enter headed by a principal warder, unlock the cell doors and forthwith report, one by one, from their different landings, that it is 'all right', by which they mean that nothing particular has occurred during the night and that none of the prisoners have escaped. Then the night officer is suffered to depart, right glad no doubt to get to breakfast and to bed after walking up and down in the bleak stone halls of the prison all night, listening to the snoring of the sleeping men, and thinking that as far as the mode of passing the night is concerned the prisoners have decidedly the best of it.

Every man is now on the alert, folding up his bed clothes and hammock and cleaning out his cell. He then washes himself and is, by the time he has completed his ablutions, quite ready for his breakfast. The breakfast, brought from the kitchen at about 6 o'clock, consists of bread and cocoa. Each man's allowance is 1 pint of cocoa and 12 oz of bread. At half past six o' clock the bell rings for morning prayers in the chapel; the service occupies about twenty minutes, and at seven o'clock all the men are on the parade ground fallen in for labour. They go off after being counted, gang by gang, to their work, which consists of clearing the stony ground around the prison and trenching it to prepare it for cultivation. At certain seasons they cut, stack and bring in turf from the bogs with which the station is surrounded. This is all the labour of which the nature of the soil will allow and the endeavours made to fertilize the earth and render it productive and remunerative, are at present, as far as we could see, anything but successful.

At twelve o'clock the gangs come in to dinner and go out to work again at quarter past one o'clock. Work is continued as long as the daylight will allow during the winter months and until half past five o'clock during the other parts of the year. The dinner allowance of the able bodied man on four days of the week consists of 6oz of boiled beef, 8oz of plain suet pudding and 1lb of vegetables or rice. On the other three days 5oz of meat, 1 pint of soup, 1lb of vegetables or rice and 6oz of bread. The supper allowance on 'soup days' is 9oz of bread and 1 pint of cocoa; on other evenings, 9oz of bread and 1 pint of oatmeal gruel. On leaving work, the men are again assembled in the chapel for divine service, after which supper is served and at eight o'clock pm the bell rings for bed. So passes the convict's day at Dartmoor.

The officers are a fine body of men and strong persons are needed here, for the duties required are very onerous and the fickle weather on the Dartmoor bogs makes the position of an officer at this station harassing to the mind and very trying to the constitution. A zealous and affectionate chaplain labours in the establishment. His duties are arduous and his efforts on behalf of his unhappy and peculiar flock are incessant and indefatigable. As our 'Day at Dartmoor' ended, and we left the prison and its vicinity, we could not forbear thinking of the manifold and manifest consequences of sin, letting fall a tear over the frailty of our common humanity and breathing forth a silent prayer … [that one day] these frowning monuments of human depravity shall be needed and known no more.

After reading this descriptive account by a visitor, consider the viewpoint of one who was confined at Dartmoor. Michael Davitt was a member of the Irish Republican Brotherhood and was involved in a failed raid on Chester Castle in February 1867 to obtain arms for a Fenian rising in Ireland. He initially evaded capture but was arrested at Paddington station on 14 May 1870 while awaiting a delivery of arms. Tried and convicted of treason felony, he was sentenced to fifteen years penal servitude and later wrote an account of his experiences in *The Prison Life of Michael Davitt* (1882) and his two-volume *Leaves from a Prison Diary* (1885):

It would be impossible for me, in the limited time at my disposal, to detail every circumstance connected with my six years and six months confinement in Dartmoor: I can, therefore, only dwell upon the most prominent incidents connected with my treatment during that period, by a simple statement of facts as to what that treatment was.

For the first week after my arrival from Millbank I was located in the penal cells, and had to make application for removal from same into some other part of the prison. The penal cells, or rather some of them, are much preferable to the ordinary or iron cells, being somewhat larger and much better ventilated but owing to their being constructed and set apart for incorrigible prisoners, men who are taught obedience by means of starvation, and consequently maddened by hunger and cold, it is almost impossible to obtain any sleep in such a place. I will have more to say about these cells by and by, as I was confined in them from August '76, until November '77. The iron or ordinary cell I was next located in, and remained an inmate of for close on five years … The dimensions of one of them will answer for that of the whole, as they are uniform in almost every respect. Length, seven feet exactly; width, four feet; and height, seven feet one or two inches. The sides or frames of all are of corrugated iron, and the floor is a slate one. These cells are ranged in tiers or wards in the centre of a hall, the tiers being one above another, to the height of four wards; the floors of the three upper tiers of cells forming the ceilings or tops of those immediately beneath them. Each ward or tier contains in length forty-two cells, giving a total of one hundred and sixty-eight for one hall. The sole provision made for ventilating these cells is an opening of two and a half or three inches left at the bottom of each door. There is no opening into the external air from any of those cells in Dartmoor; and the air admitted into the hall has to traverse the width of the same to enter the hole under the cell doors. In the cells on the first three tiers, or wards, there are about a dozen small perforations in the corner of each, for the escape of vitiated air; but in those on the top or fourth ward or, speaking more confidently, in those on that ward in which I was located a portion of my time, there were no such perforations, no possible way of escape for foul air except where most of it entered as 'pure' under the cell door. In the heat of summer it was almost impossible to breathe in these top cells; so close and foul would the air become from the improper ventilation of the cells below, allowing the breathed air in each cell to mix with that in the hall, and thus ascend to the top.

I, on one occasion, begged the governor of Dartmoor to remove me from such a situation, for the additional reason to those I have given that I had not sufficient light to read in the cell I was in, but I begged in vain. I was, however, soon after removed to a lower tier, after foul eruptions began to break out upon my body through the impure air I had been breathing … it was quite common in Dartmoor for prisoners to sleep with their heads towards the door and I have often, in the summer season, done this myself, and had repeatedly to go on my knees and put my mouth to the bottom of the door for a little air.

The light admitted to those ordinary iron cells is scarcely sufficient to read by in the daytime and should a fog prevail, it would be impossible to read in half of them. The cells are fitted with a couple of plates of thick, intransparent [*sic*] glass, about eighteen inches long by six inches wide each, and the light is transmitted through this 'window' from the hall, and not from the extern of the prison. I have often laid the length of my body on the cell floor, and placed my book under the door to catch sufficient light to read it.

The food in Dartmoor prison I found to be the very worst in quality and the filthiest in cooking of any of the other places I had been in. The quantity of daily rations was the same as in Millbank, with the difference of four ounces of bread more each day and one of meat less in the week. The quality, as I have already remarked, is inferior to that of any other prison but from about November till May it is simply execrable; the potatoes being often unfit to eat, and rotten cow-carrots occasionally substituted for other food. To find black beetles in soup, 'skilly' bread, and tea, was quite a common occurrence and some idea can be formed of how hunger will reconcile a man to look without disgust upon the most filthy objects in nature, when I state as a fact that I have often discovered beetles in my food and have eaten it after throwing them aside, without experiencing much revulsion of feeling at the sight of such loathsome animals in my victuals. Still I have often come in from work weak with fatigue and hunger, and found it impossible to eat the putrid meat or stinking soup supplied me for dinner, and had to return to labour again after 'dining' on six ounces of bad bread.

It was quite a common occurrence in Dartmoor for men to be reported and punished for eating candles, boot oil, and other repulsive articles; and, notwithstanding that a highly offensive smell is purposely given to prison candles to prevent their being eaten instead of burned, men are driven by a system of half-starvation into an animal-like voracity, and anything that a dog would eat is nowise repugnant to their taste. I have seen men eat old poultices found buried in heaps of rubbish I was assisting in carting away, and have seen bits of candle pulled out of the prison cess-pool and eaten after the human soil was wiped off them!

The labour I was first put to was stone-breaking, that being considered suitable work for non-able-bodied prisoners. I was put to this employment in a large shed, along with some eighty or ninety more prisoners but my hand becoming blistered by the action of the hammer after I had broken stones for a week, I was unable to continue at that work, and was consequently put to what is termed 'cart labour.' This sort of work is very general in Dartmoor, and I may as well give some description of it.

Eight men constitute a 'cart party', and have an officer over them, armed with a staff, if working within the prison walls, and with a rifle and accompanied by an armed guard, if employed outside. Each man in the cart is supplied with a collar, which is put over the head and passes from the right or left shoulder under the opposite arm, and is then hooked to the chain by means of which the cart is drawn about. The cart party to which I was attached was employed in carting stones, coals, manure, and rubbish of all descriptions. In drawing the cart along, each prisoner has to bend forward and pull with all his strength, or the warder who is 'driving' will threaten to 'run him in', or report him for idleness. It was our work to supply all parts of the prison workshops, officers' mess-room, cook-house, etc. with coals; and I was often drawing these about in rain and sleet, with no fire to warm or dry myself after a wetting. I was only a few months at this sort of work, as I met with a slight accident by a collar hurting the remnant of my right arm, and was in consequence of this excused from cart labour by the doctor's order. I was again set to breaking granite, and remained at that job during the winter of 1870–71.

I may remark that in June, when I was first put to stone-breaking, I was employed in a shed but during the winter I was compelled to work outside, in the cold and damp, foggy weather. I was left at this work until spring, and was then removed to a task from the effects of which I believe I will never completely recover. My health on entering prison was excellent, never having had any sickness at any previous period of my life. The close confinement and insufficient food in Millbank had told, of course, on my constitution, though not to any very alarming extent, but the task I was now put to laid the germs of the heart and lung disease I have since been suffering from. This task was putrid bone-breaking.

On the brink of the prison cesspool, in which all the soil of the whole establishment is accumulated for manure, stands a small building, some twenty feet long by about ten broad, known as the ' bone-shed.' The floor of this shed is sunk some three feet lower than the ground outside and is on a level with the pool which leaves the wall of the building. All the bones accruing from the meat supply of the prison were pounded into dust in this shed, and during the summer of 1872 (excepting five weeks spent in Portsmouth prison) this was my employment. These bones have often lain putrefying for weeks in the broiling heat of the summer sun, ere they were brought into be broken.

The stench arising from their decomposition, together with the noxious exhalations from the action of the sun's rays on the cesspool outside, no words could adequately express: it was a veritable charnel-house. It will be noted that I was at work outside the previous winter, and when the bright days and summer season came on I was put in a low shed to break putrefying bones! The number of prisoners at this work varied from thirty to six, and I may remark that the majority of these were what are termed 'doctor's men', or prisoners unable to perform the ordinary prison labour. When all the bones would be pounded, we would then be employed in and around the cesspool, mixing and carting manure, and at various other similar occupations.

I made application to both governor and doctor for removal from this bone-breaking to some more congenial task, but I would not be transferred to any other labour. After completing a term of my imprisonment which entitled me to a pint of tea in lieu of 'skilly' for breakfast, I was then removed to a hard-labour party, as, owing to my being an invalid, or 'doctor's man', I could not claim the privilege of this slight change in diet without becoming attached to some hard labour party, invalids, or 'light labour men,' not being allowed tea at any stage of their imprisonment. I very willingly consented to a heavier task, in order to be removed from the abominable bone-shed, in which I had worked and sickened during the summer.

My employment after this was various: drawing carts, bogies laden with stone, slates, etc., delving and shifting sand, at which work I was in the habit of using a pick and shovel (though not, I must fairly admit, compelled to do so), as the extreme cold made it necessary in order to keep myself from being congealed. I was next employed in winding up stones at an iron crank, during the building of an additional wing to the prison; and this was, beyond doubt, the heaviest work to which they could have put me. A crank party consisted of four men, and my being one of the four compelled me to perform as much work as either of the others, as the task would fall heavier upon them otherwise. This employment was occasionally diversified with spells at mortar-making, water-carrying for same, sand-shifting, cement-making, and various other jobs, among which carrying slates to the roof of the new prison was one not, of course, up a ladder but by a steep incline.

I may remark in passing that three prisoners lost their lives while this building was going on and in my opinion, those accidents were attributable to the ignorance of scaffolding arrangements shown by the warders appointed to superintend them. Inquests were held, of course, inside the prison; but I never learned that an intelligent prisoner was called upon to give evidence, nor what verdicts were given by what the prisoners in Dartmoor called 'the standing jury'. I may add also that my friend, Mr Chambers, fell from a scaffolding at the same building, and, on the principle that 'a man who falls deserves to be kicked for falling' he was taken to the punishment cells instead of the infirmary, and turned out to work again the following day. When my services as a mason's labourer were no longer required, I was once more put to the old job of stone-breaking, and remained thereat from about the latter part of 1873 until August, 1876.

The Prison Life of Michael Davitt (1882)

PUNISHMENTS

In prisons, staff were only too aware of the paramount requirement to maintain discipline and order. With this in mind, it is hardly surprising that the preferred candidates for the majority of positions on the prison staff were ex-military personnel, well versed in knowing how to give an order and ensure it was carried out. If a prisoner refused to work, became recalcitrant, abusive, violent or simply looked at the warder the wrong way he would be punished. If a warder took a dislike to you it could result in dire consequences, as recalled by 'A Ticket of Leave Man':

> A few months ago a poor mulatto youth was transferred to Dartmoor prison from Portsmouth. He had there got into trouble, first over a piece of tobacco not bigger than a sixpence. An officer made a 'mark' of him, seeing that he was a green hand, and got him punished over and over again. At last he carried his animosity too far. The fellow's black blood was roused, and he struck his enemy. He was flogged, and sent in chains to Dartmoor. There the whole brood of officers, or 'screws' as the 'lags' call them, got down upon him; he was reported time after time, and during the early part of this year he had existed for fifty days out of three months upon bread-and-water, and in the middle of March I left him in the hospital in a very precarious state, as the result of his punishment.
>
> *Convict Life* (1879)

Prisoners would be encouraged to behave themselves and could gain marks for good conduct which, in turn, would mount up to gain him or her privileges and remission of sentence. Minor transgressions such as talking, lateness or bad workmanship in the workshops would result in the removal of marks or a privilege, such as the denial of provision of paper or suspension of permission to write a letter home. A slightly more serious offence, such as continuing to do work to sub-standard or perceived laziness, would result in being given extra oakum to pick or an extra turn on the treadwheel or the crank.

Crank labour in a 'Separate System' cell at Pentonville. Convicts would be expected to turn twenty revolutions a minute, a typical target being a total of 10,000 revolutions in eight and a half hours.

The crank was a widely adopted means of occupying refractory prisoners in their solitary cells during the latter half of the nineteenth century. Operated by a single prisoner, the crank comprised a drum on a metal pillar or a handle set into a wall, with a dial to register the number of times the crank hande had been turned – usually about twenty times a minute, a typical target being a total of 10,000 revolutions in eight and a half hours. If the target was not achieved in the specified time, the prisoner was given no food until the dial registered the required total. A legacy of the crank remains today; if the prisoner found this task too easy the prison warder would come and tighten the screw, making the handle harder to turn, hence the prisoner parlance for a warder has, for generations, been 'the screw'.

Those who deliberately produced bad work, wilfully damaged prison property, had cross words with another prisoner or were insolent or made threatening gestures to a prison officer would often be removed to a 'Punishment Cell' otherwise known as a 'Dark Cell', a cell fitted with shutters where only minimal light or even complete darkness could be maintained throughout the day and night. In the cell only a board was provided for the convict to sleep or sit on – no mattress, sheet or blanket; no books or reading material would be provided either, privileges would be lost and the convict placed on a punishment diet of bread and water.

Mrs Maybrick recalled the most severe punishments in Woking Women's Prison:

> Solitary confinement, with loss of marks, on bread and water for three days, either in a strait-jacket or 'hobbles'. Hobbling consists in binding the wrists and ankles of a prisoner, then strapping them together behind her back. This position causes great suffering, is barbarous, and can be enforced only by the doctor's orders.
>
> To the above was sometimes added, in violent cases, shearing and blistering of the head, or confinement in the dark cell. The dark cell was underground, and consisted of four walls, a ceiling, and a floor, with double doors, in which not a ray of light penetrated.
>
> *Mrs Maybrick's Own Story: My Lost Fifteen Years* (1904)

If there ever was a leading male candidate for the dark cell, and there were many contenders, Thomas Jones was that person. A man of 'a most repulsive countenance', he was a violent and habitual criminal, nine times previously convicted and once flogged, he had been sentenced to seven years penal servitude for

A female convict in a canvas dress under punishment for tearing her clothes, Millbank Prison, 1862.

larceny at the Liverpool Sessions in 1879 when he was just 18. Serving his time at Dartmoor Convict Prison, he was brought before the governor in his office for a full hearing including magistrates and witnesses regarding an alleged attack on Assistant Warder John Staddon:

> The office, which is rather a small apartment, adjoins one of the prison corridors, where the punishment cells are situated, and strong iron railings between five and six in height run across the room so that the convict is separated from the governor. The magistrates and officials, with the exception of the warders, were inside the gates, in the office, when the order was given to bring the prisoner in.
>
> The prisoner was brought from the punishment cells to the office in the charge of two warders. He walked quietly enough to the office, apparently in ignorance of what was about to take place. Directly he was brought inside the door and was confronted with the magistrates, governor, deputy-governor and other inside the railings, he appeared stupefied for the moment and then suddenly, remembering where he was, he said to the warders in an innocent and defiant tone, 'What's the matter? What are they going to do?' He was told by the warders to be quiet and behave himself. Jones, however, violently exclaimed, 'Hang me if you like but don't shoot me,' and immediately, although he was

The solitary, dark cell for refractory prisoners, Millbank Prison, 1873.

held by two powerfully-built warders, struck out right and left, kicking at the officers and ferociously endeavouring to bite them. One warder promptly twisted his leg around Jones to prevent him kicking, a second firmly gripped his arms from behind, whilst a third, who had rushed to their assistance, grasped the nape of the prisoner's neck in order to stop his endeavour to use his teeth. Even the efforts of these three men to hold Jones was insufficient. Handcuffs were slipped on the wrists of the prisoner, who however, still resisted savagely, endeavoured to bite the officers and although held bodily by warders, continued his mad struggles.

A pair of shackles were sent for and on these being brought into the office the prisoner, who had evidently been shackled before, shuddered and struggled more fiercely than ever. He was eventually jerked upon the ground and thrown on his back where, after a most exciting struggle, the irons were tightly fastened around his legs. These measures failed to subdue the spirit of the prisoner, who violently wrestled in the hands of his keepers. A chain covered with leather was next procured and this was passed around the waist of the prisoner and then tightly secured to the iron railings running across the room. Jones then worked himself up into a towering passion and it required the combined efforts of the warders to hold his head and shoulders.

During the examination of Principal Warder Moore, the prisoner's violence was even intensified; he hissed and spat at the witness and uttered incoherent exclamations which it was impossible to understand, biting at everybody and everything like a mad dog throughout the hearing. He was eventually committed for trial at Devon Assizes and carried back to his cell, where the handcuffs and the shackles were removed. He thereupon smashed the window panes, tore his coat to shreds and attempted to commit suicide by twisting his braces round his neck. The warders rushed to the cell and on opening the door were again attacked by the prisoner. Once more the man was secured, his hands manacled behind his back and he was finally removed to a dark cell and locked in, in a condition of absolute nudity to which he had reduced himself.

Bristol Mercury, 12 April 1883

The birch was a punishment reserved mostly as a corporal punishment for wayward boys found guilty of petty offences from the medieval period up to the twentieth century. Adult males found guilty of crimes against the person, such as robbery with violence, could be sentenced to receive a flogging also known as 'the lash'; in convict parlance flogging was referred to as 'a bashing'. This punishment was also used on convicts who seriously transgressed prison rules by, for example, assaulting a prison officer; the governor could not summarily order a prisoner to be flogged, instead the case had to be brought before the Visiting Justices and the prisoner would be punished according to their order.

The birch consisted of a bundle of leafless twigs from the birch tree. No specific number of twigs appears to have been recorded for the construction of the birch but most surviving examples from provincial areas appear to have consisted of a bundle of between fifty and seventy young twigs and would have been a total of about 3ft long. The cut ends of the twigs would be bound together with cotton cord to make a handle, while the flexible twigs terminating in the natural ends made the end which would deliver the punishment. Larger examples were certainly known, most notoriously those used in some penal institutions; several versions were in use, which were often given names. For example, Dartmoor Prison's 'Senior Birch', which weighed some 16oz and measured 48in long, was used to punish male offenders above the age of 16.

Traditionally, birches were soaked in brine before use, which greatly increased the weight, flexibility and strength of the twigs, making the punishment more severe both in terms of pain and in terms of damage to the victim's flesh in the form of cuts, weals and wounds. Because of its antiseptic properties, the brine also helped prevent infection developing in the wounds following the punishment. In some prisons and reformatories a wooden apparatus known as a birching donkey or pony was specially constructed for the delivery of the punishment, but in many provincial areas offenders under the age of 16 were strapped or held down on a table and a burly officer would wield the birch.

The 'Boy's Pony' at Coldbath Fields, 1874. Young offenders would be laid face down, bare back, sometimes down to the buttocks, on this apparatus and would then be birched.

The 'Birch/Rod', Wandsworth Prison, 1862.

The Wandsworth 'Whipping Post', 1862.

The lash, or cat-o'-nine-tails, when used as a civil rather than military corporal punishment, consisted of nine knotted thongs of cotton cord, between 2ft and 2½ft long, bound to a 20in-turned wood handle, the grip bound with more cotton cord and sometimes a fabric binding above that; the 'tails' or cords fit almost flush to the shaft in grooves cut near the head of the handle with a fine cotton cord bound round them to keep them in place. The ends of the cords would either be tied or bound to prevent fraying. Most cats have three evenly spaced knots tied along each of the tails, but not all; some examples simply have a slightly thicker cord with tips bound with cotton cord and no knots.

The reason why the cat has nine tails is because traditionally the cat was made from rope rather than cotton cord. Rope is plaited and thinner rope is made from three strands of yarn plaited together and thicker rope from three strands of thinner rope plaited together. To make a cat-o'-nine-tails, a rope is unravelled into three small ropes, and each of those next unravelled, again in to three. Normally only used in prisons on convict boys and adults aged 16 years and over, the cat would be administered to a prisoner standing locked into a whipping pillory or restrained by leather straps in a standing position with arms raised and legs spread on a 'triangle'.

A commentary on the Prison Inspectors Report of 1860 discussed corporal punishment:

In the course of the last three years corporal punishment has been inflicted in 852 instances in the prisons of England and Wales. Sometimes this punishment is inflicted by order of Courts of Justice, at the Assizes and Sessions, chiefly for stealing but occasionally and not inappropriately for other offences such as assault with intent to commit rape and repeated desertion of wife and family leaving them chargeable to the parish. At other times the whipping is by order of the Visiting Justices for prison offences, which, besides insubordination and refusal to work, include such cases as attempts at suicide, breaking up all the cell furniture and setting fire to it, assaulting an officer and threatening to murder him. In most cases the punishment consists of a few lashes administered to a lad under age but occasionally older men are whipped and, for serious offences, the number extends to three or four dozen with the cat. In Dorset County Prison it is stated that men of 20, 33, 46 and even one of 53 were flogged on the bare breech. These punishments were inflicted privately but sometimes other prisoners are present for the sake of warning. In some of the cases where the whipping has been ordered by Visiting Justices, the offence is but vaguely described in the returns as 'idleness' and in one case 'sleeping in the open air'. In Tiverton Gaol all the whipping were conducted before the Mayor.

The rod seems to be most required in the North; during the three years the Visiting Justices have applied it to 84 prisoners in the New Bailey, Salford and to 37 in the City Gaol, Manchester; the quarter sessions to 53 in Walton Borough

Gaol and the Petty Sessions to 96 in the Borough Prison of Newcastle-upon-Tyne. Altogether 190 men and lads were flogged in Lancashire, 99 in Northumberland, 78 in Staffordshire, 48 in Cheshire; in Yorkshire but 15; Derby, Dorset, Suffolk, Worcestershire 5 each; in Durham, Gloucestershire, Essex, Notts and Warwickshire 4 each; in Beds, Bucks, Hants, Westmoreland 2; in Herefordshire and Cambridgeshire 1; in Cumberland and Monmouthshire none. The differences are remarkable. In Scotland there have been about 150 juvenile offenders whipped by order of Courts of Justice and in Edinburgh and Glasgow the Magistrates have power to direct corporal punishment of such persons, and this is frequently done.

During the 'Garotter' scare of the 1870s ('garotters' were originally street criminals who robbed their victims after rendering them insensible with a blow to the carotid artery, but during the scare the term soon became applied to many forms of robbery with violence) flogging appears to have been the standard punishment and detailed accounts of the enactment frequently appeared in the press. Calcraft, the hangman, carried out many of the floggings in the London and Middlesex area, a job for which he was paid an extra half a crown per performance; he features in this vivid account of a flogging at Newgate from the *Illustrated Police News* in April 1870:

William Leonard was sentenced by the Common Serjeant to seven years penal servitude and twenty-five lashes with the cat for garrotting a lady in Endell Street, Long Acre. The twenty-five lashes were administered at half past ten o'clock on Thursday morning in the old oakum room at Newgate. When Sir Joseph Causton and Mr Pattison, the Sheriffs, Mr A. Corsley and Mr A.J. Baylis, the Under-Sheriffs, accompanied by Mr Jonas the governor and Mr J.R. Gibson the surgeon of the prison entered the room the prisoner was already stripped and made fast and the hangman, Calcraft, stood, cat in hand, at his side. Leonard presented the appearance of a strong-built, muscular young fellow, apparently older than 20; his face, heavy and full, denoted unintelligence rather than ruffianism. He was short of stature, being only five feet two inches in height.

His arms were run through holes in a traverse bar and his legs were encased up to the thighs in a sort of box. The executioner, a thick-set man, apparently not taller than the prisoner, waited stolidly for the signal to begin. Then, advancing his left foot and throwing back his shoulders he, in a quiet and business-like way, brought the nine tails of the cat down transversely on the culprit's back. A prolonged cry told the blow so quietly given had been severely felt. Another lash followed and the prisoner roared outright, writhing in pain the while. The third and fourth strokes made him supplicate Calcraft to hit between the shoulders and not lower down. Calcraft, however, took no notice of the request and Leonard Shrieked out, 'Oh, for the Lord's sake have mercy! It's burning me! It is

The flogging of William Leonard at Newgate Prison, 1870.

cutting me in two! Oh, have mercy and I will pray for you! Oh, it is killing me.' The surgeon approached and put his finger on the sufferer's pulse but there was manifestly no danger to life and the ninth and tenth stokes were laid on.

Becoming desperate and bellowing for mercy the prisoner struggled frantically and actually succeeded in drawing his legs up out of the box in which they had been encased – the first time such a feat was ever accomplished. The flogging ceased and warders rushed forward and seized the offender's legs; the side of the box or case was opened and his feet were put into the sort of stocks from which they had been wrenched out. To make them additionally secure a piece of wood was inserted which the prisoner cried out hurt him. The warders eased the pressure but the prisoner evidently comprehended that any further struggles would greatly aggravate the torture. He kept crying out for mercy and promising to be quiet. Calcraft in loud and bullying tones said to him, 'Why don't you keep quiet? You are hurting yourself more than I hurt you. Hold your noise and keep easy!' This expostulation had a wonderful effect on the prisoner; hardly a cry escaped him after. The legs being again made fast, the flogging recommenced.

The back, by this time, had become pretty well scored with stripes. Along one transverse line where most of the strokes fell, the raw flesh assumed a dull red colour and some blood appeared but not much flowed. As the blows fell regularly the prisoner remained now motionless: he muttered some half audible ejaculation but it seemed as if the excessive sensitiveness of the nerves had disappeared and the pain was by no means so severe as at first.

At the twenty-second blow he turned towards the right hand, so as to change the spot on which the cat fell; the remaining blows were given and Calcraft had his arm raised again, when the welcome signal to stop was given. In an instant the prisoner's hands and legs were set free but he was unable to move; he would have fallen had not two warders caught him under the arms and supported him to a bench. He shivered and cried and appeared to give way abjectly, when a rough command 'not to go on like that' made him pull himself together. A flannel was put over his back and spots of blood coming through immediately showed that the wretch's sufferings were not all over when liberated from the stocks. He was then led away to the infirmary. Calcraft ran his fingers leisurely through the knotted cords of the cat and proceeded to dry it, so that it might be in good condition for the next operation.

Birching was maintained as a corporal punishment well into the twentieth century. County Constabulary Orders from 1901 stated:

Owing to the difference in age, nervous temperament and physical constitution, punishment must necessarily vary. The birching of children under 10 years should be less severe than in the case of older offenders. Birching to be administered by a police constable in the presence of an officer not below the rank of Inspector. Parents are to be invited to attend.

A typical sentence for a young offender under 16 years in the late nineteenth century would be the 'short, sharp shock' of six strokes of the birch and between one and three days imprisonment. Repeat or violent young offenders under the age of 16 would receive '12 stokes of the birch – red' after which they would then be sent to a reformatory or industrial school for up to three years or until they were 16. The birching of juvenile and adult offenders was finally banned in 1948, but was retained as a punishment for violent breaches of prison discipline until 1962.

Escapers

Despite penalties such as extension of sentence and flogging, there were always those among the prison population who attempted to escape – with varying degrees of success.

The year 1837, the first year of Queen Victoria's reign, did not start well for Springfield Gaol at Chelmsford in Essex. The first to escape was James Monk who, 'being diseased', was removed from his cell to a segregation area used for vagrants suffering the same condition. In the early hours of the following morning Monk succeeded in breaking away a slight window frame and forced himself between the bars. He got out to the yard, scaled the wall, let himself down the other side and 'got clear off'.

To reduce escape attempts in twilight hours, prisoners were instructed to undress and leave their clothes in the passage opposite their cell doors. However, this did not stop James Cordrey, an inmate of Springfield, who had been detained on a charge of sheep stealing. He placed his hat on the floor and covered it with his smock-frock so it appeared that the pile was his clothes. While the cells were all locked up Cordrey hid in the shadows, slipped outside and escaped by climbing over the wall.

On 22 July 1837, a large group of prisoners made an escape bid from Springfield. Their plan was to summon the surgeon on the pretext of a prisoner being ill. When the surgeon arrived he was escorted by a warder. The warder was attacked and his keys wrested from him. The prisoners then began to make their way through the doors they could now unlock to the main door and freedom. The alarm, however, was raised in sufficient time for the warders to draw pistols, blunderbusses and swords from the armoury and quell the insurrection. Reprisals were swift; many of those who dared to attempt the escape were flogged, some receiving up to fifty lashes.

Eleven years later, in April 1848, prisoners John Bryant and Edward Edwards escaped from Springfield Gaol. The prison was having new buildings erected and

A failed attempt to escape from Dartmoor Prison.

the two were being held in an old and less secure section of the prison. After being released from their cells for their daily duties, they mounted the 12ft yard wall, crossed a low roof and then dropped down between the debtor's prison and the boundary wall. Finding ropes and ladders used by the workmen on the building site, they scaled the wall with a ladder and scaffold rope and were only spotted by servants in the chaplains' house as they made their escape across the fields at the back of the prison. At the same time a prison officer noticed the ladder and rope against the wall. The alarm was raised and a pursuit was made; the fugitives were last spotted near Caton Hall.

In January 1838 Thomas Godwin was confined to Huntingdon County Gaol for debt. After visiting her son, his mother, Anne, went to a shop in the town and bought a rope, which she subsequently managed to smuggle in for Thomas. While the gaoler was away escorting a number of convicts to London, Godwin saw his chance, and managed to get up and over the prison wall; the rope, soon identified as that bought by his mother, was found hanging on the outside wall. Anne Godwin was brought to trial and faced fourteen years transportation if she had been found guilty, but although there was circumstantial evidence against her, Mr Baron Parke decided there was no solid proof and she was acquitted. By the time of his mother's appearance at the assizes, Thomas Godwin was long gone.

Some prisoners did not make it as far as the prison gates before affecting their escape. In October 1880 John Brown was sentenced to three months hard labour at Bury Quarter Sessions, Suffolk. Removed from the dock, Brown was then escorted to Bury railway station to be taken to Ipswich Gaol. After going to the toilet and leaving the facilities Brown found both warders had their backs to this exit and they were enjoying a good laugh as if Brown wasn't there. He therefore made good his escape. As the judge commented at the hearing after his recapture, '... you saw they did not care about you and you did not care about imprisonment. I can see that there is very good reason to suppose that there was a great temptation for you.' In view of these circumstances, the amount of time Brown had already served while awaiting his court appearances and the non-violence in his recapture, the judge saw fit to be lenient and sentenced him to seven days hard labour.

In September 1870, convict James Beaumont (alias Gordon), who was serving a penal servitude sentence at Portland Prison, made a daring escape. Some repairs had been made to the flooring of his cell, underneath which was an open area for ventilation. When the flooring was replaced it had not been securely fastened and Beaumont managed to remove a portion about 3ft long and 20in wide and lowered himself into the ventilation shaft. Creeping along, he came to gratings which may have impeded his progress, but he managed to force them and found himself in an open yard near the warder's quarters. Beaumont had brought with him some improvised ropes made from strips torn from his blanket, which he secured to an iron hook covered with linen to deaden any noise. Once in the yard, he climbed onto the roof of some nearby buildings then, using his linen rope, climbed to the top of the prison wall. Attaining this, he reversed the hook and prepared for his descent but found the rope was too short to carry him to the ground. In his anxiety for liberty he allowed himself to drop the remaining distance but the thud of his landing was heard by a sentry on duty nearby. Fortunately for Beaumont, owing to the darkness the sentry could not see anything untoward. The noise was heard at about twenty minutes past midnight but it was not until 2 o'clock, when the officers of the prison did their rounds, that the convict was missed.

Springfield Prison, Chelmsford, Essex, *c.* 1900.

The alarm was then raised, the troops and civil guards called up and a cannon fired as a signal to the coastguard that a convict had escaped. Rapidly, a cordon of troops and coastguard extended from Portland to the Ferry Bridge and on the railway, thus covering all the means by which the convict could leave the island. A search was then undertaken of the vicinity of the prison and the Government works. One of the civil guards fired at something which he saw moving in the dark and this being supposed to be the convict was the signal for a strong rein-forcement to be quickly on the spot, however, no convict was found. Indeed despite a thorough search of the whole area the convict eluded them.

In the press reports it was thought he must have had some accomplice who supplied him with civilian clothes rather than the prison dress he escaped in and that he had made good his escape from the island. Beaumont was described as 24 years of age, 5ft 7in tall, with a mark like a burn or summer mole over his right eye, a heart branded on his right arm and 'some mark' on his right thigh.

After being at large for about a week Beaumont was spotted near Portland bridge by a milkman between 4 and 5 o'clock in the morning. He was heading in the direction of Dorchester. Beaumont did not in fact enter Dorchester; instead, he crossed the fields to the village of Puddletown, where he was retaken while picking blackberries in a lane. He was still wearing prison shoes and stockings but had managed to obtain some other garments when he burgled a hotel in Portland and robbed a church of a priest's surplus, which he was wearing as a shirt.

An escape was reported from Millbank Prison on Thursday, 28 September 1882. Notorious housebreaker William Lovett had been under sentence of fourteen years penal servitude since the previous March for a daring burglary at Hampstead. A 'long service-man' under sentence of seven years or more was normally kept on the lower floors in Millbank, but because the prison was in the process of being shut down and most of the male convicts had been moved to Wormwood Scrubs, the usual precautions and rules were not so strictly adhered to. So Lovett, contrary to the usual practice, was placed in an upper-storey cell which overlooked the governor's garden. Lovett's trade was that of stonemason and he was employed in the prison in this capacity in part of a yard attached to the prison. Somehow he acquired a rope – probably one used for hauling his stone about – wound it round his body and secreted it in his cell. He retired as per regulations before 9 p.m. on Wednesday night but the following morning he was found to have made his escape by making a hole in the roof of his cell, climbing out and then lowering himself down into the governor's garden by means of the rope. He then took some of the same rope and lashed together two boards which he placed against the brickwork of the boundary wall and fled to freedom over the top. Upon examination of his cell, it was discovered that he had secreted a tool for loosening the brickwork in the roof of his cell and had worked to this end for some time, replacing the material he scraped out every night with chewed bread to avoid detection when his cell was inspected.

Lovett had escaped dressed in his convict's uniform of broad arrows but contractors Mowlem & Burt had premises nearby and it was though he could have obtained workmen's clothing from there and made good his escape wearing them. As soon as the escape was discovered, a special cordon of police was placed around the prison and a team of detectives was sent in all directions. A reward of 5s was also offered for information that led to the apprehension of Lovett, but there was a warning in the police appeals; Lovett was a desperate man and a career criminal who ten years previously, during his incarceration in Portland Prison serving a term of penal servitude, was flogged for a murderous assault on a warder (it was commented that 'He still bears the marks of his punishment'). He was described as '33 years old, 5ft 3in tall, hair brown, eyes grey and complexion fresh', he was also said to be made distinctive by a number of birthmarks.

Wormwood Scrubs Prison had not been completed when its first prisoner escaped in September 1883. John Rourke (31) was a twice-convicted burglar who had completed eighteen months of a twelve-year sentence and had been removed to Wormwood Scrubs from Pentonville for over a year. Rourke's cell was in one of the upper stories of the prison. Up to the time of his escape he had endeared himself to prison authorities, had earned remission marks and was engaged, during the day, in outdoor labour. While so engaged he had managed to obtain three small pieces of hoop iron, one of them not longer than a forefinger, and by means of these scraped away at the mortar around the bricks of his cell wall and managed to make a hole large enough for him to squeeze his body through. Rourke had fashioned a rope from his bedclothes and with this he lowered himself 30ft to the ground. Managing to elude the vigilance of the armed sentries on duty around the building, he scaled the outer wall by availing himself of the scaffolding poles being used in the building works for the rest of the prison and made off. It was suggested he had found shelter and a change of clothing 'in some of the low haunts surrounding the canal banks' in the vicinity. The escape was discovered a short while later by a night watchman, who found the bedclothes of the convict fluttering from his cell window.

In April 1885 the Metropolitan Police published an appeal to find the whereabouts of John Oxley, alias Adams (32). Oxley was a notorious burglar who had been convicted at the Old Bailey on a charge of warehouse breaking and sent down for eighteen months the previous September. He had already made a determined bid for freedom from the police when they went to arrest him at Westminster. After successfully getting onto the roof of a building, he made a jump for it but broke both his ankles in the process and was taken into custody when he had recovered sufficiently. After being found guilty, he was taken to Holloway Prison and gave the officials there no trouble, nor aroused suspicion that he was planning another escape bid. On 7 April Oxley was in the prison hospital, but when the prison officers did their unlocking and rounds on the following morning Oxley was found to be missing and the lock had been removed from his

ESCAPE FROM WORMWOOD SCRUBS CONVICT PRISON

The *Illustrated Police News'* depiction of John Rourke's escape from Wormwood Scrubs, September 1883.

door. A piece of iron which had been fashioned into the shape of a screwdriver was discovered concealed in his bed. Oxley had left behind his cap, jacket and boots, thus it was assumed he made his escape wearing just a prison vest and drab trousers. After removing the lock, he had let himself out of a window and down to the prison yard with the aid of several bandages that he had been given to use for his legs. Then he had hauled himself up to the top of the partition wall where he could reach the top of the outer wall, clambered over and descended to a piece of waste ground by means of another rope. These ropes were found and, upon examination, were proved to have been made from pieces of string, rags and the counterpane of his bed.

Despite a reward being offered for information leading to his re-capture and keen enquiries, the police found no one had seen Oxley escape and they had to admit to the reporter that 'having evaded his re-apprehension up till the present he will probably not be captured until he is taken on some other charge.' Oxley was described as 'Aged thirty-four years, height five feet, thick set, complexion dark, hair dark. On his arms and body there are several tattoo marks.'

Oxley was, in fact, found by the City Police the very same day he escaped, in a house at Bath Place, Haggerston. The police surrounded the house and, even though his ankles had not fully recovered, Oxley jumped from the window, managed to elude the constables and ran off to a neighbouring timber yard. There he scrambled 'like a cat' to the top of a wood stack that stood about 50ft high and then down the opposite side and made off again. The constables caught up with him near the canal, where he threw himself in and swam across. After a pursuit of nearly half an hour, Oxley was finally captured by Detective Hunt of the City Police with Detective Sergeants Sage and Newby of G Division close behind.

Detective Inspector Peel of G Division commented that he had experienced one of Oxley's previous escape attempts. He had caught him in the nick of time just as he was about to escape through a hole in a door from Old Street police station. Oxley had begun his escape bid with no other implement than his empty drink can. With this he had taken the hinges off an inner door of the cell, afterwards using them to break down the outer panels.

Bought before the Middlesex Sessions on 13 May 1885, Oxley pleaded guilty to escaping from Holloway but argued in mitigation that he had made his escape because he had 'never been so cruelly treated' than in Holloway. The assistant judge ordered him to be kept in penal servitude for an extra five years; to commence at the expiration of his present sentence.

Escapes were not limited to London prisons and, as this particularly violent instant from late May 1888 illustrates, the provincial prisons certainly faced the

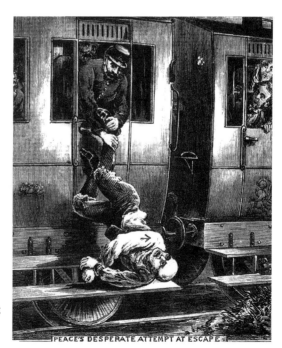

Charles Peace evades his escorts and throws himself from a moving train in a last desperate attempt to escape the gallows, 1879.

same dangers as their metropolitan counterparts. Notorious housebreaker John Jackson (alias Edward Graham), aged 33, who claimed to be a native of Nottingham and a plumber by trade, was being held in Strangeways Prison, Manchester. He had been convicted at the previous Salford Sessions for housebreaking at Eccles but was also wanted in connection with offences at Hull, Huddersfield, Oldham and Bradford. Jackson had been working under the supervision of warder Webb and as soon as Webb turned his back, Jackson sprang up and struck a terrible blow to the back of his head with a hammer, knocking him to the ground insensible. Jackson then exchanged his boots with those of the warder and managed to climb onto the roof and down onto the top of a lower building before reaching the wall, where he had a drop of about 10ft to the street. Shortly afterwards, Jackson was spotted by two boys going down Red Bank, 'a densely populated part of the city and near resort of habitual criminals and low lodging houses.' During that same night a number of burglaries were committed in Oldham, including the theft of clothing, no doubt the work of Jackson who had made his escape wearing prison clothes.

Warder Webb died about three hours after the attack, an inquest was called and verdict of murder recorded against Jackson. The police really were up against it to apprehend Jackson; his features were described as 'commonplace' and 'not very distinctive' to the degree that it was suggested in the *Illustrated Police News* 'any tramp or loafer of medium height with stumpy whiskers and moustache was in some danger of arrest.'

The manhunt continued for several weeks, but was brought to a conclusion when Jackson was arrested in Bradford, after breaking into a house. Tried for murder at the Manchester Assizes and found guilty, he was returned to Strangeways under sentence of death and was executed on 7 August 1888.

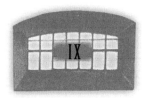

IX

ROGUES GALLERY

What follows are a selection of representative cases which, although not infamous, are nonetheless insightful, that profile many of the common types of crime brought before the provincial Magistrates' Courts and County Assizes of the Eastern Circuit during the nineteenth century. These stories not only illustrate the crime but also give an insight into the background stories and types of convicted criminal that commonly occupied our county gaols, convict prisons or were transported to our penal colonies. These cases also demonstrate that it was often not the law but the luck of the draw, lack of advanced forensics, a good defence barrister, or the constraints of old draconian laws that would determine your fate and your sentence. Until its abolition in 1868, transportation for a variety of durations (dependant on the offence) was the sentence pronounced for more serious crimes and repeat offenders. A typical example is the case of the Suffolk Summer Assizes of 1847, when Edward Coots, aged 15, a labourer from Framlingham, was charged with having broken into and entered the house of John Oakley at Framlingham. Accused of stealing a tea chest, two silver caddy spoons and a variety of other articles, he was found guilty and, because it was not his first offence, he was given ten years transportation. At the same assize, Ipswich labourer George Barker (27) was found guilty of the wilful murder of Elizabeth Jager in the parish of St Margaret in Ipswich. He was sentenced to twenty years transportation.

Trouble with Poachers

One of the most frequent offences brought before rural magistrates were cases of poaching, which could still receive sentences under the early nineteenth-century game laws, thus the exchanges between gamekeepers and poachers attempting to evade arrest were often violent and led to far more serious offences. On 4 March 1856 brothers James (29), William (22) and Thomas Thurgood (23) and

BOROUGH OF NORTHAMPTON.

A

CALENDAR of PRISONERS

TO BE TRIED AT THE

General Quarter Sessions of the Peace,

TO BE HOLDEN AT NORTHAMPTON,

On WEDNESDAY, the 21st day of November, 1888.

BEFORE

JOHN HIBBERD BREWER, ESQ., BARRISTER-AT-LAW,

RECORDER.

JAMES BARRY, ESQUIRE, MAYOR.

WILLIAM SHOOSMITH, GENTLEMAN, CLERK OF THE PEACE.

NOTE.—(N.) signifies neither read nor write: (R.) read only; (Imp.) read and write imperfectly; (Well) read and write well; (Sup.) superior education.

WILLIAM MARK, Printer, 27, The Drapery, Northampton.

The Calendar of Prisoners brought before the Borough of Northampton Quarter Sessions in November 1888. Two men stood trial; Charles Hall was accused on three counts of stealing clothing and boots, while William Freeman stood accused of stealing a horse, trap and harness worth a total of £42.

James Guiver (30), all labourers and 'athletic young men', were brought before the Essex Assizes on the charge of wilfully murdering gamekeeper William Hales. The last three fellows breathed a sigh of relief when it was announced the Grand Jury had dropped the capital charge against them, but the case should be confined to James Thurgood.

It emerged as the evidence was given that William Thurgood suggested their group go at night to Sir John Tyrrell's wood for a bit of poaching. Walking across the fields to Boreham and Duke's Wood, each man had a gun. Joseph Wesby, his father James and William Hales were all gamekeepers watching the woods. Upon hearing the shots they walked towards the sound, Hales went a slightly different direction but was soon to be heard call, 'Come on mates, here they are!' Joseph Wesby was closest to Hales when he heard a report of a shotgun and saw Hales fall. The poachers then took flight. The Wesbys managed to catch hold of James Thurgood and took him back to Duke's Head Farm and when he was secured there they returned to the wood. When they found Hales' body his clothes were still smouldering. At the inquest Mr Copeland the surgeon agreed Hales had not stood a chance with a shot fired that close to him.

At the trial it could not be proved beyond reasonable doubt that James Thurgood actually fired the fatal shot, but he was found guilty of being an accessory to the murder and was sentenced to death. Thurgood was not the least affected and replied in impudent tone, 'Thank you sir; God Bless you all!' His sentence was later commuted to transportation for life. The other accused were acquitted of the murder but immediately faced charges of night poaching, they all pleaded guilty and were given four years penal servitude each.

In a similar case, on 18 November 1872 Thomas Dudley, gamekeeper to Sir Thomas Western, Lord Lieutenant of Essex, was fatally shot by poachers while he patrolled the estate at Great Braxted. Dudley's fellow gamekeepers knew who to suspect and summoned the police. Three men were arrested; the man considered to have fired the fatal shot was William Bundock. Evidence was all over his house; wet clothes, powder and shot in jacket pockets and a shotgun under his bed. All his were removed to Witham police station.

At the inquest a verdict of wilful murder was pronounced against Bundock. At the trial it was decided that the gun was discharged in panic at being discovered and not with intent to murder. Bundock was an old offender and he was lucky to be acquitted of the capital charge and the judge told him so, but finding him guilty of poaching with violence he sentenced him to five years penal servitude. Bundock's non-violent accomplices, Challis and Miller, both received four months with hard labour.

In March 1870, David Heffer (21) and James Rutterford (27) were brought before Suffolk Assizes charged with the murder of gamekeeper John Hight on the Eriswell Estate on 31 December 1869. Rather than being tragically shot in an exchange with fleeing poachers, it was plain Hight had been knocked to the ground and mercilessly beaten to death. PC Peck had been on duty just a short distance away that night and had exchanged words with Rutterford and Heffer. When the murder was discovered the two poachers were soon arrested and appeared on trial at the Suffolk Winter Assizes. With a mountain of evidence against them, Heffer turned Queen's Evidence and saw Rutterford sentenced to death as he walked free. Much to the indignation of local people Rutterford did not keep his appointment with the hangman. Due to a large burn on his face and neck which caused a malformation, it was considered wise not to hang him and he was sentenced to penal servitude for life. Neither of the murderous poachers evaded death for long though; Rutterford died in prison three years later and Heffer of a 'broken blood vessel' in 1885.

Seeking Gainful Employment

On 9 January 1888, George Thurgood of Wickhambrook, Suffolk, was brought before Haverhill Petty Sessions charged with searching for work in workhouse clothes. Mr James Hale, the master of the Kedington Workhouse, stated that Thurgood had left the workhouse wearing a suit of clothes, property of the Risbridge Union, valued at 15s, he also pointed out that this was not the first time Thurgood had left the workhouse without permission. Despite his insistence that he was just looking for gainful employment, Thurgood was sentenced to fourteen days with hard labour.

Money for Old Rope

On 21 January 1880, Thomas Garwood (39) was brought before Lowestoft Police Court, Suffolk, and pled guilty to having stolen 14 stone of old rope and 2 stone of salt beef to the value of 27s from the schooner *Albion*, the property of John Grindell. Garwood had sold the rope to Samuel Bagshaw, a marine store dealer, for 12s. In reply to the Bench, the prisoner said he had no defence and knew he deserved punishment. He received two months imprisonment with hard labour.

Juvenile Offenders

In October 1871 Alfred Amos (13) was caught stealing apples from an orchard by Head Constable Sach of Sudbury Borough Police. Tried and found guilty of this crime, the boy was sentenced to one month imprisonment with hard labour.

John James Neavecy (10) stole four pairs of stockings, valued at 3s, belonging to Elizabeth Wilton, a widow lady of 10 Victoria Terrace, Kirkley in April

1880. Easily apprehended, young John appeared before Lowestoft Police Court, Suffolk. James Peto, chair of the Bench, commented that the boy was a very badly behaved lad, having appeared in court on a number of previous occasions and it was only just over a week since he had had a few days in prison and had been whipped. He was sentenced to Norwich Castle Gaol for ten days and then to a reformatory for five years.

In March 1901, the Lowestoft Police Court, Suffolk heard the case of four boys named Sharman, Morter, Larter and Abramson, who were charged with stealing a jar of jam from the Star Tea Company. All boys pleaded guilty. Superintendent Shipp stated that Sharman's mother had died when he was four years old. He was taken care of by his aunt, who sent him to the workhouse in October 1899. His father and brother 'declined to have anything to do with him. Not long back, he left the workhouse and was discovered sleeping in a rabbit hutch and because of his filth and chilblains his toes were rotting away.' In the interests of the lad, Superintendant Shipp asked to have him sent away. And thus Sharman was sent to the workhouse for a week so arrangements could be made for his removal. Abramson was sent to a reformatory until he was 16, while Larter and Morter were bound over for three months under the First Offenders Act.

Young Arsonists

On 18 July 1844, Samuel Baxter (10) was brought before the Huntingdon Assizes and pleaded guilty to an indictment for setting fire to four stacks of straw, the property of Captain Daintree at Hemingford Abbotts. The boys' father was the farm bailiff for Captain Daintree and there seemed to be no motive for the child's actions. All that was stated in court was a conversation between the boy and the captain where young Baxter said he thought the farm house as well as the stacks would be burned 'and then we must go and live in the village'. In passing sentence the learned judge, Mr Baron Alderson, expressed his very great regret in having to do so upon a boy of such tender years but it was 'absolutely necessary that the law should make the same example for boys as it did for men' and hammered down that the boy should be sentenced to fifteen years transportation and his Lordship earnestly hoped that other boys would take notice and be warned by it.

In November 1879 John Douglas Spence (13) and Henry Silver (14) were brought before the Essex Assizes charged with attempting to set fire to the training ship *Shaftesbury* on the nights of 2 and 4 August. No evidence was offered against Silver, who was ordered to be discharged. No reason could be assigned to the actions of the boys; the captain even wrote a letter stating the previous good character of Spence. He was sentenced to ten days imprisonment, twelve strokes of the birch rod and afterward to be sent to a reformatory for three years.

For Swearing

In December 1887 Charles Beavis was heard using obscene language on Haverhill High Street in Suffolk by PC Ransom. The policeman had cautioned Beavis about the swearing whereupon Beavis repeated the language and walked away. At the Haverhill Petty Sessions the Bench was 'determined to put a stop to the use of such vile language' and Beavis was duly sentenced to fourteen days without hard labour.

Beavis was not alone; being brought before the Bench for using profane and threatening language in public was a common occurrence and was not restricted to the lower orders in the late nineteenth century, as Major Frank Fisher of the King's Own Scottish Borderers found out in October 1892 when he was brought before the Cambridge Police Court. Major Fisher had recently appeared in court on charges of using threatening language to his wife, this time he was charged with using obscene language in St Andrew's Street, which he strenuously denied and threatened to bring his 'harsh treatment' at the hands of the local police to the notice of his relative, Colonel Howard Vincent. Unmoved by such bluster, the magistrates were satisfied PC Perry and a number of witnesses spoke the truth and, finding the major guilty, sentenced him to fourteen days imprisonment – without hard labour. Major Fisher asked if he could pay a fine instead but the Bench stuck with a committal and Major Fisher was taken down as he attempted to prevaricate and demand an appeal.

Opposite, clockwise from top left:
Charles Mason (30) of Woodhurst, Huntingdonshire; committed to Wisbech Prison for stealing an overcoat in 1872. His sentence was to serve seven years penal servitude, then to have seven years under police supervision. He was soon transferred to Pentonville Prison. His sentence was hard because he was a repeat offender with a record dating back to 1853 with such crimes as vagrancy, stealing a sack, stealing a drawer and money and larcency.

Isaac Davies (14) of Wisbech was convicted of breaking into a warehouse and stealing twenty oranges and a packet of Brazil nuts in 1872. He was sentenced to three calendar months with hard labour.

William Lines, alias Bloom, (21), Donkey Dealer of Stowmarket, Suffolk, 1872. Tried and convicted of assault, having, with associates, thrown a man violently into a river. He was sentenced to three calendar month with hard labour.

William Samuel Edwards (10) of South Brink, Wisbech was found guilty of stealing and causing wilful damage to vegetables in July 1877. He was sentenced to one week in prison and five years in a reformatory.

FROM THE WISBECH PRISON BOOK

Rural Disquiet

Rural disquiet at the poor treatment and mean wages for agricultural labourers was often expressed by instances of rioting, anonymous threatening letters being sent and stack burning.

In mid-nineteenth-century Suffolk, strong-arm tactics were maintained against any of those who would transgress the laws of person or property. At Suffolk Assizes in July 1844 the stance of the judiciary is well evinced on this day when Robert Grimwade (29) of Polstead was sentenced to ten years transportation for sending a letter threatening to burn down the property of three local landowners. Grimwade had followed Faber Copsey (19) of Glemham, who was transported for life for firing a barn, and William Gill of Drinkstone, who received the same for setting fire to a stack of Barley; both of whom were sentenced at the previous March Assizes. In the 1820s the men found guilty of firing the stacks would almost certainly have gone to the gallows.

On 24 July 1862, James Boatman, a deaf labourer, was brought before the assizes charged with maliciously setting fire to a stack and a shed in the occupation of the Guardians of the Billericay Union at Great Burstead, Essex. Boatman was shown the assize calendar with his charges listed, to which he replied, 'I did it, I was tired of working for 5*d* a day and a loaf of bread'. It appeared that the final straw was when he was refused a pair of shoes. He was sentenced to three years penal servitude.

In December 1864, John Williams, a labourer, was brought before the Essex Winter Assizes charged with setting fire to a stack of wheat and two stacks of straw at St Osyth. Found guilty of the crime and reprimanded by the judge for his actions, he was sentenced to fifteen years penal servitude. The unrepentant Williams, on hearing his sentence, said, 'Thank you my Lord, it's the best day's work I ever did in my life.'

Even in 1899, the final year of the nineteenth century, firing stacks was still a form of protest and the punishments remained severe, as Charles Dennis found to his cost when he was found guilty of setting fire to a stack of wheat straw at Fordham in Cambridgeshire. Mr Justice Wills commented, 'it was a most wanton and wicked thing to do. It was a most dangerous crime,' and he sentenced Dennis to four years penal servitude.

Drunken Thief

In May 1881, William March appeared before the Petty Sessions at Sudbury, Suffolk charged with the theft of a gallon of whisky from the Bull Inn in the town. Witnesses stated he was seen coming out of the tap room with a bottle of whiskey and promptly left the pub. Mary Ann Elliott, the housekeeper, seeing this summoned the tap-boy and sent him after March and he was brought back, with the whiskey, to the pub. Found to be in a state of intoxication he was handed over to the constable. In court, March claimed no recollection of the entire incident. The bench were not amused. The mayor, Mr G.G. Whorlow, put the blame squarely on March's drinking habits and proclaimed this was however 'no excuse' and sent March down for two months with hard labour.

Stealing from the Royal Mail

In December 1859, George Currey (29), a Post Office letter carrier at Braintree, pleaded guilty at the Essex Winter Assizes to stealing a letter containing three half sovereigns. The justice was keen that an example be made of Currey and sentenced him to four years penal servitude.

January 1880 saw Thomas Waller (11) appear at court in Ipswich, Suffolk. The boy had observed a postman putting letters in a tradesman's box. Pushing his slender arm and small hands through the letterbox he extracted one of the letters. Opening it, he discovered a cheque for £82 and suggested to one of his pals they go to London on a spending spree. His pal didn't like the idea and, his conscience pricked, the boy confessed all to his mother. Justice was, however, seen to be done and, described in court as 'a proper subject for the birch', the boy received six strokes of the birch rod and served three days imprisonment.

In June 1894 a number of cases of alleged mail robberies were brought before Suffolk Summer Assizes at Bury. Mary Smith (18) was indicted for stealing a postal order to the value of 7s 6d from the postmaster at Stanton. Justice Knight stated that Smith 'had shown a great deal of low cunning ... and for her own sake [he] must give her a term of imprisonment which would give her time to reflect upon her conduct.' He hammered down ten months with hard labour. William Ellis Norman, a postman, was also charged with three counts of stealing letters and 10s in money. As a postal official and one 'who had abused his position of trust' he was sentenced to twelve months with hard labour.

Prostitution and Robbery

In February 1888, a case was brought before the Suffolk Assizes of a robbery in a house of ill-fame. In a beautifully phrased address by the prosecution it was stated, 'On the night of 5 February, Mr John Roberts, the master of the barge *John of Faversham*, fell in with a woman named Elizabeth Girkin and went with her to her house in Asylum Court.' After falling asleep his watch was put into a cupboard for safety. In the middle of the night John Reeve (29), the man Girkin co-habited with, came in and threatened to murder her if she didn't turn the man out and then he stormed out. Returning with Jonathan Marsh (23), they turned Roberts out of the house. Subsequently missing his watch and the contents of his purse, Roberts informed the police and the items were found on the prisoners. It appears Marsh was acquitted but Reeve, who had been previously convicted, was sent down for five years penal servitude.

Highway Robbery

Although often not committed on horseback, highway robbery did not die with Dick Turpin in the eighteenth century. The case of Robert Allen (20) in 1879 is a typical example. Brought before the Cambridge Assizes charged with highway robbery with violence, it transpired that Allen and another man had stumbled out of a public house at Eversden on 8 October, both of them in an inebriated state. After walking about a mile up the road Allen tripped up his compatriot and kicked him, threatening to kill him and throw him over the hedge. As the man lay on the floor Allen rifled his pockets for the purse he had spotted on the man in the pub. Allen claimed he had only picked the man out of the ditch and left him by the side of the road; he swore he did not take the purse. It was proved that Allen had been seen after the attack with the purse and the two half sovereigns his victim had claimed were in it. The jury convicted Allen of larceny only, but as Allen had a previous conviction he received ten months imprisonment with hard labour.

Opposite, clockwise from top left:
Harriet Cornwall (40) of Wisbech, pleaded guilty to fraudulently obtaining £2 and was sentenced to six calendar months with hard labour in 1873.

John Kennedy (68) was a habitual criminal with a record including over fifteen convictions for felonies in Norfolk, Lincolnshire and Cambridgeshire dating back to 1842. In May 1873 he was discovered in an enclosed yard and arrested. Found guilty of intent to commit another felony, he was sentenced to six weeks with hard labour.

Charles Frost (22), a Suffolk labourer, was found guilty of stealing a foal in 1872. He was sentenced to three calendar months with hard labour.

William Anthony (36) of Buckland, Hertfordshire was sentenced to one year with hard labour for stealing in 1875. He had a long criminal record for felonies. In 1854 he had received three days solitary confinement and thirty-six lashes, followed by increasingly longer custodial sentences with hard labour in 1870, 1872 and 1874.

FROM THE WISBECH PRISON BOOK

Concealment of Birth

On 6 March 1867, Elizabeth Dann (23), a domestic servant and 'imperfectly educated', was brought before the Essex Spring Assizes charged with the wilful murder of her illegitimate child. The court was lenient as there was no direct evidence of foul play; as the judge pointed out, she had concealed the birth of her child and so only she would have known if the child was born alive or dead. To give her time for reflection and instruction in religion and, above all, to set her up as 'a warning to those who indulge in vice', she was sentenced to eighteen months imprisonment, with hard labour.

In February 1888 at the Suffolk Winter Assizes held at Ipswich Shire Hall, Clarissa Ford (17) pleaded guilty to concealing the birth of her child at Ipswich and was sentenced to be imprisoned without hard labour for one fortnight.

A Most Unusual Case – Impersonation of a Priest

In July 1888, the case of George Wilfred Frederick Ellis (35) was heard at Suffolk Winter Assizes, held at Bury. Ellis was appointed curate at Wetheringsett in 1883. A popular priest with the locals, he performed baptisms, marriages, funerals and regular services in the village until, by chance, he was found out and exposed as a fraudster impersonating a priest. Ellis's paperwork proved to be forged and he was apprehended by Inspector Bly of Eye in March 1888. In a trial where no lesser luminary than the Lord Bishop of Norwich gave evidence, the jury were left in no doubt of the answers given on oath and returned a verdict of 'Guilty' without leaving their box. Ellis was sentenced to seven years penal servitude in Dartmoor Prison.

The matter left a legacy behind in the village. Where did the people stand who had been married by Ellis over the five years of his tenure? Were they still married or not and did this make their children bastards? A special Act of Parliament had to be drawn up recognising all of Ellis's marriages 'as valid as if the same had been solemnised before a duly ordained clergyman of the Church of England'.

No Mercy for the Repeat Offender

On 17 July 1863, Francis King (alias George Smith) was brought before the assizes for the theft of a horse worth 5s, the property of his own father and brother. The horse had been kept on Bentley Common and was found in the possession of King, who made false statements about it. His brother and father both gave evidence, the old man being a particularly sad and broken sight in the box; he was so overcome by the cross-examination that he collapsed in the witness box. King was found guilty of this offence and a further charge of burglary. It appeared he had already been convicted of some similar felony and had served four years penal servitude – he had committed these fresh offences as soon as he was released. King was therefore sentenced to fourteen years penal servitude.

Mugging

On the evening of the 1842 Cambridge Pot Fair, William Haslop was at his stall when he met a woman he knew and they left the stall together for a stroll in the moonlight along the banks of the Cam. As they walked along they were passed by a group of three men who initially walked by but then suddenly rushed back. Mr Haslop was tripped up, a hand was put over his mouth and another over his eyes and he was held on the ground while one of the men rifled through his pockets, removing all of the seven shillings he had about him. Haslop's female companion raised the alarm by running off screaming 'Murder!' and calling out for a policeman. As soon as the ruffians had removed the cash from their victim they ran off, one of them leaping a hedge into a private garden which, unfortunately for him, turned out to be a dead-end and as he returned he fell into the arms of a police constable. Taken into custody and charged, William Freeman was brought before the county assizes the following month on charges of assault and stealing on the Queen's Highway. Despite denying he was involved, it was a pretty open-and-shut case for its day. Found guilty by the jury, Mr Justice Williams sentenced Freeman to prison with six months hard labour.

Assaulting a Police Officer

In March 1844, Constable William Brown, the village bobby of Isleham in Cambridgeshire, had called at the Harp Inn and cleared out the last of the drinkers. They left quietly but a number of them loitered outside 'kicking up a row' to the nuisance of the neighbourhood. Constable Brown asked the men to disperse; they would not. He ordered them to go home but they argued they had as much right to be on the highway as anyone else, so the constable threatened them with the cage. The men argued they would not be placed there by anybody in Isleham. The exchange grew heated and one of the aggressors pulled down the constable and kicked him. Constable Brown called for assistance 'in the Queen's name', to which one of the men told him to go to hell and delivered him a violent blow. The men then set about the constable with fists and kicks as he writhed on the ground and then left him lying in the dirt.

The landlord of the Harp helped the beaten constable inside and tended to his wounds, then, not sated by their last attack because they had not 'done for him', the men came into the pub and gave the constable a few 'parting salutes' and even lingered outside to give him some more when he came outside again. Constable Brown was in such a bad way he was put up on a bed and the village surgeon was called. His injuries about the head threatened such pressure on his brain that he was lucky to keep his life.

The men who assaulted Constable Brown were all known to him and soon Charles Whiterod and Joseph and Elijah Brown were arrested and brought before the assizes for their part in the assault. Found guilty of the attack, these violent men were sentenced to be transported for fifteen years.

Wounding with Intent

On 23 April 1867, Frederick Watkins (23) was out walking with his sweetheart, Matilda Griggs (16), at Buckhurst Hill. She had already borne him a child but they lived apart, she with her parents and he working in London, although he visited a few days each week. Now she was 16 it was anticipated, at least by Matilda and her family, that they would marry, but Watkins seemed reluctant to set a date. While walking out together on this fine evening he began to accuse her of flirting with other men, this she confidently and immediately denied. Appearing to calm down, Watkins suggested they cross over the palings into a field. Without warning Watkins then drew out a lead weight on a string and struck her about the head until the string broke. He then took out a dagger and stabbed her several times. In his haste he did not realise he had not removed the knife from its sheath. Despite this horrific attack the wounds did not kill Matilda, who managed to lift herself up and struggle to a fence, where she was discovered a few hours later and taken to her home.

Watkins gave himself up at Epping police station at 5 a.m. on the morning after the attack. Convinced he had killed her, he was surprised when he was charged with cutting and wounding with intent to murder. By the time his trial came to court Matilda Griggs was well on the road to recovery but Watkins' parents had paid her off to disappear so she could not give evidence at his trial. Despite the lack of Matilda's evidence, he was found guilty of 'unlawful wounding with intent to do grievous bodily harm' and was sentenced to twenty years penal servitude. In the end, Matilda did not wait for her beau; she married a Leytonstone tailor, joined him in the trade and bore him three children.

Unlawful Wounding

On 19 September 1871, James Bass Mullinger, a Cambridge graduate with 'some literary distinction', visited Annie Haslam, his stepbrother's wife, who was staying with a relative, Mrs Barnard, at Harlow. During the visit Mullinger appeared to be seized with some mania, took up a knife from the supper table and struck Annie Haslam on the left side. Fortunately, the knife was old and worn and Mrs Haslam's dress was padded to the degree that the knife did not penetrate, but such was the force with which she was struck the blade of the knife broke. Mullinger, undeterred, picked up another knife and delivered some eighteen wounds to her throat, face and hands before she could get away with Mrs Barnard. Mullinger was then seen to calmly pick up his hat and coat and walk back to his father's house, also in Harlow.

The police were summoned and Mullinger was arrested. Luckily, over the following weeks, Mrs Haslam recovered from her wounds. The case was brought before the Winter Assizes. A number of witnesses spoke favourably of Mullinger's academic prowess. Dr Bateson, Master of St John's College, stated that the prisoner had obtained a number of prizes, including the Le Bas and Hulsean essays. In an appeal to the jury his defence counsel argued that Mullinger was lame and, like Byron and other literary doyens, so sadly afflicted by it, combined with his devotion to study and literary work, a temporary mania had manifested itself on the fateful evening. Mrs Haslam pointed out she had no vindictive feeling towards the prisoner and that rather than a charge of attempted murder a lesser charge would be preferable. A verdict of unlawful wounding was returned and Mullinger was sentenced to twelve months without hard labour.

Aggravated Burglary

At 1 a.m. on 12 December 1880, Charles Murrells (56), Caleb Farran (40) and William Gaskin (45) broke into the home of Thomas Cole, a butcher, residing at Hare Green, Great Bromley, Essex. Mr Cole heard the sound of smashing glass and went to the door just in time to see one of the men put his hand through the smashed pane and begin to turn the key in the lock. As they made their way to the sitting room, Cole saw that each of the burglars was disguised with a black net over their face. Cole attempted to escape but was spotted and tripped by a fourth man and struck on the head with a thick stick by a fifth, whom he later identified as Farran. Cole was taken inside and his money detected and taken with intimidation.

Murrells was the first of the burglars to be caught. The day after the burglary he was in a pub and made it known he had a sovereign and a bit of paper (a £5 note). As he was only an occasional cattle market drover he could hardly have come by the money legitimately. It was soon found he had made enquiries about Cole's business in the days before the burglary. Apprehended a few days later, he made a desperate attack on the arresting officer with a knife. Two of the other burglars were soon in custody and the three were brought to trial at the January Assizes. The case against Gaskin was very circumstantial and he was acquitted. Farran was given fifteen years and Murrell, who had a number of previous convictions including a sentence of fifteen years for aggravated burglary, was sent down for life.

Robbery with Violence

Maurice Dyer (24), Harry French (18) and David Deaves (19), all of whom were labourers, were brought before the Suffolk Summer Assizes in June 1894 charged with stealing a stick and 2½d in money from Thomas Hayward at Little Coman the previous April. The judge noted that the men had robbed an old man with considerable violence and their punishment would reflect this. Dyer was given three calendar months imprisonment and was ordered to be 'at once flogged, receiving twenty lashes of the cat.' Deaves received two months and eighteen lashes and French one month and fifteen lashes.

Opposite, clockwise from top left:
Sophia Doughty (13) of Emneth, Norfolk was sentenced to twenty-one days in prison and three years in a reformatory in 1873 after being found guilty of the theft of a pair of women's drawers.

Thomas Chase (11) of Wisbech was found guilty of stealing 1s 6d from Mr Chapman in July 1873. Chase was sentenced to twenty-one days imprisonment followed by five years in a reformatory.

Martha Key (26) was of 'known bad character' when she was sent down for seven years for felony in 1875. Over the previous twelve years she had served time, often with hard labour, on a number of occasions for felonies, including being a rogue and a vagabond, being drunk and riotous.

Ann Edwards (17), a domestic servant of March, Cambridgeshire was found guilty of firing a stack of wheat straw in 1874. She was sentenced to six calendar months with hard labour.

FROM THE WISBECH PRISON BOOK

Robbers' Desperate Struggle with Police Officers

On 10 June 1851, police were observing the home of Mr Cook at Twinstead (Great Henny), Essex. Their vigilance paid off as three men entered the premises obviously intent on burglary. PCs John Eldred, John Jonas, William Humphrys and PC Cross challenged the intruders and one of the policemen was immediately struck down with a blow from a chisel by one of the burglars. Another robber was tackled by John Flower, one of Mr Cook's labourers. A desperate struggle ensued, fists and hand weapons flew, there was even a shot loosed off, which later resulted in the amputation of John Flower's arm. The blood splattered up the walls to the degree that it was described by officers who examined the scene as being akin to a slaughterhouse. All of the intruders were eventually brought in and were identified as Stephen Pryke, William Poole and James Dawson. Poole's head had been badly cut in the melee and he later died of his wounds. Dawson was sentenced to death (later commuted to life imprisonment) and Pryke was transported for ten years.

Pub Brawl

During a quiet night in the Woolpack Inn at Haverhill in October 1888, the landlord, Fuller Chamberlain, was in the tap room with Frank Farrant when local labourer, Arthur Hall (20), called for beer. When presented with his pint Hall stated he only had three-halfpence in his pocket to pay. Chamberlain took the beer back and reminded him he had been refused credit for bad debts in the pub before. Hall stated he wanted a quiet word with Chamberlain – the landlord said speak on. Hall asked if the landlord remembered him hitting him, to which Chamberlain said, 'I don't want any of your nonsense tonight.' Hall levelled up close to Chamberlain, stating, 'You *******, I'll rip your ******* ********* up!' Putting down his pint pots, Chamberlain saw Hall had a knife in his hand. The landlord hit Hall, knocking him to the floor, but the ruffian got up again, lunged at Chamberlain and tried to draw the blade across his neck. In the ensuing struggle Hall's fingers ended up in Chamberlain's mouth, 'trying to rend it.' Chamberlain bit with all his might and managed to keep Hall pinned to the floor until the constable arrived to take him into custody. The jury at the Suffolk Assizes found Hall guilty of wounding with intent to do bodily harm and he was sentenced to twelve months penal servitude with hard labour.

Drunken Assault

In July 1892, William Clay (36) was brought before Huntingdon Assizes indicted for the manslaughter of Thomas Parkinson at Woodstone. Both men had been employed at the railway wagon works at Peterborough. On the evening in question they were drinking at the Cross Keys when they started arguing. When they left the pub Clay lashed out at Parkinson, punching him twice and knocking him to the ground. Parkinson was knocked insensible and died the following morning from 'suffusion of blood on the brain' the result, the doctors deposed, of two violent blows on the temples. Clay was found guilty and sentenced to sixteen months with hard labour.

Attempted Murder

In March 1864, Letitia Newman (24) was tried at Suffolk Assizes. Newman, a housekeeper to William Keeble, a Baddingham butcher, had been given notice to quit. As a parting shot she put arsenic into the mug of porter Keeble was drinking. Fortunately her surreptitious action was noticed and Keeble was prevented from drinking the now fatal brew. Found guilty of attempted murder, she was sentenced to penal servitude for life.

Domestic Violence

Two Suffolk cases from 1876 show the courts robust attempts to tackle the age-old problem of violence in the home. Frederick Gayfer (19) of Ipswich was charged with 'unlawfully wounding' his mother-in-law in a reprisal attack after an argument. At the Winter Assizes the judge told Gayfer that he was 'a very dangerous person – a person with vindictive and bad feeling who will go to any length to satisfy your vengeance.' Gayfer was sent down for seven years penal servitude.

Also in 1876, John Taylor (66), a thatcher of Debenham, Suffolk, a well-known drunkard who was known to have argued with his wife Maria on a regular basis, raised his gun to within inches of her head and fired. The shot shattered Maria's bonnet but she remained physically unharmed. No doubt believing he had killed her, Taylor retreated to his cottage and barricaded himself in, so the situation became a siege, with Taylor threatening instant death to anyone who dared to enter. The report in the *Norfolk & Suffolk Journal* explored the expedients and suggested that to extricate him: 'one thought the fire engine would dislodge him, for as a devoted worshipper of Bacchus he had a mortal hatred of pure water. Another suggested smoking him out by burning brimstone; but one who knew him better than the rest suggested beer.' Beer aplenty was brought to Taylor until he was so drunk an entry was forced and Taylor was arrested. On leaving the house Taylor received a true rogue's march to the lock-up as villagers lined the way, each with a kick, punch or scratch for him. Brought before the assizes, Taylor was found guilty of attempted murder and sentenced to penal servitude for life.

This final case relates the story of a hot-headed young man prone to drink-fuelled aggression. In December 1881 Joseph Watson (21), a navvy, was the boyfriend of Mary Anne Squirrell (22). Mary was living with her parents (Mr and Mrs Bumpstead) in Ipswich after she had separated from her husband.

Returning home one afternoon, Mrs Bumpstead found Watson asleep on the couch with her daughter sat on a stool beside him. A row broke out; Mrs Bumpstead wanted Watson out of the house and he left with Mary. Joe and Mary spent the rest of the day in two pubs, Mary spending most of her time trying to dissuade the drunken Watson from 'doing something on his mind.' At 11 p.m. they were seen by the docks and witnesses recall hearing a woman's voice call out, 'Don't be so cruel Joe; oh don't,' and a man replying, 'I'll be ****** if I don't drown you,' and a splash was heard. Witness Alice Tricker stated she saw Watson throw his arm round Mary's waist, raise one of the quay chains with his other hand and then both stooped and rested on the quay for a moment, the woman on the man, then they rolled into the water. Cries were then heard from the water from each to save the other. Poor Mary drowned and Joe Watson was brought to trial at the assizes. The jury found him guilty of murder but with a recommendation for mercy. Initially sentenced to death, Watson's date with the hangman was later cancelled and his sentence commuted to penal servitude. Having served his term, Watson was released on 10 July 1892.

Beyond the Pale

On 24 July 1849, George Shaw, described as 'a man of unusual stature and strength', was arraigned at the Crown Court charged with murdering Ann Simms by knocking her down and kicking and trampling upon her at Melbourn in Cambridgeshire. Testimony was given by a number of Melbourn residents; first was Joel King, who stated, 'I was at Melbourne Feast. I was coming down the village at one in the morning with Ellis Bysoath. I saw the prisoner and a woman with him. Near Mr Wood's house I saw the prisoner knock the woman down … He kicked her several times, and said, "I will kick your damn guts out". He kicked her with all his strength and then said to her, "Get up will you".' After a short exchange he dragged the woman up. According to Joel, she appeared 'very weak then … when we got within 100 yards of the Bull's Head Inn, we heard a noise. We heard a man's voice swearing and then we heard a woman scream out, "Pray George, do not kill me, perhaps I may do better next time".' Joel and Ellis walked on but still heard shouts from across the allotments. Ellis gave evidence next and confirmed Joel's story.

Joseph Prior, the landlord of the Bull, gave his statement; after being disturbed by his dog barking he went to the front window:

> I saw a man hunting a woman round the horse trough. It was the prisoner. The trough is six yards from the house and stands a yard from some palisades, so he could just catch her across it. He kept striking her, till he knocked her down. She kept crying out, 'Don't George, don't hit me,' and crept under the horse trough. The poor thing crept under it like a dog … I opened the window and said to him, 'You leering hound you – do you mean killing the woman?'

In reply, Shaw clawed up a few stones as if ready to hurl them up and threatened to smash out Prior's brains if he said another word. Shaw then dragged the woman out from under the trough and set off up the road kicking and cursing her.

Maria Howe nursed poor Ann over the following days; it was her who had sent for the doctor, but poor Ann died from her beating a few days later. Neighbour Eliza Almer had seen Shaw threaten, beat and even attempt to lock Ann in a cupboard. Shaw clearly did not care if poor Ann lived or died; the day before Ann died he had gone to Sandy Fair, and shortly after her death he was at Stamford races, where he was apprehended by William Robinson.

John Deighton, the town surgeon, attested to the wounds and bruising which confirmed the beating Ann had suffered, but stated in the days that followed she appeared to make some recovery. The post-mortem revealed that she died of 'an effusion of blood on the brain'. After a long speech for the defence and summing up from the judge the jury retired and returned a verdict of guilty of manslaughter. Shaw burst into tears. Even the justice seemed surprised at the verdict and with steely eyes congratulated Shaw on evading the capital charge. But then he addressed the prisoner in the most solemn tones, reminding Shaw that morally he had committed 'the most atrocious offence toward the victim of his violence' and that 'Under these circumstances it was the duty of the Court to remove him for ever from the country which he had polluted with his crimes.' Shaw was sentenced to be transported to a penal colony for the rest of his life.

On the Grounds of Insanity

On 26 May 1870, Martha Finch was found dead in bed with her throat cut at the home she shared with her husband and family at Sandon, Essex. Her husband, Isaac, was missing and a search discovered him wandering in the fields. When he realised he was being pursued he threw himself into a ditch, but when the searchers approached he climbed out and went quietly with them. In his pocket was found a Bible with a leaf turned down at a page where it stated King David stood upon the body of the Philistine, and took out his sword and cut off his head. In the coalhole a bloodstained billhook, undoubtedly used in the crime, was discovered.

Isaac was taken into custody and stood trial for murder at the Summer Assizes. It emerged his family had a history of mental illness. Finch had been in a state of deepening depression and mention was made of how he had left the Church of England to join another sect known as the 'Ranters'. Mrs Finch had been worried to the degree that she had confided with friends about the way Isaac 'turned up his eyes' and 'made her feel quite ill with alarm'. Found not guilty of wilful murder on the grounds of insanity, Finch was ordered to be detained at Her Majesty's pleasure and was removed to Broadmoor Criminal Lunatic Asylum.

Some Infamous Prisoners

The more infamous the case the more intense the clamour to learn about the behaviour of the accused while in prison and, if found guilty of a capital crime, their last hours in the condemned cell and their final moments on the gallows. When Queen Victoria ascended the throne in 1837, the infamous eighteenth-century gaol breaker 'Slippery Jack' Sheppard and thief taker Jonathan Wild were still the subjects of broadsheets, books and melodramas, while infamous crimes such as the Ratcliff Highway murders (1811) and the Red Barn Murder (otherwise known as the Polstead Slaying), committed by William Corder upon Maria Marten in 1827, sold over a million broadsheets. And then there was James Greenacre, who murdered and dismembered his fiancée Hannah Brown, dumping her torso on the Edgware Road (1836). Their names were renewed to successive generations of children with threats like – don't do that or Greenacre will get you! There were to be many more bogeymen *and women* before the end of the reign of Queen Victoria.

James Blomfield Rush (1848)

The first crime to really capture the public's imagination during Victoria's reign were the killings that became known as the Stanfield Hall Murders, committed by James Blomfield Rush at Stanfield Hall in Norfolk in 1848. In fact it was to become one of the most infamous crimes of the nineteenth century and contained all the potent factors to provoke Victorian attitudes of shock, horror and outrage. Books and broadsheets recounting every dramatic and lurid detail of the murder sold in unprecedented numbers; the broadsheet account of 'Sorrowful Lamentations' of the murderer sold an incredible two and a half million copies across the country. Columns, pages and whole supplements were given over to it in both local and national papers. Queen Victoria was recorded as taking a personal interest and even one of the greatest authors of his day, Charles Dickens, visited the scene and recorded his impression that it had 'a murderous look that seemed to invite such a crime'. Simply the name of the location would stimulate talk of the crime and the dastardly deeds connected with it – Stanfield Hall.

James Blomfield Rush, the perpetrator of the murders, fitted the bill of a classic Victorian villain, not only in physical appearance in both build and dress but in his behaviour, manners, morals and sinister schemes that were exposed at his trial. His wax image 'taken from life at Norwich' was undoubtedly the star attraction in Madame Tussauds' Chamber of Horrors in the last year of her life. Visitors were recorded as looking into his cold, glassy eyes 'with the most painful interest'. The notoriety of James Blomfield Rush ensured his figure was on display in the Chamber for over 120 years.

Rush was not born into a family with a criminal background, but he was born to Mary Blomfield out of wedlock, in a time when scorn was poured on illegitimacy. James was baptised in Tacolneston Church on 10 January 1800. His father, William Howe, was successfully sued for breach of promise and Mary was awarded enough damages to provide the foundation of a good dowry when she married Old Buckenham farmer John Rush in 1802. John seemed to have taken to young James; he allowed him to assume the name of Rush and paid for him to receive a good education at the grammar school of Mr Nunn at Eye in Suffolk.

In the publications, written with hindsight after his execution, Rush was condemned as 'always a bad one', a debauched deceiver and swindler, some even went so far as to record that they 'had always said Rush will be hanged'. The problem was that Rush was always trying to find legal loopholes and wrangles to get himself out of debt or bad financial commitments, he also failed to defend suits brought against him for seduction and bastardy by more than one complainant. Rush was to meet his match in a far better educated and higher-status man named Isaac Jermy, the Recorder of Norwich. However, Jermy was not a well-liked man. Many felt Jermy had obtained his home of Stanfield Hall by legal wrangle to the cost of the less well educated branch of his family, who were, in fact, the rightful heirs. Jermy was a man who knew the law and finance and was not afraid to use it to his advantage. As a short aside, both Rush's wife and father had died in what could be construed, certainly in the light of later events, as 'suspicious circumstances'.

W. Teignmouth Shore, the editor of 'Trial of J. Blomfield Rush' in the classic *Notable British Trials* series, eloquently sums up the dire situation Rush was in by November 1848:

(a) Pecuniarily Rush was *in extremis*
(b) Rush would shortly have to pay his landlord (Isaac Jermy) the mortgage on Potash Farm etc., a sum which he could not possibly raise
(c) He possessed documents from Thomas Jermy and John Larner, which if they

should succeed in their claim to the Stanfield Hall and Felmingham estates would establish him again in security

(d) He hated Isaac Jermy

(e) Also, he held the forged agreements between Isaac Jermy and himself, which would be valueless unless the former died within a few days

To be precise, the loan on Potash Farm was due for settlement on 30 November 1848. On the night of Tuesday, 28 November 1848, a telegraph was received by the Norwich City Police stating that Mr Isaac Jermy and his son had been murdered. Upon their arrival at Stanfield Hall the scene was one of 'utter dismay' and the story of the night's events soon unfurled. Between 8.15 p.m. and 8.30 p.m. Isaac Jermy Jermy (29), Sophie, his wife and one of Recorder Jermy's daughters, Isabella (aged about 14), were in the drawing room about to sit down for a game of piquet. Recorder Jermy had, as was his habit after dinner, gone from the dining room to the entrance porch in front of the Hall to take in the evening air. A gunshot was heard and the butler, James Watson, came out of his pantry to investigate. Just as he reached the turn of the passage, to his horror, he was confronted by the figure of 'a man in a dark cloak, of lowish stature, and stout, apparently with a mask on his face and something on his head'. The figure pushed the slightly built butler to one side, as he did so the butler noticed what be believed to be 'two pistols, one in each hand'. Fearing for his life, Watson cowered at his pantry door as the figure strode on.

Jermy had also heard the shots and had run out of the drawing room and, across the staircase hall, to the door of the passage. Watson saw the cloaked man draw back a pace, level his gun at young Mr Jermy and shoot him at about 3ft distance through the right breast, causing his body to fall backwards onto the mat of the staircase hall. The assassin then crossed this hall toward the dining room. Upon hearing the second shot Mrs Jermy rushed out of the drawing room. She was horrified to see her husband lying on his back in a spreading pool of blood. She ran into the small square passage calling for Watson the butler and other servants where she met the housemaid, Eliza Chastney, who had heard the shots and ran to the calls of her mistress. The killer saw them and fired two shots in quick succession, the first catching Mrs Jermy's upper arm, the second wounding Eliza Chastney in the groin and thigh. The murderer then made his exit by the side door. After medical examination it was thought Eliza had received 'a whole charge' that causes a compound fracture of the bone. The wound to Mrs Jermy's arm eventually resulted in amputation.

Eliza testified: 'I saw the head and shoulders of the man who shot me. There was something remarkable in the head; it was flat on the top – the hair set out bushy – and he was wide shouldered. I formed a belief at the time who the man was, I have no doubt in my own mind about it.' She identified the man as James Blomfield Rush. She qualified her belief: 'Mr Rush has a way of carrying his head which can't be mistaken. No person ever came to Stanfield with such an appearance, beside himself.'

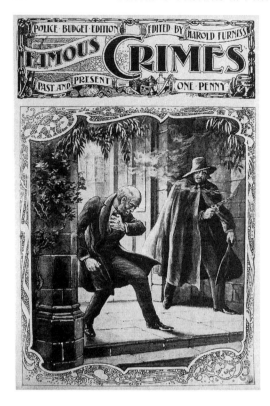

The *Famous Crimes* cover picture of the shooting of Isaac Jermy, the Recorder of Norwich at Stanfield Hall, by the heavily disguised James Blomfield Rush.

Rush was arrested at Potash Farm and removed to the nearby Wymondham Bridewell. On Thursday 30 November summonses were issued for a jury to hold an inquest at the King's Head, Wymondham. The jury returned a verdict of 'wilful murder' against James Blomfield Rush and the coroner issued his warrant accordingly. After the magistrates' hearing on 14 December 1848, Rush was committed to trial and he was removed to await his appearance at the assizes in Norwich Castle Gaol.

The trial opened on 29 March 1849 before Baron Rolfe. Rush had arrogantly turned down offers of legal counsel and opted to defend himself. He was often belligerent and attempted to intimidate the prosecution witnesses. The press and broadsheet sellers were having a field day, with extended accounts and illustrated supplements. The large crowds who gathered in front of the Shire Hall confirmed the vast public interest in the case. The drama was heightened still by the arrival of the injured housemaid, Eliza Chastney, who was carried to court upon a palanquin by police officers to give her evidence. From her canopied bed this brave young lady repeated her account of the night and confidently identified Rush as the murderer. Eliza's evidence and her identification of Rush by his build, gait and shape of head were corroborated by Watson, the butler, and Martha Read, the cook.

James Blomfield Rush, drawn
from life in the dock, 1848.

   On the fifth day of the trial, Rush, looking every bit the melodrama villain
– bulky, aggressive and conceited, and dressed all in black – lumbered over from
the dock to the witness box to deliver his defence. He was to speak, in total, for
a marathon fourteen hours. More blustering, aggressiveness, fabrications, half-
truths and barefaced lies typified his address, with sanctimonious intercessions
opening with such proclamations as 'God Almighty will protect me' and 'God
Almighty knows I am innocent'. His five witnesses were hardly worthwhile, even
damning; notable amongst them was Maria Blanchflower, a nurse at Stanfield
Hall. She stated that she had seen the disguised murderer but did not recognise
the figure as Rush, despite having run past within a few feet of him. Rush asked,
'Did you pass *me* quickly?' perhaps an unfortunate slip of the tongue, especially in
open court!
   After six days there had been a vast amount of evidence to digest, Rush had not
helped himself with his convoluted and often irrelevant cross-examinations, but
with the weight of evidence pressed against him he stood little chance of acquit-
tal. The jury returned their verdict after just ten minutes deliberation – 'Guilty'.
Rush burst out: 'My lord, I am innocent of that, thank God Almighty.' When
asked why the death sentence should not be pronounced upon him, the prisoner
remained silent.

Baron Rolfe assumed the black cap and pulled no punches in a tirade against Rush. His vitriol is well evinced by his remarks; 'There is no one that has witnessed your conduct during the trial, and heard the evidence disclosed against you, that will not feel with me when I tell you that you must quit this world by an ignominious death, an object of unmitigating abhorrence to everyone.' During this final pronouncement Rush only spoke once, when the judge chided him for not making good his promise to Miss Sandford that she may well have invoked her legal right to refuse to testify against her husband. Rush, petty to the bitter end, replied, 'I did not make any promise.' Rush said no more, the sentence of death was passed, and he apparently regained his composure and was removed from the dock 'with a smile and an unfeeling observation' to the condemned cell of Norwich Castle Gaol to await his fate.

The behaviour of Rush in Norwich Gaol was very much the same as it was during the trial. He adopted the airs and phraseology of piety apparent in a devoutly religious man, but in Rush's case, without the dignity. His act fooled no one. The clergymen who attended him listened to Rush in his hours of need and 'sincere' protestations of innocence but after Rush's execution a sketch of Rush's demeanour and conduct was provided by the prison chaplain, the Revd James Brown, Hon. Canon to the Cathedral and Minister of St Andrews. His opening comments sum up his opinion: 'Rush, from the first moment of his apprehension, undertook a character which he was totally unable to support. He assumed the lofty and confident bearing of innocence; but he so unnaturally overacted his part, as to enable the most casual observer to see through the flimsy veil which he attempted to throw over his real feelings.' Assiduously attending every religious service, reading the Bible and demanded regular attendance by the prison chaplain, Rush requested Holy Sacrament to be administered to him in private, but as Rush refused to be penitent or offer a confession for his crime, this latter request was refused. Displeased with the prison chaplain, Rush requested attendance from two other ministers known to him, namely the Revd W.W. Andrews and the Revd C.J. Blake. Rush also became increasingly belligerent towards these men as they could not promise to intercede on his behalf.

Rush had ensured he ate well in prison: refusing the prison food, he ordered his meals in from a nearby inn. In a letter dated 24 March 1849 to Mr Leggatt of the Bell Inn, Rush laid out his requirements:

Sir,-
You will oblige me by sending my breakfast this morning, and my dinner about the time your family have theirs, and send anything you like *except beef*; and I shall like cold meat as well as hot, and meal bread, and tea in a pint mug, if with a cover on the better. I will trouble you to provide for me now, if you please, till after my trial, and if you could get a small sucking pig in the market to-day, and roast it for me on the Monday, I should like that cold as well as hot after

Monday, and it would always be in readiness for me … Have the pig cooked the same as you usually have, and send plenty of plum sauce with it. Mr Pinson will pay you for what I have of you. By complying with the above,

You will very much oblige,
Your humble and obedient servant, James B. Rush

The execution of James Rush was set for noon on Saturday, 21 April 1849. Rush prepared himself on the morning he was going to meet his doom with the breakfast of 'a little thin gruel' that he had requested, followed by a visit to the prison chapel. The service finished at 11.40 a.m., leaving the prison chaplain and Revd Andrews with Rush. They urged Rush to repent, but he only became irritated and said, 'God knows my heart; He is my judge, and you have prejudged me … the real criminal will be known in two years.' Rush then began to lose his temper, and, upon hearing Rush's raised voice, the governor, Mr Pinson, personally removed Rush from the chapel and Rush cooled himself down by washing his face, hands and neck with water from the pump in the prison yard.

From the prison yard he was conducted inside the pinioning room, where Rush met his executioner, William Calcraft. Upon seeing Calcraft, Rush gruffly asked, 'Is that the man who is to perform this duty?' to which Mr Pinson replied he was. Calcraft asked Rush to sit down and began to pinion his hands, Rush said with a shrug, 'This don't go easy; I don't want the cord to hurt me.' Calcraft loosened the restraint a little and Rush confirmed he was comfortable and joined the procession to the gallows.

The day of Rush's execution had dawned cold, dismal and cheerless. Small groups had collected on Norwich Castle Hill from an early hour. Most of these early arrivals were members of the farming community. A contemporary account stated, 'They eyed, at a respectful distance, the dreadful apparatus of death, and in little knots, with bated breath, talked over the fate of the wretched man, whom many of them [had] no doubt known and bargained with, and whose occupation in life had been similar to their own.' As the hour of execution approached the sun broke through the clouds and shone down as a crowd of thousands, including children, assembled to view the execution. Shortly before noon the number of spectators was swelled further as a large crowd arrived from the specially chartered trains from London and East Anglia. The usual viewing points bulged to capacity, house tops and even the tops of one of the city's square-towered churches were seen to be occupied by the many who wanted a glimpse of the final act of the Stanfield Hall murderers.

Broadsheet sellers and those with barrows of hot pies, potatoes and drinks did a roaring trade – as did the pickpocketers! The short space between the Castle Prison gate and the scaffold was lined by the magistrates of the county on one side and representative of the press on the other. Shortly after the appointed

THE

LIFE and EXECUTION

OF

James Blomfield Rush,

For the MURDERS at Stanfield Hall, on the

Bodies of ISAAC JERMY and

JERMY JERMY, his son,

Who was Executed on the Castle Hill, on Saturday last, in April, 1849.

James Blomfield Rush, is the natural son of the daughter of a farmer, near Wymondham, by a farmer residing near the parish in or near which she lived, to whom she was engaged. From some cause the engagement was broken off, and an action was brought by her for breach of promise of marriage, and heavy damages obtained. Mr. Rush, of Aylsham, not long afterwards married the prisoner's mother. From this year until 1834, Rush's father occupied a farm at Felmingham, the property of the late Rev. George Preston, and subsequently of the late Mr. Jermy, where he died, his death having been attended by somewhat extraordinary circumstances. He was found dead in his kitchen in the day time, with a shot wound behind his ear, a discharged gun lying near him. Several reports were spread respecting this affair, and amongst them, one that a number of persons had been summoned to the house by the son, and when the Coroner arrived, he found his jury as it were ready to his hand. The verdict was Felo-de-se.

The prisoner was brought up by his mother's husband, and put to school with Mr. Nunn, at Eye, in Suffolk. In 1834 he commenced farming at Aylsham, under the Rev. Samuel Pitman, from whom he rented for about four years, 120 acres of land. In 1828 he married the second daughter of a highly respectable yeoman, in the neighbourhood of Aylsham, and took the Wood Dalling hall farm, under W. E. L. Bulwer, Esq. where he expended a considerable sum in improvements. The husband of Rush's mother held a farm at Felmingham, under the Rev. George Preston. Times were very hard for farming, and he often talked of giving up his farms, and he said I should have what part I liked when he did so, but should prefer my taking the whole; in the mean time, one of his tenants at Felmingham would not hold under him any longer; he wished me to take that, he did so, under an agreement for 18 years, from Michaelmas, 1835, at £110 per annum.

He took the Stanfield hall farm for 21 years, at £500 per annum; In 1837 the Rev. George Preston died; Mr. Jermy, his son, the late Recorder, discovered the leases were not legally made, and this was the beginning of disputes between Mr. Rush and Mr. Jermy.

At the letter part of his occupation of Wood Dalling Hall Farm, Rush commenced and continued the business of valuer and auctioneer, in which he met with some success.

The Potash farm, which was the property of Mr. Calver, was for sale, and as it lies between the Stanfield Hall and Bethel properties of Mr. Jermy, that gentleman had a wish to possess it, as it would have made the property a compact

whole. Rush consulted Mr. Jermy about its purchase, and the latter deputed him to buy it at a certain sum. However, the estate was run up to a higher sum than Mr. Jermy had directed Rush to bid, and Rush bought it for himself. The price was about 130l. above Mr. Jermy's bid. Rush informed Mr. Jermy, that although he (Rush) had purchased it, he did not possess the means to pay for it, and requested Mr. Jermy to pay for it, and requested Mr. Jermy to lend him the sum he required on mortgage, 3500l. was advanced for which interest was to be paid. After this two more sums were advanced, making 5000l, which was not to be called in until ten years after. This term expired two days after the murder.

The daughter of the prisoner, whose decease was confidently reported on saturday, had an interview with her father; she and the rest of the family are as well as under these melancholy circumstances can be expected. Miss Rush, and the younger branches of the family are still at Felmingham; with the exception of one son, who with his eldest brother, Mr. James Rush, is at Potash. The prisoner has nine children.

THE EXECUTION.

This morning the above unhappy culprit paid the forfeit of his life to the offended laws of his country. No execution of late years has attracted so large an assemblage of spectators, some thousands being present. About nine o'clock he took some refreshment, and shortly afterwards the sheriff arrived at the castle, and immediately proceeded to the condemned cell. The usual melancholy preparations having been completed, Rush was brought to the room where he was to be pinioned. He appeared to be quite calm and collected, and walked with a firm step. The melancholy procession then proceeded towards the scaffold, which he mounted without any assistance, and in less than a minute the drop fell, and the wretched malefactor was launched into eternity,

---

O Lord! receive my sinful soul, have mercy on my guilt;
The blood of Christ have made me whole, for me that blood was spilt!
All you that go around me stand, may this a warning be;
Unto the word of God attend, and shun bad company.
You see me here a wretched man; but short will be my stay;
Yet on my Saviour I'll depend, to wash my sins away.
Pray for my soul, good people all, and pity my sad fate;
A moment hence the drop will fall, I have not long to wait.
And may the blood of Jesus Christ, atonement for me make;
On his dear name my comfort rest, he died for sinners' sake.

WALKER, PRINTER, CHURCH STREET, ST. MILE'S, NORWICH.

The broadsheet sold after the execution of James Blomfield Rush on Saturday, 21 April 1849. So intense was the interest in this case that over a million copies were sold of the various Rush broadsides.

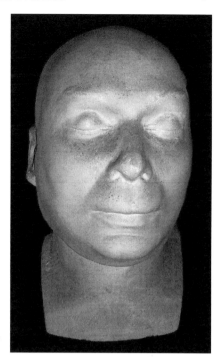

The death mask of James Blomfield Rush.
The cast of Rush's head was made by Mr
Bianchi of St George's Middle-Street, Norwich,
on the afternoon after the execution.

hour the great door opened and the sheriffs, attended by their javelin men, led
the solemn procession, followed by Colonel Oakes the Chief Constable of the
County Police, followed by the chaplain, reading loud and clear the appropriate portion of the burial service. The chaplain was followed by Rush, attended
on one side by Mr Pinson, the governor of the Castle Gaol, and Calcraft the
executioner on the other, with a number of the turnkeys following behind. The
bell of St Peter Mancroft tolled the death knell and the procession moved almost
in time with each slow, mournful toll. As they strode out, Rush's tread and composure was remarkably firm. Rush was attired in the same black suit and patent
leather boots he had worn for his trial, the collar of his shirt, remarked upon as
being 'scrupulously clean', was turned over for the purpose of freely adjusting
the noose. His head bare, Rush's features were keenly observed; it was noted they
had undergone no perceptible change since his trial, 'perhaps a little paler, but his
determined expression had not changed.'

　　Upon seeing the scaffold, Rush lifted his eyes to Heaven and raised his pinioned hands as far as he could and shook his head mournfully from side to side
once or twice. Rush was led up the steps of the gallows and placed himself under
the fatal beam. An eyewitness recorded that, 'The wretched creature looked for
an instant on the vast mass of spectators, whose earnest gaze was upon him and
on every movement he made, and then turned himself round and faced the castle
– his back being towards the populace.' Clearly Rush could not resist one last

defiant gesture! He shook hands with the governor; Calcraft then drew the white hood over Rush's head and, having fastened the rope to the beam, set about adjusting the noose around Rush's neck. Unable to resist a last whinge, a voice snapped at the executioner from under the hood, 'This does not go easy! Put the thing a little higher – take your time – don't be in a hurry!' These were to be Rush's last words. As the chaplain read the section requested by Rush, 'The Grace of our Lord Jesus Christ …' the signal was given and the bolt was drawn, releasing the gallows trap door 'and the scene of life closed upon this malefactor, almost without a struggle.' The crowd maintained an eerie silence, excepting a few faint shrieks as the trap fell; the sound of the falling trap and the tightening rope was audible over some considerable distance.

Rush was left to hang for the obligatory hour. When the body was taken down it was removed to the prison on a wheeled litter. In the afternoon Rush's head was shaved and a 'death mask' cast was taken by Mr Bianchi of St George's Middle-Street in Norwich. The remains were then buried within the precincts of the prison and a stone tablet bearing his initials and the year of his execution set into the wall above.

The Tichbourne Claimant, 1871

Arthur Orton (aka Thomas Castro), known to history as 'The Tichbourne Claimant', was the nineteenth century's most notorious fraudster. He had appeared after the Dowager Lady Tichbourne placed appeals in newspapers all around the world searching for news of her son, Sir Roger Charles Doughty Tichbourne, who was believed to have been lost at sea after boarding a ship from Rio de Janeiro in April 1954. Her ladyship's pleas were answered in 1863 by Orton (a butcher's son from Wapping), who, having been bankrupted in England, had emigrated to Wagga-Wagga, Australia. After reading her advertisement he wrote a letter claiming to be her son and asked for money. Despite the letter containing spelling mistakes uncommon to men with the real Sir Roger's education she sent the money and begged her 'son' to come home. Considering he had nothing to lose but everything to gain, Orton returned to England in 1866 and assumed the imposture of Sir Roger Tichbourne. When his lordship had last been seen he had weighed just 9 stone, but the man who walked off the boat was an impressive 27 stone. Then there was Sir Roger's Stonyhurst accent – no trace of it remained, but Lady Tichbourne accepted him regardless and was delighted to have her son back.

Orton boldly laid claim to the family estates but relatives and friends of Sir Roger were not so easily fooled and they began legal actions to stop him. Proceedings began in 1867 but it was four years before the trial opened on 11 May 1871, held in the Court of Common Pleas before Sir Alexander

Arthur Orton (aka Thomas Castro),
'The Tichbourne Claimant'.

Cockburn. Orton had prepared himself well and memorised a huge amount of information about the man he was impersonating, indeed, he convinced over 100 people to vouch, in court, for his identity as Roger but his trump card, Lady Tichbourne, died shortly before the trial opened and the case put up by his opposition was compelling: for example, despite Sir Roger spending much of his young life in France, Orton spoke little French, in fact Orton was caught out again and again. Most telling was the testimony of Lord Bellow, a school friend of Sir Roger, who stated that Tichborne was known to have a small tattoo on his left forearm – Orton had nothing there. Orton was convicted on two counts of perjury on 28 February 1874, and was sentenced to fourteen years hard labour.

It had been the longest fought case in British judicial history – a total of 1,025 days. The legal costs amounted to £200,000 (this equates to about £10 million in modern currency). Orton had been modelled during his trial by Tussauds and had promised that he would provide a fresh suit of clothes for his model in the exhibition. In fulfilment of his promise, after the sentence had been passed upon him, he beckoned from the table at which he was seated in court to an attendant, and handed him the suit of clothes, saying: 'Please see to these being delivered at Madame Tussauds, as they are expected there.' When his wax figure was put on display crowds queued outside to have a good look at him. The public interest in his behaviour behind bars continued well past his admission:

Since his incarceration in Newgate the 'Claimant' had done his best to keep up the delusion that he is the missing heir to the baronetcy and estates. He stoutly refuses to answer to the appellation of Orton or Castro but willingly responds to the name of Tichbourne. Otherwise he has accepted his fate, submitted to the prison regulations and accommodated himself to his changed position with as much ease and tact as he had shown before in passing from the life of a bushranger to the life of a baronet. The prisoner seems to have been most impressed with his fall when he had to don the prison apparel … His convict garb is a light brown woollen suit with knee breeches, ribbed worsted stockings, common leather shoes and a cap with a little knob a-top without a peak.

It is scarcely necessary to say this suit required some expansive dimensions. The shirt sleeves are 37 inches round, the muscle of the arm being 27 inches and the chest 56 inches. When it was shown to Orton he faltered a little but the feeling was only momentary, he quickly regained his usual self-possession. In this altered dress, close shaven and hair cropped short, the huge bulk of the prisoner only remains to identify him with the defendant of the Queen's Bench.

Lloyd's News, 8 March 1874

'A Ticket of Leave Man' followed shortly behind Orton into Dartmoor Prison. He heard the impressions and opinions of the 'Claimant' from his fellow convicts and recounted them in *Convict Life*:

The 'Claimant' had left Dartmoor for Portsmouth before my arrival at the former place. I heard a good deal about him of course. He is said to have given an infinity of trouble. His applications to address the Home Secretary, and to have interviews with Directors, governor, doctor, and priest were incessant. He applied to be admitted to the church choir for two reasons; he obtained a more comfortable seat, and he was excused labour on Saturday mornings that he might attend practice. The organist assured me that he had no notion of singing, and that the noise he made was something between the chirp of a crow and the croak of a raven.

He was doing his best, by the aid of French school-books furnished him by the priest, to master the French language. When the Claimant first went to Dartmoor he seems to have had a good friend in the gentleman who was at that time governor of the prison. He was extremely troublesome, constantly breaking prison rules, and being reported for doing so; but so long as the Major remained in command, he was never punished, and, when he received visits from his friends, the visits took place, contrary to regulations, in the governor's office, and extra time was allowed him.

The advent of Captain Harris as governor was a misfortune for the Claimant. I may here take the opportunity of doing an act of simple justice to Captain Harris. I am quite sure that if the son or brother of the Secretary of State were a prisoner under his control, he would be treated with precisely the same indulgence as every other prisoner, and no more. The Claimant when next he received a visit did so behind the bars, and within the time specified by the rules. When reported for insolence he was sentenced to two days' bread and water, and he got a second punishment for the same offence and some others. By the doctor's orders he had 8oz of additional bread per day and 8oz of potatoes, and on meat and soup days he had increased rations.

I presume his friends induced the Home Secretary to have him transferred to Portsmouth, where, I am told, he is fetching a tolerably easy 'lagging'. Perhaps the air there is not so bracing, but at Dartmoor his appetite was enormous. I know men employed in the tailor's shop who did not need all their food, and who gave him some constantly; and the orderlies who carried round the bread were in the habit of yielding to his entreaties to shy him a loaf, if a 'good screw' happened to be on duty. By the way, a 'good screw', amongst prisoners, means a man who does not do his duty. I knew a little Irishman who told me that one day he was able to give the Claimant six 6oz loaves, and that he came very near getting three days as a reward for his good nature.

The big man was very unpopular with some of his neighbours, who say that he was a bad sleeper, and used to puff and blow, and grunt and groan all through the small hours. He was unpopular with the warders because it was with the greatest difficulty he could be got to scrub his cell, or keep his cell-furniture clean.

Convict Life (Wyman & Sons, 1879)

A number of newspapers ran the Press Agency story of the later stages of the prison life of the 'Claimant' on the announcement of his imminent release:

On his removal to Portsmouth Orton was employed in the tailor's shop, but never took kindly to the work and after some time he petitioned to be sent out on the public works. The confinement he had endured in the mean while, though exceedingly irksome to him, had the effect of considerably reducing his weight, which is now not more than 18st 7lb. His conduct was always marked 'first-class exemplary' and as a result of this, he was permitted on entering his last year to wear the Blue Dress which is the highest privilege a convict can aspire to as it entitles him to an additional week's remission of sentence and ensures him an extra £3 from the government on his discharge.

He has never been mentioned in reports, although his remonstrances with his fellow-prisoners on the subject of excessive industry; he on one occasion almost infringed the regulations. His request to be sent on the public works, that he might enjoy fresh air, was readily acceded to and he was for a time employed in the stacking ground in Portsmouth Dockyard, though in this class of labour he did not greatly distinguish himself. He soon discovered that he was here the subject to be gazed upon by workmen and others in the

Incidents of the case and the prison life of Arthur Orton; published by the *Illustrated Police News* shortly after his release in 1884.

dockyard and to the least semblance of this practice he always showed the most deep-rooted antipathy.

His next move was to the Carpenter's Shop which was more secluded. It was not anticipated that he would prove a better carpenter than a tailor but he has turned out a very skilful workman and would have no difficulty in earning his living at this handicraft ... During his stay at Portsmouth the 'Claimant's' bulky frame gave as much concern to the authorities as it did elsewhere, difficulty being experienced in providing him with adequate quarters. Eventually the problem was solved by sending him to one of the punishment cells where he had the advantage of being under the care of the most experienced warders, specially told off for this class of work.

Orton served ten years in prison and was released from Pentonville, the final prison he was removed to prior to release, on ticket-of-leave in 1884. After writing to John de Morgan asking to be employed by P.T. Barnum and being turned down because 'the Claimant would not prove attractive in the United States' he joined Sanger's Circus and toured the country telling his story. He alternately confessed and then counter-claimed he was innocent but aroused little interest in his later years and died in poverty in April 1898.

W.T. Stead

One of the most famous public figures to become a prisoner in the late nineteenth century was W.T. Stead, the editor of the *Pall Mall Gazette*. In the interests of investigative journalism he had set about the sensational exposure of white slavery in Britain. In 1885, with the help of Josephine Butler and acting at all times under the proprietorial supervision of Bramwell Booth of the Salvation Army, Stead got in touch with Rebecca Jarrett, a reformed prostitute and brothel-keeper and with her help bought a 13-year-old virgin named Eliza Armstrong from her alcoholic mother for £5. Stead published the story as a series of articles in the *Pall Mall Gazette* as the 'Maiden Tribute of Modern Babylon'. The story exposed a disgusting trade and caused outrage across the nation and soon Parliament was discussing what was to be done about this abominable business, but despite all propriety being shown and the fact that Miss Armstrong remained untouched, the act of procurement and charges of abduction brought by the girl's father (his permission had not been asked) landed Stead and some his compatriots involved in the procurement in court. Booth was given a stern warning by the judge but he and a number of others were acquitted while a total of four others, including Stead, were sentenced to terms of imprisonment. Stead was sentenced to three months. He was first sent to Coldbath Fields Prison for three days then to Holloway as a first-class inmate for the rest of his sentence.

W.T. Stead, social campaigner
and editor of the *Pall Mall
Gazette.*

What follows is an edited version of Stead's own account of his prison
experiences, which he published as three penny pamphlets entitled 'My First
Imprisonment' shortly after his release in 1886:

Sentence was pronounced; a buzz of eager conversation filled the crowded
court. Friends were pressing round the dock, where we had spent so many
exciting days, to say good-bye. All was movement – a feverish murmur of
many voices. The long tension had given way, last words were being hurriedly
exchanged – 'Good-bye, good-bye, God bless you!' 'I'd rather be in your place
than in that of your judge' – it was Mr Waugh who said that, although I did not
know his voice at the time from other voices rising from below. 'Once more,
good-bye.' And waving my hand to the excited throng I descended the steps,
with a confused vision of horse-hair wigs, eager faces, and a patch of scarlet still
lingering on my retina. Down we went Jacques and I –Rebecca and Madame
Mourez had preceded us – and we were prisoners. We had been below for a
few minutes every day of the trial, but now we went further afield. Newgate
is a deserted gaol. The long corridors, like combs of empty cells, stand silent
as the grave. As we were marched down passages and through one iron gate

after another, I experienced my first feel of a gaol. Those who have not been in prison will understand it when they in their turn receive sentence of imprisonment. It is a feel of stone and iron, hard and cold, and, when, as in Newgate, the prison is empty, there is added the chill and silence of the grave. The first thing that strikes you is the number of iron gates that are to be locked and unlocked, and the word turnkey first seems real to you. Overhead the tiers of cells, with their iron balustrades and iron stairs, rose storey after storey. It was as if you were walking at the bottom of the hold of some great petrified ship, looking up at the deserted decks.

What a sepulchre of hopes it once was, and how many ghosts of the unhallowed dead must walk these aisles and corridors, where rings now but the echo of the clang of the iron gate, or the spring of the lock as the warder passes his prisoners along the via dolorosa that leads to the condemned cells. When we reached these grim chambers we turned to the left and entered the warder's office. It was bright and cheerful, and the fire glowed from the grate like a live thing, after the deadly chilly murk of the prison. There we sat and waited, and as the minutes passed, and we waited and waited, some faint sense of the change came over me. At last, after years of incessant stress and strain, and after six months in which every hour had to get through the work of two, I had come to a place where time was a drug in the market – where time was to hang heavy on my hands, where, after being long bankrupt in minutes, I was to be a millionaire of hours. It was a sudden transition from the busy, crowded, stirring excitement of an existence exceptionally full of life and interest to the dull monotony of a gaol. Suddenly I was summoned out. The manager of the *Pall Mall Gazette* had got an order to see me, and I was marched back through the unending passages to a small room, where the interview was permitted. He told me that the sentence began from the first day of the trial, and that consequently I should be out on January 18th.

My visitor left. I was re-conducted to the warder's room. At last the prison van was ready and we climbed aboard – not for the first time. We had ridden out from Bow Street in it before, but then all the compartments were full of prisoners. Now we were alone locked in with the warders. A lamp at one end shed a dim light down the centre. At last we started. As we drove through the prison gates we heard the hoarse roar of the crowd which had waited to give us a parting yell of execration as we left the scene in which for so many days we had been the central figures. It was the last sound from the outside world which we heard. After ten minutes' drive we arrived at Coldbath-in-the-Fields. Jacques and I alighted, and the van drove on to Millbank – the woman's prison, where Rebecca and Madame Mourez are still awaiting the expiry of their sentences; Rebecca in good spirits, taking all things patiently, knowing, as she says, that she deserves the punishment for the many bad deeds she had done in her life, although it is rather odd it should be given her the only time she ever tried to do anything good. Madame Mourez, they say, is dangerously ill of erysipelas in the hospital at Millbank.

Jacques and I were made to stand in line, and then marched off through echoing corridors and the usual endless series of grated gates to the reception room, where some dozen or more fellow-prisoners were already assembled waiting till the dregs had drained into this human cesspool from all the contributory police-stations. We were seated on forms fronting an officer, who entered our names, emptied our pockets, labelled us, and sent us across the room to select caps and shoes. The night was raw and cold. There was a glorious fire close to the officer, but so far from us as to make us only colder for its sight.

Prisoners are allowed to select their own hats and shoes out of a miscellaneous assortment of all sizes. Whether the ordinary criminal head is abnormally small, or whether the persons who had preceded us that day were abnormally big-headed men, I do not know; but I found nearly all the hats – dun-yellow glengarries without buttons or tails – too small for me. At last, after trying some twenty hats which had been going in succession round the score of my fellow-prisoners, I found one which was luckily split open a little, so that by wearing it with the back to the front I could get a tolerable fit. The shoes were another difficulty. They were fearfully and wonderfully patched. Some of them were monuments of careful industry. By careful selection I got two misfellowed ones which I thought would fit. When I came to lace them, however, I found them nip my feet so badly that, after trying them two days, I had to get them changed. My new pair were so large I had to fill them up with oakum when I went for exercise, and then stumbled along as best I could. When we had all been entered up, we marched in single file downstairs along passages until we came to the bath and dressing room. Here we were halted, and sent to bath in detachments. I squirmed a little at the thought of the bath from the description of the Amateur Casual, but I was agreeably surprised. The bath was filled fresh for each prisoner; the water was clean and although it might have been pleasanter if a little more of the chill had been taken off, for it was nearly nine at night in mid-November, there was nothing to complain of. Your own clothes are then taken away, and a prison suit given you. The suites are allotted in sizes. Jacques, being large and stout, was ill to fit, and his toilette took him a long time. As we had come in with drawers and flannels, we were allotted underclothing – fairly comfortable, although the drawers are short in the leg. Braces are superfluities of civilization. So are cuffs, collars, and neckties. The prisoners' complete outfit is as follows: – Cap and shoes, selected in the reception room; a pair of worsted stockings, even more monumental specimens of industry and ingenuity than the boots – which was darn and which was original stocking no one could tell, and in the darning one of the heels had somehow managed to stray half down the foot towards the toe; flannel shirt and drawers; a blue-striped cotton shirt; trousers, waistcoat, coat, pocket handkerchief, and stock. The stock is a narrow strip of cloth, which

W.T. Stead in prison. Upon his release he asked for and was allowed to keep his uniform and he wore it every year on 10 November, the anniversary of his conviction, as a proud remembrance of what he had done and his time in 'Happy Holloway'. This he did until his death in 1912, when he went down with the *Titanic*.

buttons round the neck and over which the shirt collar folds. There is only one pocket in the suit, into which the large, coarse pocket handkerchief is thrust. The trousers are held in situ by the waistband. At Coldbath the band had only one buckle, and a hole pierced to receive it. The girth of prisoners differs so much that if there were three holes an inch apart it would conduce much both to comfort and seemliness. Where there is only one hole, and the prisoner is slim, he has continually to be hitching up his breeches. At Holloway the waistband has the ordinary double sharp-pronged buckle, which makes its own holes, and this, of course, is the best. When dressed complete a small pocket comb is given you and a pair of leather boot laces, an article I never possessed since I gave up wearing a leather bootlace as a watchguard. When the last loiterer had finished his toilette we tramped back to the reception room, where, after a time, we were taken off to our cells. Before we went, however, a tin looking like an old American beef tin with something like paste at the bottom of it and a small loaf of hard whole-meal brown bread were handed to each of us. I thought of the waiter at the London Club, where I had dined the night before, and valorously put the tin to my lips, following the example of my neighbours. The viscous fluid crawled slowly down the tin and touched my lips. And there it stopped. Gruel at the best is an abomination. But prison gruel without any salt is about as savoury a beverage as the contents of the editorial paste pot. There was salt in my cell, I was told, and carrying our skilly and our bread in our hands, we were marched off to the reception wing, where we were to sleep that night. The warder who conducted us was a decent fellow. 'You had better say good-bye,' said he; 'you will not see each other again.' In this, however, he was wrong. We went to the doctor's together next morning and also to the governor.

Here was my cell. As I entered it my first sensation was one of pleasant satisfaction. There was the plank bed. I had heard so much about it from Irish members, and had so often alluded to it in my campaign in the north, that it seemed almost like an old acquaintance standing up there against the wall. The gaoler explained the whereabouts of the various articles, handed me the bed-clothes and a mattress about an inch thick, and then left me to my meditations. The cell was better than I expected – that is to say, it was larger, loftier, and not a bad kind of a retreat, immeasurably superior to all the hermit's cells I had seen or heard of. There was a jet of gas, turned off and on by a tap outside the cell, the clean scrubbed wooden table and stool, and there also was the wooden salt cellar. Prison salt cellars are of wood, and there is no stinting of quantity. I salted my skilly, and broke the bread into it to soften it, fished it out with my wooden spoon, and tried to eat a piece or two. I unrolled my bedclothes, laid my plank bed down, stretched the mattress, and felt thoroughly glad to be alone after all the turmoil. Here was quiet at least. After a little time I laid down and slept. I woke once or twice and heard the chimes of a clock in some distant spire, and dozed again, with a strange kind of consciousness of the pres-ence of an immense multitude of friendly faces all around me. The enthusiastic audiences that I had addressed in the north were visible as you see things in a camera obscura, on this side and on that, and I heard the din and ghostly echoes of their cheers in the otherwise unbroken silence of the prison. At a quarter to six the bell rang, and everyone was on the alert. A warder opened the door and gave me instructions. I was only in a reception cell, R2/7, that is to say, in the seventh cell on the second floor of the reception wing. I would have to be taken to my destined abiding place in the course of the day, I need not, therefore, clean out my cell, or attend chapel, until I got into my regular cell. A prisoner swept out my cell. Then one of the principal warders came round. He was a big, kindly man. 'You may have made a mistake,' he said, 'but you have done a good work.'

The breakfast of bread and skilly had been served out, my bedclothes had been rolled up, and I sat alone in the darkness. A dense fog lay heavy upon the outside world. In the cell nothing but darkness was visible. It was a strange and somewhat weird experience. Yesterday the crowded court, with letters, tel-egrams, enthusiastic friends; to-day, darkness as of Egypt, in a solitary cell. There was nothing to do. It was too dark to read. And as the hours stole on the cold made itself felt, and I shivered in the cell. Might I wrap myself in the blankets? Yes, if I liked, although it was contrary to regulations. After a while we were marched to the doctor; he weighed us. In prison costume I weighed 9st. 11lb. I complained of the cold. 'The cells,' said he, in the usual dry official way, 'are heated to a temperature of 60 deg.;' and there was an end of that.

Before we saw the doctor we were inspected by the governor. Captain Helby is a retired naval officer, pleasant and sympathetic, he addressed me very kindly.

'Whatever sympathy I may have,' he said, 'with you and your work (and in my private capacity I sympathise very much with you), I can only treat you as an ordinary criminal convict prisoner, who must be subject to the ordinary rules and regulations laid down for the treatment of criminal convict prisoners. I hope, therefore, that you will conform yourselves thereto, and that you will not subject me to the painful necessity of subjecting you to discipline.'

'Sir,' I replied, 'I think I understand the position in which I am placed, and to the best of my ability I will conform to the regulations laid down for my guidance.' I have often wondered since then what on earth he thought I was likely to do that might necessitate the infliction of discipline, which, being interpreted, I suppose meant crank, treadwheel, 'cells,' bread and water, and I know not what else. Editors no doubt are somewhat rare birds in Coldbath-in-the-Fields, but even editors could hardly be expected to assault their warders, or refuse to pick oakum or to wash out their cells.

At twelve o'clock the door of the cell was opened, and a tin pot and the usual brown little loaf handed inside. At the bottom of the tin was a tough, gluey composition, which on reference to the dietary scale I found was called a suet pudding. I pecked a little hole in it, tasted it as a kind of sample, and then desisted. More hours passed then came Dr Clifford, armed with a Home Office order; I had to vacate almost immediately. I was taken away to the B wing, and there placed in cell No. 8 in the second floor. I got a new label, B2/8, and had a brass number sewed upon the other side of my coat. Jacques was taken off to another wing, and I saw him to speak to no more. I was placed under the charge of a warder whose name I think was Smithers, a kindly, courteous official, whom I regretted not being able to thank when I was so unexpectedly carried off to Holloway.

What a welcome change it was to my new cell can only be appreciated by those who have shivered for hours in an unwarmed cell. For my new cell was really heated up to 60 deg., and the pleasure of the change was immense. All pleasures are comparative. If you feed a man on bread and water he will rejoice more over skilly than an epicure over a Lord Mayor's banquet. The great secret of enjoyment is to do without for a time. I never thought I could have hungered and thirsted so keenly for a bit of chop as after my three days on low diet. As for a cup of tea, that seemed a beatific vision of unattainable bliss. My pleasure at the warmth was somewhat damped by the announcement that I was to have no mattress. Criminal convicts must sleep on bare boards. I winced a bit, but I remembered poor William's receipt, and took courage. As some may not have seen that receipt, I will repeat it here. When you have to sleep on bare boards you will discover that the weight of your body rests almost entirely on your shoulders and your hip joints. Wrap your coat round your shoulders, your breeches round your loins, and, if you have no oakum, put your waistcoat in your hat for a pillow, and you will be able to sleep without waking at midnight

The main gate of Coldbath Fields Prison, Stead's first place of incarceration.

with aching bones. If you are found out you will be reported; you are not allowed to sleep in your clothes. There is a peephole in the door of every cell through which the warder looks to see that you are all right according to regulations, but unless he has a spite against you he will not, as a rule, discover that your clothes are round your hips instead of being outside the bed.

I enjoyed my two days in B2/8 very much. The change from the cold of R2/7 was very great. The dense fog lifted, and I could see to read. There was in the cell a Bible, a Prayer Book, and a library book, Dean Vaughan's 'Consolation for the Sorrowful'. Then, again, I was allowed the luxury of having something to do. I scoured out my cell in the morning with hearty goodwill, and scrubbed my table and stool. Then I set to work to pick oakum. It was not the proper oakum, but coir fibre. I had to pick from ten ounces to one pound. It is an excellent meditative occupation. But it is hard at first on the finger-nails. Mine wanted trimming; for, if the nails are not short, the leverage on the nail in disentangling the fibre causes considerable suffering. 'How do prisoners do when they want their nails cut?' I asked. 'Bite 'em,' laconically replied the warder. You don't know how strange it feels to have neither knife nor scissors, nor pens, nor pencils, nor pockets, although of course it may be said that you don't need pockets if you have nothing to put into them. Those who say this forget that even prisoners use hands.

The Ventilator, which can be opened and closed at will, is under the window. The gas jet is over the table. The plank bed is raised from the floor just high enough to allow mice free space to frolic under the planks. The bed-clothes are rolled up tight every morning and the roll stood on end on the highest of these shelves in the corner. There is a little whitening for polishing the drinking can, the can itself, a piece of soap, and the salt cellar!

In No. 7 was an elderly man, not there for the first time, who was in for stealing a pail. He sang a good deal by himself. His voice was good, and he seemed to have many hymns by heart. On the other side was a young fellow who had eighteen months for passing counterfeit coin. He had been there six months, and had still twelve more to serve. Six months! What a contrast between his last half-year and mine! He was a kindly soul, and his sympathetic word to me as we trudged to chapel in single file, that my 'three months would soon be done,' was very pleasant. On the whole I liked my fellow-prisoners, with one or two exceptions, very much, and I felt a strange new sense of brotherhood with convicts and criminals, which was in itself a boon worth coming to gaol to gain.

This was the order of our day at Coldbath. At a quarter to six the bell rang. You rise and dress in the dark. At six the warder opens the door, and you throw your bedclothes over the polished iron balustrade that runs round the corridor outside the cells. The door is locked again, and you scour out your cell. Then the door is unlocked, and you bring in your bedclothes and roll them up, strap them tightly, and set them away on the shelf. You are asked if you have any applications to make for the governor, doctor, or chaplain, and your application is duly noted and reported. Then you take your oakum, picked and unpicked, to the warder who weighs it, examines its quality, and gives you out a fresh quantum for the day. It is a strange sight, a great gaol all stone and iron, with innumerable gas jets twinkling down the corridors and the prisoners moving to and fro with their bundles of oakum. When people run all round the world in search of novel sights and strange sensations, what a mine of unexplored novelties they neglect in London gaols! At eight o'clock your skilly and bread are handed in, and then about half-past eight the summons comes for chapel. You turn out of your cell, put on your hat, and stand with your face to the door of your cell till the word is given to march. Then you face about and march in single file along the corridors, upstairs, and along many passages. The road to chapel is like the road to heaven – it is a narrow way, and it winds upward still. Both at Coldbath and Holloway the chapel is perched as near the sky as the building permits. Chapel at Coldbath was a mockery. We filed in, and took our seats about a couple of feet apart; very few prisoners brought their Prayer-books or their Bibles. A distant and more or less inarticulate sound as of reading is heard. Now and again we stump down on our knees, but do not bend our heads, or close our eyes, or take part in any responses. Oh! how I longed for a stave of song, or even for the melodious music of the inarticulate organ. But there was not a sound, save the voice of chaplain Stocken a-droning away from the desk. When that ceased, we were marched back again to our cells, where we picked oakum. At eleven the governor or the chief warder came round. You have to stand with your back to the wall with your hat in your hand, and answer any questions that are put to you. The inspection is brief. If your cell is clean and neat and you have no complaint to make, it is almost momentary, and the door is locked. The door is locked and unlocked about twelve times in the day. After inspection, or sometimes after dinner, you go out for exercise. We marched in single file round and round the exercise ground. It was a pleasant sight for me to see the sky again, and the green grass, and to hear from over the high walls of the prison the welcome sounds of common life. The rumble and the roar of the traffic, the cries of the street sellers, and even the strains of a barrel organ sounded pleas-anter to the prisoner and captive than they do to the free man outside. Dinner is served at twelve – once we had soup which tasted well but did not digest, and another day two whole potatoes boiled in their jackets, together with the unvarying 6 oz. of whole meal bread. Supper – bread and skilly – comes at five, and then your gas is lit, and you can read till eight. You are not allowed to go to bed before the bell rings, why, I don't exactly know. I have a somewhat weak spine, and my back ached so badly sometimes; but a stretch, even on a plank bed, is forbidden till a quarter past eight.

My brother came to see me to get some cheques signed, and to read me a very kind message of sympathy from Cardinal Manning, who throughout has ever been the kindest and most thoughtful of friends. My solicitor called about pending cases, and swore a good comfortable oath at the 'degradation' of my costume. I did not feel degraded one whit. All the same I enjoyed the sympa-thy much more, I fear, than I condemned the morality of the oath. At last, after being three days in Cold-bath, I was summoned to receive another visitor, who brought me news that the Home Secretary had decided to transfer me to Holloway without waiting to communicate with the judge. An hour after-wards I had doffed my prison garb, and was driving in a hansom to Holloway Gaol.

This stately building with its castellated keep and its spacious wings I had seen many years ago from the top of the Monument, and wondered what it was, little dreaming that the next time I saw it I was about to enter its gates as a pris-oner. Here, as in an enchanted castle, jealously guarded by liveried retainers, I was kept secure from the strife of tongues, and afforded the rare luxury of jour-nalistic leisure. From the governor, Colonel Milman, to the poor fellow who scrubbed out my room, everyone was as kind as kind could be. From all parts of the Empire, even from distant Fiji, rained down upon me every morning the benedictions of men and women who had felt in the midst of their lifelong labours for the outcast the unexpected lift of the great outburst of compas-sion and indignation which followed the publication of the 'Maiden Tribute.' I had papers, books, letters, flowers, everything that heart could wish. Twice a week my wife brought the sunlight of her presence into the pretty room, all hung round with Christmas greetings from absent friends, and twice a week she brought with her one of the children. On the day after Christmas the whole family came, excepting the little two-year-old, and what high jinks we had in the old gaol with all the bairns! The room was rather small for blind man's buff, but we managed it somehow, and never was there a merrier little party than that which met in cell No. 2 on the ground floor of the E wing of Holloway Gaol, which last Christmas was in the occupation of a certain 'misdemeanant of the first division', named Stead. Mr Talbot, my minister at Wimbledon, whose thoughtful kindness has never varied, came once a week, while I had visitors from my staff every other day. The magistrates placed a veto upon the visits of all persons who had taken part in the recent agitation. If anyone wished to see me, I had to submit his name to the governor, who submitted it to the visiting magistrates, and when they gave it their sanction, the person named was allowed to visit me, not in my room, but in the ordinary visiting cell, for half an hour between two and five.

I was warmer in Holloway Gaol than I have been since I came out of it. I was immeasurably quieter … my 'little room', as the good chaplain always euphemistically described our cells, is a double cell, just like a college room. I had the same cell as Mr Tates, of whom traditions still linger in the gaol. I was well supplied with flowers and fruit. I got some lovely boxes of flowers from the South of France, bunches of fragrant violets from Glasgow in the north and Devon in the south. Pots of lilies of the valley, forced into premature bloom, sweetened, and gay tulips and graceful cyclamen brightened the cell.

Until I was in gaol I never knew what a racket a single mouse can make. A little midget that would hardly fill a couple of thimbles can keep you awake all

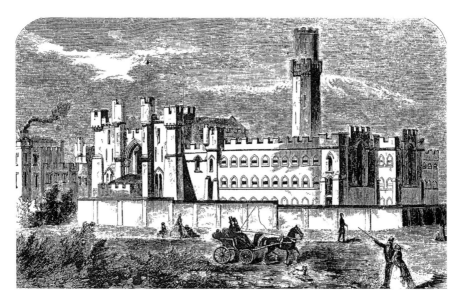

The grand vista of Holloway Prison, described by Stead as an 'enchanted castle'.

night, as it practises gymnastics among your empty boxes, and dances quadrilles upon your newspapers. Lively little fellows were the brown-coated companions of my solitude. I could take exercise when I pleased, as long as I pleased, in the daytime, but always in one appointed place – round and round the prison hospital, a neat and commodious structure, built by the present governor almost entirely with prison labour. The walk round the hospital is about one-eighth of a mile, and when there was any sun it was sunny on one side. At Holloway I paid 6s. a week for the rent of my room, 3s. 6d. a week for service, and 2s.6d. a week I believe for something else – possibly fires and gas. I had my own little kettle and made my own tea: fresh eggs were sent me by some unknown benefactor in Dunville in Ireland, and anything in the shape of food was ordered outside. The hours were the same as at Cold-bath. But instead of planks I had a comfortable bed. I was allowed my own hearthrug and easy chairs, as well as a writing desk and a cosy little tea table.

I enjoyed chapel immensely at Holloway. 'Best attended place of worship in Holloway,' said one of my warders, and no congregation takes more vigorous part in the services. Some mere boys were there, whose appearance touched me much. The prisoners in appearance are as respectable-looking as members of Parliament. Some of course are worse, but some are better but what struck me most was the absence of old men. There were not half a dozen grey heads in all the congregation. And didn't they sing! Contrasted with the miserable mockery of the dead-alive drone at Coldbath, the service at Holloway was full of sweetness and light. All of us that could read brought our hymn-books and Prayer-books, and there was nothing that was more humanizing and more pleasant than the twenty minutes' service in gaol. The chaplain, Mr Plaford, a sincere, strenuous Evangelical, with a famous voice and a kind heart. He was librarian also of a well-assorted library of some two or three thousand books, and, although he lamented in the pulpit the taste of his readers for fiction, he did not deny them the enjoyment which he condemned. My surety-servant told me he was reading 'poor Robin Crusoe', and the sympathetic tone in which he referred to Defoe's hero was very impressive. What a gift a man leaves the world who writes a good book!

The bell rang for bedtime at twenty minutes past eight. At half-past the warder shuffled round in list slippers, and peered through the peephole in the door to see if we had gone to bed. The gas was turned down from the outside, according to regulations, but as I turned my gas down myself inside, before the warder's round, the outside tap was not interfered with. Thus when, as often happened, I woke at two, three, or four in the morning and could not sleep, I could get up and write. As a rule, I slept well, but nine hours in bed was sometimes more than I could manage. From the day I received notice that in consideration of certain circumstances not specified, but not very difficult to imagine, her Majesty had been pleased to grant me a pardon conditional on my

conforming to the rules and regulations laid down for the guidance of a misdemeanant of the first division, my position was almost ideal. My only regret was
that I could not share some of the gladness and peace which made hard work
restful with those who were left in the hurly-burly outside. I have ever been the
spoiled child of fortune, but never had I a happier lot than the two months I
spent in happy Holloway.

Mrs Florence Maybrick (1889)

Florence 'Florie' Maybrick was a pretty American girl from a good family who
married James Maybrick, an English cotton broker, some twenty-three years her
senior, in 1881. They made their home at Battlecrease House in the Liverpool
suburb of Aigburth. James Maybrick was, apparently, not the easiest of men to
live with, he was known to take concoctions of drugs and maintained a number
of mistresses, one of whom bore him five children. The disenchanted Florie took
to having a few clandestine liaisons of her own, including a dalliance with her
husband's brother, Edwin. Her affair with local businessman Alfred Brierley was
the one that reached the ears of James and after a violent row during which he
assaulted Florie, Maybrick demanded a divorce.

In April 1889, Florie bought fly papers that she knew contained arsenic and
soaked them in a bowl of water to obtain the poison for cosmetic use. On 27
April 1889 James was taken ill, the doctor was called and he was treated for acute
dyspepsia, yet his condition declined and he died at Battlecrease on 11 May 1889.
Suspicious of the cause of death, Maybrick's brothers requested James's body be
examined and traces of arsenic were detected, not enough to prove fatal, but they
were present and Florie was arrested and tried for murder at the Liverpool Assizes
held in St George's Hall on 31 July 1889. The evidence against her was flimsy;
there was no way of proving that it was 26-year-old Florie who had administered
the arsenic to James but it seems her private life and affairs drew condemnation
and she was found guilty, more for lack of morals than by direct evidence of
murder. The case was a sensation that drew great public interest on both sides of
the Atlantic. Mr Justice Stephens took two days to sum up the case, and after an
absence of nearly three quarters of an hour, the jury returned. Florence Maybrick
takes up the story in her own words:

Judge: 'And do you find the prisoner guilty of the murder of James Maybrick
or not guilty?'
The Foreman: 'Guilty.'
A prolonged 'Ah!' strangely like the sighing of wind through a forest, sounded
through the court. I reeled as if struck a blow and sank upon a chair. The Clerk
of Arraigns then turned to me and said: 'Florence Elizabeth Maybrick, you have

Mrs Florence 'Florie'
Maybrick.

Mr James Maybrick.

been found guilty of wilful murder. Have you anything to say why the court should not pronounce sentence upon you according to the law?'

I arose, and with a prayer for strength, I clasped the rail of the dock in front of me, and said in a low voice, but with firmness: 'My lord, everything has been against me; I am not guilty of this crime.'

These were the last words which the law permitted me to speak. Mr Justice Stephen then assumed the full dress of the criminal judge – the black cap – and pronounced the sentence of the court in these words: 'Prisoner at the bar, I am no longer able to treat you as being innocent of the dreadful crime laid to your charge. You have been convicted by a jury of this city, after a lengthy and most painful investigation, followed by a defence which was in every respect worthy of the man. The jury has convicted you, and the law leaves me no discretion, and I must pass the sentence of the law. The court doth order you to be taken from hence to the place from whence you came, and from thence to the place of execution, and that you be hanged by the neck until you are dead, and that your body be afterward buried within the precincts of the prison in which you shall be confined after your conviction. And may the Lord have mercy upon your soul'

Utterly stunned I was removed from the court to Walton Jail, there to be confined until this sentence of the law should be carried into effect. The mob, as the Liverpool public was styled by the press, before they had heard or read a word of the defence had hissed me when I entered the court; and now that they had heard or read the evidence, cheered me as I drove away in the prison van, and hissed and hooted the judge, who with difficulty gained his carriage.

In all the larger local English prisons there is one room, swept and ready, the sight of which cannot fail to stir unwonted thoughts. The room is large, with barred windows, and contains only a bed and a chair. It is the last shelter of those whom the law declares to have forfeited their lives. Nearby is a small brick building in the prison-yard that has apparently nothing to connect it with the room; yet they are joined by a sinister suggestion.

For nearly three terrible weeks I was confined in this cell of the condemned, to taste the bitterness of death under its most appalling and shameful aspect. I was carefully guarded by two female warders, who would gladly have been spared the task. They might not read nor sleep; at my meals, through my prayers, during every moment of agony, they still watched on and rarely spoke. Many have asked me what my feelings were at that awful time. I remember little in the way of details as to my state of mind. I was too overwhelmed for either analytic or collective thought. Conscious of my innocence, I had no fear of physical death, for the love of my Heavenly Father was so enveloping that death seemed to me a blessed escape from a world in which such an unspeakable travesty of justice could take place; while I petitioned for a reconsideration of the verdict, it was wholly for the sake of my mother and my children.

I knew nothing of any public efforts for my relief. I was held fast on the wheels of a slow-moving machine, hypnotized by the striking hours and the flight of my numbered minutes, with the gallows staring me in the face. The date of my execution was not told me at Walton Jail, but I heard afterward that it was to have taken place on the 26th of August. On the 22nd, while I was taking my daily exercise in the yard attached to the condemned cell, the governor, Captain Anderson, accompanied by the chief matron, entered. He called me to him, and, with a voice which – all honour to him – trembled with emotion, said: 'Maybrick, no commutation of sentence has come down today, and I consider it my duty to tell you to prepare for death.'

'Thank you, governor,' I replied; 'my conscience is clear. God's will be done.'

He then walked away and I returned to my cell. The female warder was weeping silently, but I was calm and spent the early part of the night in my usual prayers. About midnight my exhausted nature could bear no more, and I fainted. I had barely regained consciousness when I heard the shuffle of feet outside, the click of the key in the lock – that warning catch in the slow machinery of my doom. I sprang up, and with one supreme effort of will braced myself for what I believed was the last act of my life. The governor and a chaplain entered, followed by a warder. They read my expectation in my face, and the governor, hastening forward, exclaimed in an agitated voice: 'It is well; it is good news!' When I opened my eyes once more I was lying in bed in the hospital, and I remained there until I was taken to Woking Convict Prison.

Mrs Maybrick's Own Story: My Lost Fifteen Years (1904)

There had been a public outcry at the death sentence pronounced upon Florence; the public were simply not convinced of her guilt. Petitions of reprieve poured in from across Britain, half a million from the Liverpool Exchange alone, there were also petitions from medical practitioners who complained about the lack of medical evidence. James Maybrick had taken arsenic on a regular basis as it was regarded by some men at that time to be an aphrodisiac and tonic; a city chemist confirmed that he had supplied the dead man with quantities of the poison and a search of Battlecrease House later turned up enough to kill at least fifty people. The Home Secretary, Henry Matthews and Lord Chancellor Halsbury concluded: 'that the evidence clearly establishes that Mrs Maybrick administered poison to her husband with intent to murder; but that there is ground for reasonable doubt whether the arsenic so administered was in fact the cause of his death' and her death sentence was commuted to life imprisonment.

Florence recalled her arrival at Woking Prison:

As we approached the prison the great iron gate swung wide, and the cab drove silently into the yard. There I descended. The governor gave an order, and a woman – who I afterward found was assistant superintendent – came forward.

The Maybrick case as featured in the *Illustrated Police News*, August 1889.

Accompanied by her and an officer, I was led across a near-by yard to a building which stood somewhat apart from the others and is known as the infirmary. There a principal matron received me, and the assistant superintendent and the chief matron returned to their quarters.

In the grasp of what seemed to me a horrible nightmare, I found myself in a cell with barred windows, a bed, and a chair. Without, the stillness of death reigned. I remained there perhaps half an hour when the door opened and I was commanded by a female warder to follow her. In a daze I obeyed mechanically. We crossed the same yard again and entered a door that led into a room containing only a fireplace, a table, and a bath. Here I was told to take off my clothes, as those I had travelled in had to be sent back to the prison at Liverpool, where they belonged.

When I was dressed in the uniform to which the greatest stigma and disgrace is attached, I was told to sit down. The warder then stepped quickly forward and with a pair of scissors cut off my hair to the nape of my neck. This act seemed, above all others, to bring me to a sense of my degradation, my utter helplessness; and the iron of the awful tragedy, of which I was the innocent victim, entered my soul. I was then weighed and my height taken. My weight was one hundred and twelve pounds, and my height five feet three inches.

Once more I was bidden to follow my guide. We re-crossed the yard and entered the infirmary. Here I was locked in the cell already mentioned. At last I could be alone after the anguish and torture of the day. I prayed for sleep that I might lose consciousness of my intolerable anguish. But sleep, that gentle nurse of the sad and suffering, came not. What a night! I shudder even now at the memory of it. Physically exhausted, smarting with the thought of the cruel, heartless way in which I had been beaten down and trodden under foot, I felt that mortal death would have been more merciful than the living death to which I was condemned. In the adjoining cell an insane woman was raving and weeping throughout the night, and I wondered whether in the years to come I should become like her.

The next day I was visited by the governor on his official rounds. Then the doctor came and made a medical examination, and ordered me to be detained in the infirmary until further orders. My mind is a blank as to what happened for some time afterward. My next remembrance is being told by a coarse-looking, harsh-spoken female warder to get ready to go into the prison. Once more I was led across the big yard, and then I stood within the walls that were to be for years my tomb.

Mrs Maybrick's Own Story: My Lost Fifteen Years (1904)

Florence served her sentence at Woking and Aylesbury prisons. Her case became a *cause célèbre* but she was only released in January 1904. She published *Mrs Maybrick's Own Story: My Fifteen Lost Years* the same year she was released and after her return to the United States she earned a living on the lecture circuit. In the end though Florence became a tragic recluse and died in poverty in 1941. Found among her few remaining possessions was a tatty family Bible. Pressed between its yellowed pages was a scrap of paper which had written upon it, in faded ink, the direction for soaking flypapers for use as a beauty treatment.

Oscar Wilde

Following the exposure of his homosexual practices in his relationships with Alfred Taylor and Lord Alfred Douglas in the press and during a high profile libel trial, poet and playwright Oscar Wilde was arrested in 1895 and charged with 'gross indecency' under Section 11 of the Criminal Law Amendment Act (1885).

Oscar Wilde.

His trial opened on 26 April 1895 and very soon it became a sensation in the press. The first trial jury were unable to agree a verdict and Wilde was brought up for a second trial presided over by Justice Sir Alfred Wills. On 25 May 1895 Wilde was convicted of gross indecency and sentenced to two years penal servitude with hard labour. Even though he had just handed down the maximum sentence allowed for the charge, Justice Wills was still not satisfied and commented that the sentence was 'totally inadequate for a case such as this.'

Wilde was imprisoned first in Pentonville and then in Wandsworth Prison, where he proclaimed in *De Profundis*: 'I longed to die. It was my one desire.' After two months in the infirmary Wilde was transferred to Reading Prison. While Wilde was in Reading, Charles Thomas Wooldridge (30), a trooper in the Royal Horse Guards who had killed his wife in a fit of jealousy, was executed on 7 July 1896. After his release, the memories of that event remained bold and indelible upon the mind of Wilde and he wrote the 'Ballad of Reading Gaol'. Wilde had observed Wooldridge in the exercise yard of the prison during the time Wooldridge was detained there and dedicated the poem to him with the initials C.T.W. only. Wilde wrote of Wooldridge:

He walked amongst the Trial Men
In a suit of shabby grey;
A cricket cap was on his head,
And his step seemed light and gay;
But I never saw a man who looked
So wistfully at the day.

I never saw a man who looked
With such a wistful eye
Upon that little tent of blue
Which prisoners call the sky,
And at every drifting cloud that went
With sails of silver by.

I walked, with other souls in pain,
Within another ring,
And was wondering if the man had done
A great or little thing,
When a voice behind me whispered low,
'That fellow's got to swing.'

The Ballad of Reading Gaol (Smithers, 1898)

Known as prisoner C33, Wilde was not initially allowed paper and pen but a later governor was more amenable. Shortly after his release from prison in 1897 Wilde wrote to the editor of the *Daily Chronicle* in the case and dismissal of Warder Martin, with especial regard to the treatment of children in prison, it also reveals much about the things Wilde witnessed and his own experiences while incarcerated:

Sir,
I learn with great regret, through the columns of your paper, that the warder Martin, of Reading Prison, has been dismissed by the Prison Commissioners for having given some sweet biscuits to a little hungry child. I saw the three children myself on Monday preceding my release. They had just been convicted and were standing in a row in the central hall in their prison dress, carrying their sheets under the arms, previous to their being sent to the cells allotted to them.

They were quite small children, the youngest – the one to whom the warder gave the biscuits – being a tiny little chap, for whom they had evidently been unable to find clothes small enough to fit. I had, of course, seen many children in prison during the two years during which I was myself confined. Wandsworth Prison, especially, contained always a large number of children. But the little child I saw on the afternoon of Monday the seventeenth at Reading, was tinier than any one of them.

I need not say how utterly distressed I was to see these children at Reading, for I knew the treatment in store for them. The cruelty that is practised by day and night on children in English prisons is incredible, except to those who have witnessed it and are aware of the brutality of the system.

The present treatment of children is terrible, primarily from people not understanding the peculiar psychology of a child's nature. A child cannot understand a punishment inflicted by society. It cannot realise what society is. With grown up people it is, of course, the reverse. Those of us who are either in prison, or have been sent there, can understand, and do understand, what that collective force called society means, and whatever we may think of its methods or claims, we can force ourselves to accept it.

The child consequently, being taken away from its parents by people whom it has never seen, and of whom it knows nothing, and finding itself in a lonely and unfamiliar cell, waited on by strange faces, and ordered about and punished by representatives of a system that it cannot understand, becomes an immediate prey to the first and most prominent emotion produced by modern prison – the emotion of terror.

The terror of a child in prison is quite limitless. I remember once, in Reading, as I was going out to exercise, seeing in the dimly-lit cell right opposite my own, a small boy. Two warders – not unkindly men – were talking to him with some sternness apparently, or perhaps giving him some useful advice about his conduct. One was in the cell with him, the other was standing outside. The child's face was like a white wedge of sheer terror. There was in his eyes the terror of a hunted animal.

The next morning I heard him at breakfast time crying and calling to be let out. His cry was for his parents. From time to time I could hear the deep voice

The gate of Reading Gaol, *c.* 1900.

of the warder on duty telling him to keep quiet. Yet he was not even convicted of whatever little offence he had been charged with. He was simply on remand. That I knew by his wearing his own clothes, which seemed neat enough. He was, however, wearing prison socks and shoes. This showed that he was a very poor boy, whose own shoes, if he had any, were in a bad state. Justices and magistrates, an entirely ignorant class as a rule, often remand children for a week, and then perhaps remit whatever sentence they are entitled to pass. They call this 'not sending a child to prison'. It is, of course, a stupid view on their part. To a little child whether he is in prison on remand, or after conviction, is not a subtlety of social position he can comprehend. To him the horrible thing is to be there at all. In the eyes of humanity it should be a horrible thing for him to be there at all.

Every child is confined to its cell for twenty-three hours out of the twenty-four. This is the appalling thing. To shut up a child in a dimly lit cell for twenty-three hours out of the twenty-four is an example of the cruelty of stupidity. If an individual, parent or guardian did this to a child he would be severely punished. The Society for the Prevention of Cruelty to Children would take the matter up at once. There would be on all hands the utmost detestation of whomsoever had been guilty of such cruelty. A heavy sentence would, undoubtedly, follow conviction. But our own actual society does worse itself.

Inhuman treatment by society is to the child the more terrible because there is no appeal. A parent or guardian can be moved, and let out a child from the dark lonely room in which it is confined. But a warder cannot. Most warders are very fond of children. But the system prohibits them from rendering the child any assistance. Should they do so, as Warder Martin did, they are dismissed.

The second thing from which a child suffers in prison is hunger. The food that is given to it consists of a piece of usually badly-baked prison bread and a tin of water for breakfast at half-past seven. At twelve o' clock it gets dinner composed of a tin of coarse Indian meal stirabout, and at half-past five it gets a piece of dry bread and a tin of water for its supper. This diet in the case of a strong grown man is always productive of illness of some kind, chiefly of course, diarrhoea, with its attendant weakness. In the case of a child, the child is, as a rule, incapable of eating the food at all. Anyone who knows anything about children knows how easily a child's digestion system is upset by a fit of crying, or trouble and mental distress of any kind. A child who has been crying all day long, and perhaps half the night, in a lonely dimly-lit cell, and is preyed upon by terror, simply cannot eat food of this coarse, horrible kind.

In the case of the little child to whom Warder Martin gave the biscuits, the child was crying with hunger on Tuesday morning, and utterly unable to eat the bread and water served to it for its breakfast. Martin went out after the breakfasts had been served and bought the few sweet biscuits for the child rather than see it starving. It was a beautiful action on his part, and was so recognised by the child, who, utterly unconscious of the regulation of the Prison Board, told one of the senior warders how kind this junior warder had been to him. The result was, of course, a report and dismissal.

As regards the children, a great deal has been talked and written lately about the contaminating influence of prison on young children. What is said is quite true. A child is utterly contaminated by prison life. But the contaminating influence is not that of the prisoners. It is that of the whole prison system – of the governor, the chaplain, the warders, the lonely cell, the isolation, the revolting food, the rules of the Prison Commissioners, the mode of discipline as it is termed, of the life. Every care is taken to isolate a child from the sight even of all prisoners over 16 years of age. Children sit behind a curtain in chapel, and are sent to take exercise in small sunless yards, sometimes a stone-yard, sometimes a yard at back of the mills – rather than that they should see the elder prisoners at exercise. But the only really humanising influence in prison is the influence of the prisoners. Their cheerfulness under terrible circumstances, their sympathy for each other, their humility, their gentleness, their pleasant smiles of greeting when they meet each other, their complete acquiescence in their punishments are all quite wonderful, and I myself learnt many sound lessons from them.

I am not proposing that the children should not sit behind the curtain in chapel, or that they should take exercise in a corner of the common yard. I am merely pointing out the bad influence on children is not, and could never be, that of the prisoners, but is, and will always remain, that of the prison system itself.

There is not a single man in Reading Gaol that would not gladly have done the three children's punishment for them. When I saw them last, it was on the Tuesday following their conviction. I was taking exercise at half-past eleven with about twelve other men, as the three children passed near us in the charge of a warder, from the damp, dreary stone-yard in which they had been at exercise. I saw the greatest pity and sympathy in the eyes of my companions as they looked at them. Prisoners are, as a class, extremely kind and sympathetic to each other.

It is not the prisoners who need reformation. It is the prisons.

Of course no child under 14 years of age should be sent to prison at all. It is an absurdity, and, like many absurdities, of absolutely tragic results. If, however, they are to be sent to prison, during the daytime they should be in a workshop or schoolroom with a warder. At night they should sleep in a dormitory, with a night-warder to look after them. They should be allowed exercise for at least three hours a day. The dark, badly ventilated, ill-smelling prison cells are dreadful for a child, dreadful indeed for anyone. One is always breathing bad air in prison. The food given to children should consist of tea and bread-and-butter and soup. Prison soup is very good and wholesome.

A resolution of the House of Commons could settle the treatment of children in half-an-hour. I hope you will use your influence to have this done. The way that children are treated at present is really an outrage on humanity and common sense. It comes from stupidity.

Sir, your obedient servant,

Oscar Wilde

May 27th 1897

Daily Chronicle, 28 May 1897

During his time in prison, Wilde wrote a 50,000-word letter to Lord Alfred Douglas, which he was not allowed to send while still a prisoner but which he was allowed to take with him at the end of his sentence. On his release, he gave the manuscript to Robert Ross, who published a heavily abridged version of the letter in 1905 (five years after Wilde's death) under the title of *De Profundis*. Wilde reflected on his experience of prison:

> When first I was put into prison some people advised me to try and forget who I was. It was ruinous advice. It is only by realising what I am that I have found comfort of any kind. Now I am advised by others to try on my release to forget that I have ever been in a prison at all. I know that would be equally fatal. It would mean that I would always be haunted by an intolerable sense of disgrace, and that those things that are meant for me as much as for anybody else – the beauty of the sun and moon, the pageant of the seasons, the music of daybreak and the silence of great nights, the rain falling through the leaves, or the dew creeping over the grass and making it silver – would all be tainted for me, and lose their healing power, and their power of communicating joy. To regret one's own experiences is to arrest one's own development. To deny one's own experiences is to put a lie into the lips of one's own life. It is no less than a denial of the soul.
>
> *De Profundis* (Ross, 1905)

Mrs Amelia Dyer

In the latter half of the nineteenth century British society was the epitome of upright morality and sturdy values, but behind those well painted and highly polished doors debauchery was rife. Out of these times grew a hideous business all too indicative of the times it was practiced in; it became known as baby farming and its most infamous practitioner was Mrs Amelia Dyer.

The method was simple: If one of the servants or daughters of the house was found unwed and pregnant there were a number of horrible options to 'deal with the situation', but only one method really appealed to Victorian sensibilities. The method was simple. Scan the national newspapers for advertisements such as:

ADOPTION: A good home, with a mother's love and care, is
offered to a respectable person, wishing her child to be entirely
adopted. Premium £5 which includes everything. Apply to Mrs-----
by letter only ...

After a short exchange of letters terms would be agreed (the woman who was
contacted would no doubt have given assurances of a good family where the
baby would be found an adoptive home), a short train ride to a large conurbation
such as London, a meeting, a cash transaction, baby handed over; problem gone,
out of sight out of mind. The problem was that despite the dangers of child-
bearing and high rates of child mortality the supply of unwanted children far
outweighed the demand. As more and more operatives indulged in the foul trade,
the hideous business of baby farming began to be exposed. First indications of the
crime and its scale appeared in official reports like that of the Registrar General,
who stated in the 1860s:

> In the last five years within the metropolitan district alone, at least 278 infants
> were murdered; above 60 were found dead in the Thames or the canals and
> ponds about London and many more than 100, at all events were found dead
> under railway arches, on doorsteps, in dustholes, cellars and the like.

The first high-profile prosecution of a baby farmer was that of the 'Brixton Baby
Farmers'; Margaret Walters and her sister Sarah Ellis in 1870. Sarah was lucky to
get off with 18 months with hard labour – Margaret kept an appointment with
the executioner.

Amelia 'Annie' Elizabeth Dyer (56) was trained as a nurse but found baby-
farming to be a far more lucrative business. In return for a one-off payment,
which in her case could range from an average of about £10-£20, plus the provision of adequate clothing for the child to sums in excess of £50 if hush money
was paid. In her advertisements and meetings with clients, she assured them that
she was respectable, married (in fact the Dyers were separated), and that she
would provide a safe and loving home for the child.

Dyer did not initially kill her tiny wards but rather left them to die from
neglect or untreated childhood illnesses. She eluded the interest of the police
and the inspectors of the newly-formed NSPCC for quite some time, but she
was eventually caught in 1879 after a doctor was suspicious about the number
of infant deaths he had been called to certify for young children in Dyer's care.
Instead of being convicted of murder or manslaughter, she was sentenced to six
months hard labour for neglect. During her stay in prison and with exposure to
the hard labour of her sentence it appears her mind had become unstable.

After her release, Dyer attempted to resume her nursing career but failed miser-
ably and ended up being admitted for short periods in asylums due to her alleged

Mrs Amelia Dyer, 'babyfarmer'.

mental instability and suicidal tendencies. To earn some money she returned to her old trade but, having learned the hard way that involving doctors could lead to detection, she began murdering the babies and disposing of the bodies personally. Dyer also got more professional in her dark business and began moving around the country, using many aliases to avoid attracting the interests of the police or any families attempting to reclaim or check on the progress of the baby placed in her care.

In 1895, Dyer moved to Caversham, Berkshire with her associate, Jane Smith, and her daughter and son-in-law, Mary 'Polly' and Arthur Palmer, moving again that same year to 45 Kensington Road, Reading, Berkshire. Mrs Dyer was finally traced to this last address after a baby wrapped in a brown paper parcel had been pulled out of the water by a bargeman at Caversham Lock. The infant had been strangled by a piece of fabric tape tied under the left ear. Dyer had made her fatal mistake, she had wrapped the baby in paper from a parcel sent to her at her old address of 20 Pigott's (spelt Wigott's on the parcel) Road, Caversham. She had also been spotted before the horrible discovery by a witness on the Caversham tow path with a parcel under her arm. The waters were searched and a further six bodies were found. The home of Mary and Arthur Palmer was also searched and more baby clothes were found there; their complicity in Dyer's evil trade was suggested but at the inquest there was no evidence forthcoming to connect them to any crime.

Arthur Palmer was discharged as the result of a confession written by Amelia Dyer. In Reading Gaol she wrote (her own spelling and punctuation have not been corrected):

Sir will you kindly grant me the favour of presenting this to the magistrates on Saturday the 18th instant I have made this statement out, for I may not have the opportunity then I must relieve my mind I do know and I feel my days are numbered on this earth but I do feel it is an awful thing drawing innocent people into trouble I do know I shal have to answer before my Maker in Heaven for the awful crimes I have committed but as God Almighty is my judge in Heaven a on Hearth neither my daughter Mary Ann Palmer nor her husband Alfred Ernest Palmer I do most solemnly declare neither of them had any thing at all to do with it, they never knew I contemplated doing such a wicked thing until it was to late I am speaking the truth and nothing but the truth as I hope to be forgiven, I myself and I alone must stand before my Maker in Heaven to give a answer for it all witnes my hand Amelia Dyer.

April 16, 1896

Dyer's own daughter did not hesitate to deflect any blame and condemnation onto her mother and she was eventually acquitted, but Mrs Amelia Dyer was found guilty; the jury returned the verdict in under five minutes, and she was sent to the gallows.

Because the female wing of Newgate Prison was no longer in use and had been partly dismantled, the condemned cell occupied by Mrs Dyer was situated directly under the infirmary on the male side. It was constructed by knocking through two cells and making one which measured some 14ft long and 18ft wide. This cell's previous occupant was Mrs Pearcey, who had been executed for the murder of Mrs Hogg and her baby in 1890. It was heated by steam pipes and the floor was covered by cocoanut matting and furnished with a square table and chairs for the wardresses and the condemned. From the time of sentence Mrs Dyer was watched night and day; a task performed by five wardresses, two of whom were on duty for eight hours at a time. At night a third officer was placed on duty outside the cell door to be ready in case of emergency, 'the convict being a powerful woman'.

During her three weeks in the condemned cell, she filled five exercise books with her 'last true and only confession'. Among this vast statement, Dyer ensured her daughter was absolved and in doing so revealed her cold and callous methods:

I can safely say my daughter had nothing to do with it. I feel sure in my own mind she has said a great deal to screen me and now she is only suffering for it herself – suffering for what I myself have done. But I am certain now she will tell the truth of the whole matter. No matter what I have done, I never let my daughter or her husband know the truth of what I did do. I am telling the truth in this matter. They never did know. I had entirely forgot to mention the last two children, Dorris Morman and Harry Simmons. The statement my daughter made to the Magistrates is perfectly true. Neither Mary Ann Palmer nor her husband ever had anything in the world to do with either of those children …

Dyer stated she had told her daughter she had placed little Doris Marmon with a family; she had in fact killed the child and wrapped her in paper with a napkin folded around and hid it under the sofa until she could dispose of it. She continues:

As regards the child Harry Simmons, I am quite sure my daughter went to her bedroom to wash and dress and I was left in the sitting room alone. I locked the sitting room door and I am speaking truthfully when I say no-one was in the room with me or knew what I was doing. I then unlocked the door and laid the little boy on the sofa and wrapped him up in a large plaid shawl and made it appear if he was asleep. Arthur had not then come home and when I tied that boy I was in the room alone, so I am certain no one ever saw what I had in the bag and I can speak truthfully and say not in any one case have they helped me or knew what I was going to do. What was done I did do myself. My only wonder is I did not murder all in the house when I have had these awful temptations upon me.

A number of newspapers reported her behaviour in the cell as 'most peculiar':

She has sat for hours with her eyes riveted first on one of her attendants and then on the other, without speaking, or betraying any emotion. She manifested such a dislike to one of her attendants that another had to take her place. The convict has not been heard to utter one prayer in her cell by her attendants. In a letter she wrote to her daughter, Mrs Palmer, last week, she said: 'I have no soul; my soul was hammered out of me in Gloucester Asylum.'

Leeds Mercury, 11 June 1896

The day before her execution, Milsom, Fowler and Seaman were executed together on the Newgate gallows. In order to spare Mrs Dyer the pain of hearing the tolling bell and the bustle incidental to the execution, she was temporarily removed from Newgate to Holloway Gaol and was returned the same evening, but before reaching her cell she had to proceed up a walkway that would have clearly shown the disturbance of the stones of the newly-made graves for the executed men. Executioner James Billington and his assistant William Warbrick remained in Newgate and prepared the scaffold for Dyer the following morning.

The chaplain visited her the night before her execution and asked her if she had anything to confess and in reply she offered him her exercise books with the

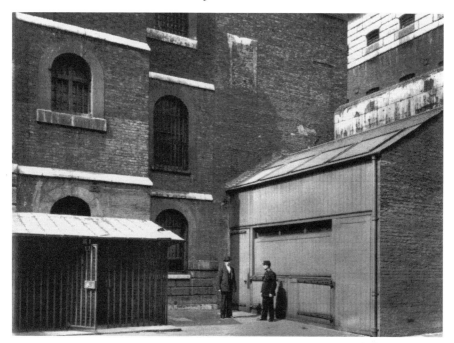

To the right of this picture is the shed that contained the Newgate gallows, where Mrs Dyer and many others kept their appointment with the executioner.

question 'isn't this enough?' She remained in a 'wretched and agitated state' and passed a very restless night. The chaplain joined her again early on the morning of Wednesday, 10 June 1896. Colonel Milman the prison governor, Mr Ruston the Under-Sheriff of Middlesex and Dr Scott the medical officer all arrived at the prison shortly before nine o'clock. Mrs Dyer had told one of her warders shortly after her conviction that she would never walk to the gallows and that was almost the case.

In some accounts of her last moments in the condemned cell it is claimed Dyer made a feeble attempt to strangle herself by twisting a handkerchief around her throat, whether this dazed her, or whether she feigned collapse, witnesses stated:

At the appearance of Billington, who carried in his hand the strap with which to pinion the arms, Mrs Dyer, wearing her gown only and with her hair twisted up ball fashion at the back of her head leaving her neck quite free, suddenly collapsed. She had made but a poor attempt at breakfast, being even then faint and ill but as the last moments of her life were at hand all the self composure which she had maintained so well during her incarceration left her, and she had to be supported by the female warders while her arms were fastened. This was but the work of a moment and almost immediately the procession had set out.

Chief Warder Scott
(right) by the inner
gate at Newgate,
c. 1895.

The cell she occupied was but a few paces distant from the shed in which
the final work was to be performed but even across this short distance the
condemned woman had to be carried by the warders. Indeed, she seemed
altogether unconscious now of what was taking place. Almost within a minute
she was under the beam, still supported by the warders and while Billington's
assistant strapped her dress around her legs, Billington himself drew the white
cap over her face and adjusted the noose. The chaplain who had preceded the
condemned woman from the cell was still reading the burial service when, at a
signal from the Under-Sheriff, the hangman pulled the lever, the drop fell and
Mrs Dyer was dead.

Illustrated Police News, 20 June 1896

Other press reports carried the story that the Under-Sheriff had informed a press representative that when asked by the governor at the final moment before the hood was pulled down whether she had anything to say, Dyer appeared to recover herself and reply, 'No sir, I have nothing to say,' and even went on to thank the governor and the female warders for their kindness to her.

Mrs Dyer was not the last woman to be hanged in Britain for baby farming; she would be followed by Annie Walters and Amelia Sachs – the first women to be hanged in the new women's prison at Holloway in February 1903 – and finally Rhoda Willis (aka Leslie James), who was executed at Cardiff Prison by Henry and Tom Pierrepoint on 14 August 1907. But Mrs Dyer's notoriety exceeds them all by far, a real Victorian bogeywoman; the icy glower of Mrs Dyer's cold eyes sent a shudder down the spines of visitors to Madame Tussauds for generations after her crimes. It is impossible to ascertain the precise number of her victims, but at the time of her arrest Mrs Dyer had been carrying on her trade, on and off, for about twenty years and it could be safely assumed that the number of babies entrusted to her 'care' numbered dozens, perhaps even over fifty; the chances are many of their tiny bodies will never be found. Chillingly, when Mrs Dyer was asked about the identification of her victims, she replied, 'You'll know mine by the tape around their necks.'

Prison warders are not prone to flights of fancy but when Robert Thurston Hopkins made the acquaintance of Chief Warder Scott of Newgate he was fascinated to hear his recollections of Mrs Dyer during her stay in the prison and her final words to him on the morning of her execution: 'Meet you again some day, sir.' Then Scott explained how her spirit did not rest quietly:

One night just before Newgate was closed down for good several of the warders were having a bottle of whisky together to celebrate the final week of duty in the prison. They were sitting in the Keeper's room next to the Women Felon's Yard. There was a door with a glass observation wicket looking out to the yard. Suddenly Scott felt aware that someone's eyes were fixed on him and he heard a voice ringing in his head 'Meet you again … meet you again some day, sir …' Then he looked towards the door and Mrs Dyer's face was framed in the grill. There was no mistaking her oily benevolent smile, the little dark, snake-like eyes and the thin lips trying to look kind and harmless. She gave Scott one sad enigmatical look and passed on. Scott jumped up and opened the door and saw nothing except a woman's handkerchief which fluttered at his feet on the wet flagstones. There was no woman convict in the prison at that time – indeed the reception of women had been discontinued for some years.

R. Thurston Hopkins, *Adventures with Phantoms* (1946)

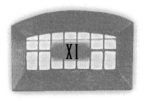

EXECUTION

Early Victorian executions contained elements of both civic occasion and public entertainment and they drew vast crowds who ate, drank, revelled and jostled for the best view of the felon's final moments 'on the drop'. Executions were reported with apparent relish and with every lurid detail recorded, even for the more provincial hangings. A fine and quite typical example of the reportage for a 'Hanging Day' recounts the execution of Elias Lucas (25) and his sister-in-law Mary Reader (20), who were hanged in front of Cambridge Castle on 3 April 1850 for the murder of Elias's wife Susan by the administration of two drams of arsenic. It was the old story of an illicit affair and their desire to remove the obstacle to their union, this time made more perverse because the unwanted wife and mistress were sisters. Susan's food was poisoned at a meal she had shared with Elias and Mary. Complaining the food tasted bitter, she was soon vomiting and forced to take to her bed. Dr Frederick Cramer was called but Susan was dead by the time he arrived. The symptoms shown by the deceased suggested cholera or poisoning, Cramer suspected the latter. Tests were carried out and arsenic was detected in her body. Elias and Mary were arrested. Tried before Mr Justice Whiteman at Cambridgeshire Assizes, both were found guilty and sentenced to death.

The Times of Monday 15 April related:

Long before daybreak, every street and road leading into this town exhibited the appearance of a fair day. From 6 o'clock until the hour appointed for the execution, 12 o'clock, the streets were one living mass. The place where the gallows were erected was in front of the debtor's door of the county gaol, which is situated on the Castle-hill. It is surrounded by a large green, in the centre of which is an extensive mound from the base to the summit [that was] crammed with spectators, nearly two thirds of whom were women and children ... A few minutes before 12 o'clock it was announced to the unfortunate

THE DYING WORDS and CONFESSION OF

Elias Lucas AND Mary Reader,

Who were Executed this morning (April 13) in front of the County Goal at Cambridge, for the wilful MURDER of SUSAN LUCAS.

LIFE, CHARACTER, &c.

TRIAL and CONVICTION.

CONFESSION.

EXECUTION.

COPY OF VERSES

The dying words and confession broadside for Elias Lucas and Mary Reader, sold on the day of their execution, 13 April 1850.

culprits that the fatal hour had arrived. They received the intelligence without the slightest emotion.

Calcraft the executioner was then summoned to pinion the prisoners and as the clock struck the hour the solemn procession emerged from the governor's House. A party of javelin men headed the procession; next followed three or four of the county magistrates, bare headed; next the Under-Sheriff, bearing a white wand; then the officiating chaplain, reading the burial service in a very solemn tone; next came the executioner, followed by the officers of the gaol who conducted the male prisoner. He walked with a firm step and without the least assistance, and as he passed, smiled on recognising an acquaintance standing by. The female prisoner followed. She also walked to the scaffold with a firm and unwavering step. A number of county magistrates closed the mournful procession.

Lucas first ascended the scaffold and on reaching the first flight of steps he paused for a moment, as if startled by the immense crowd which had assembled opposite. He soon, however, recovered himself and actually ran up the remaining steps with a firm and elastic tread and placed himself under the fatal beam. Calcraft, who had followed him up the steps, hastily pulled the cap over his face and adjusted the rope. Whilst his office was being performed the female culprit stood at the bottom of the steps and appeared as unconcerned as possible. She walked up as tranquilly as can be conceived, without the least assistance and, while the rope was being adjusted around her neck, the Rev. H. Roberts proceeded to read the proper service. At its conclusion the Rev. gentleman said in a clear voice – 'God Almighty bless you both!' At the same time the male prisoner whispered to Calcraft, 'I am going to God.' The next moment the executioner loosened the fatal bolt, the drop fell and the two unfortunate wretches were launched into eternity. Neither of the culprits struggled much and a slight convulsion of the legs and hands was all that was visible. As the drop fell shrieks were heard proceeding from some women in the crowd and the cry of 'Hurrah!' from a single voice was heard in the immediate vicinity of the scaffold. The bodies having been suspended the usual time, they were taken down, conveyed into the gaol and buried within its precincts.

The hanging of Lucas and Reader was to be the last public double execution at Cambridge Castle. It was estimated that about 40,000 people had attended; stands had been erected for those wanting a good view and a local landlord put up scaffolding in a nooking commanding a view of the drop and let these prime seats at 5s each.

The executioner, William Calcraft, had taken up the position of public hangman in 1829 and served continuously for the next forty-five years, becoming Britain's longest-serving public hangman. Born at Great Baddow, Essex in 1800, he was the first of twelve children. Maintaining his trade as a cobbler,

William Calcraft, Britain's longest
serving hangman.

Calcraft worked all over the country and did so in front of crowds of thousands.
He hanged both men and women, sometimes swinging three or four at the same
time in the early years of his career. During his long career Calcraft executed
many of the nineteenth century's most notorious criminals, among them James
Greenacre, Mr and Mrs Manning, Dr Pritchard, Franz Muller – the first man to
commit a murder on a railway – and James Blomfield Rush, the Stanfield Hall
murderer (*see* page 143).

By far the most infamous place of execution in Victorian Britain was outside
the debtor's door of Newgate Prison – the immediate successor of, and every bit
as infamous as the old Tyburn Tree. So let us gain a glimpse of one such execution,
that of Francois Benjamin Courvoisier, on Monday, 6 July 1840. Valet to Lord
William Russell, Courvoisier had been found guilty of and subsequently confessed to the murder of his master after Russell had discovered the theft of some
silverware and ordered Courvoisier to resign from the household. Rather than
lose his position, Courvoisier decided to murder Russell while he slept in order
to conceal the matter. Recorded directly by one who was there:

> As early as 8 o'clock on Sunday evening groups of persons began to assemble in
> front of the prison and boys were seen walking up and down soliciting custom-
> ers to buy places commanding the best views of the gallows, some fetching as
> much as five guineas. At one of the houses immediately opposite the drop the

windows were taken out in order to allow their occupants a more complete view of all that passed. At a later hour in the evening the Old Bailey resembled a fair and the number of persons continued to increase until midnight, when some returned to their homes to take rest between that time and the morning while others resolved to remain in the street all night rather than lose the chance of a commanding position. Men stood smoking their pipes and relating stories of previous unfortunate souls they had seen suffering upon the drop while women stood with infants in their arms listening to their narratives.

Shortly after St Paul's clock had struck 12 the carpenters began to arrive in the yard of Newgate and forthwith proceeded with their preparations for the erection of barriers in the street to ensure the public safety against the pressure of so large an assemblage of persons as was anticipated would be brought together to witness the death of the wretched man. At two o' clock the apparatus of death was brought out of the prison yard and fixed in its proper place. The carpenters were occupied rather more than two hours in completing it. The sound of the hammer ceased as the bells of St Sepulchre chimed the quarter past four o'clock. The completion of the work was signalised on the part of the mob by a shout of triumph. Shortly after the carpenters began fixing the scaffolding a body of 60 City Police constables marched to the Old Bailey for the purpose of preserving order and at a later hour in the morning 60 more arrived.

The crowd did not much increase until six o'clock, when numbers began to arrive from all points of the metropolis and long before the hour appointed for the execution the whole line of view from Giltspur Street Compter down to Ludgate Hill presented one great mass of human heads. The general hum of conversation which was heard among the crowd, a stray hat or bonnet excited merriment as it was tossed among the crowd and the loud and heartless laugh which ever and anon struck the ear would have induced a person ignorant of the object which had called them together to have supposed that they had come out for a holiday or to witness a passing pageant, rather than behold a fellow creature sacrificed upon the scaffold.

Within the walls of the prison, inside the condemned, cell Courvoisier had slept with little disturbance from Sunday night to Monday morning, indeed it had been commented upon that during his time in the condemned cell 'His conduct never altered throughout; during his waking hours he never gave way to violent grief, nor did he ever manifest any remarkable degree of excitement or agitation at the approach of death. Only in his sleep would he occasionally groan and gnash his teeth.'

Courvoisier's conduct within the last three or four days preceding his execution was remarkable for its firmness but he did articulate his regrets many times, 'Oh God! How could I have committed so dreadful a crime? It was madness. When I think of it I can't believe it.'

He was woken, as per his own request, at 4 a.m. on the morning of his execution by a turnkey, immediately rose and dressed himself and was occupied until the arrival of Mr Carver in writing letters in French to some of his relatives. At 6.30 a.m. Mr Newman, the principal turnkey of Newgate, was ordered to take the sacramental bread and wine into the prisoner's cell. After the conclusion of the rite, Calcraft the hangman entered the cell with a black bag containing a rope with which Courvoisier's arms were to be pinioned. The prisoner complied by clasping his hands together and the rope was bound around his arms and wrists. The prison chaplain continued to pray with him for some time and put several questions to him as to whether he was fully penitent for the crime he had committed and whether he believed in the atonement of the Saviour; to which he replied in the affirmative 'in barely audible whispers, accompanied by an expression of countenance which but too plainly showed the deep anguish of his soul.' As he spoke he wrung his hands and, as far as the ropes with which he was bound would allow, raised them upwards towards the heavens. A little before seven the Swiss minister who had also attended Courvoisier went to the condemned cell and they prayed together (the Swiss minister stayed with Courvoisier and was one of the two clerics who accompanied him to the scaffold).

Our eyewitness picks up the story:

At five minutes to 8 o'clock the dismal sound of the prison bell struck upon the ear and immediately the vast multitude uncovered their heads and their eyes directed toward the procession approaching the gallows. Mr Cope the governor led the way, followed by the Sheriffs, the Under-Sheriffs, the two clergymen and the murderer, who upon arriving at the foot of the ladder shook hands with the Sheriffs and ascended the platform at two minutes after 8 o'clock, advancing to the centre of the platform without looking round him. He was followed by the executioner and the Prison chaplain, the Rev. Mr Carver. On his appearance a few yells of execration escaped from a portion of the crowd but the general body of the people, great as must have been their abhorrence of his atrocious crime, remained silent spectators of the scene which was passing before their eyes. The prisoner's step was steady and collected and free from agitation. His countenance was indeed pale and bore the trace of much dejection but it was at the same time calm and unmoved. While the executioner was placing him on the drop, he slightly moved his hands (which were tied in front of him) and strongly clasped one within the other, up and down two or three times and this was the only visible symptom of any emotion or mental anguish which the wretched man endured. His face was then covered with the cap, fitting so closely as to conceal the outlines of his countenance and the noose adjusted. During this operation he lifted up his head and raised his hands to his breast as if in fervent prayer. In a moment the fatal bolt was withdrawn, the drop fell and in this attitude the murderer perished. He died without violent struggle.

A mid–nineteenth-century execution outside the debtor's door of Newgate Prison.

In two minutes after he had fallen his legs were twice slightly convulsed but no further motion was observable, excepting that his raised arms, gradually losing their vitality, sank down from their own lifeless weight. After hanging one hour the body was cut down and removed within the prison for burial.

In many prisons it was still the custom to parade the inmates of the prison in the yard and have the body carried through in an open coffin as a warning to all. Pressure to abolish hanging had gathered momentum since the early nineteenth century. In 1810 an unprecedented 220 offences carried the death penalty for crimes so diverse as highway robbery, burglary, arson, piracy and sodomy to pick-pocketing above the value of 1s, shoplifting goods above the value of 5s, firing hay stacks or destroying a pond containing fish. As the century progressed the number of offences that carried the death penalty was reduced but the pressure against the vile spectacle of public execution and the behaviour of the crowd gathered weight from some influential personalities and was riled against by some of the literary giants of the day.

Dickens had been among the thousands present at the execution of Courvoisier and riled against the scene. Another who attended was the novelist William Makepeace Thackeray, who wrote an anti-capital punishment essay, *On Going to See a Man Hanged*. Thackeray commented:

Courvoisier bore his punishment like a man, and walked very firmly. He was dressed in a new black suit, as it seemed: his shirt was open. His arms were tied in front of him. He opened his hands in a helpless kind of way, and clasped them once or twice together. He turned his head here and there, and looked about him for an instant with a wild imploring look. His mouth was contracted into a sort of pitiful smile. He went and placed himself at once under the beam, with his face towards St. Sepulchre's. The tall grave man in black twisted him round swiftly in the other direction, and, drawing from his pocket a night-cap, pulled it tight over the patient's head and face. I am not ashamed to say that I could look no more, but shut my eyes as the last dreadful act was going on which sent this wretched guilty soul into the presence of God ... If a public execution is beneficial – and beneficial it is, no doubt, or else the wise laws would not encourage forty thousand people to witness it – the next useful thing must be a full description of such a ceremony, and all its entourages, and to this end the above pages are offered to the reader. How does an individual man feel under it – in what way does he observe it – how does he view all the phenomena con-nected with it – what induces him, in the first instance, to go and see it – and how is he moved by it afterwards? The writer has discarded the magazine 'We' altogether, and spoken face-to-face with the reader, recording every one of the impressions felt by him as honestly as he could.

I must confess, then (for 'I' is the shortest word, and the best in this case), that the sight has left on my mind an extraordinary feeling of terror and shame. It seems to me that I have been abetting an act of frightful wickedness and violence, performed by a set of men against one of their fellows; and I pray God that it may soon be out of the power of any man in England to witness such a hideous and degrading sight.

Along with his friend the illustrator John Leech, Dickens attended the execu-tion of Frederick and Maria Manning 'the Bermondsey Murderers' at the Horsemonger Lane Gaol on 13 November 1849. The Mannings, husband and wife, had murdered Maria's former lover, Patrick O'Connor, and buried his body under the kitchen floor. Maria Manning became known as 'the woman who murdered black satin' because she wore a black satin dress for her own hanging; such material was shunned by English women for years thereafter.

Just like at Courvoisier's execution, and just about every other hanging day, a huge crowd had gathered the previous evening to ensure they had a good view of 'the drop', and revelled all night. By dawn it is estimated that 30,000 had gathered to watch the double hanging. Dickens was horrified at the carnival atmosphere of public executions. He immediately wrote a letter to *The Times*, published the following day:

I was a witness of the execution at Horsemonger Lane this morning. I went there with the intention of observing the crowd gathered to behold it, and I had excellent opportunities of doing so, at intervals all through the night, and continuously from day-break until after the spectacle was over ... I believe that a sight so inconceivably awful as the wickedness and levity of the immense crowd collected at that execution this morning could be imagined by no man, and could be presented in no heathen land under the sun. The horrors of the gibbet and of the crime which brought the wretched murderers to it faded in my mind before the atrocious bearing, looks, and language of the assembled spectators. When I came upon the scene at midnight, the shrillness of the cries and howls that were raised from time to time, denoting that they came from a concourse of boys and girls already assembled in the best places, made my blood run cold. As the night went on, screeching, and laughing, and yelling in strong chorus of parodies on negro melodies, with substitutions of 'Mrs. Manning' for 'Susannah', and the like, were added to these. When the day dawned, thieves, low prostitutes, ruffians, and vagabonds of every kind, flocked on to the ground, with every variety of offensive and foul behaviour. Fightings, faintings, whist-lings, imitations of Punch, brutal jokes, tumultuous demonstrations of indecent delight when swooning women were dragged out of the crowd by the police, with their dresses disordered, gave a new zest to the general entertainment. When the sun rose brightly – as it did – it gilded thousands upon thousands of upturned faces, so inexpressibly odious in their brutal mirth or callousness, that a man had cause to feel ashamed of the shape he wore, and to shrink from himself, as fashioned in the image of the Devil. When the two miserable crea-tures who attracted all this ghastly sight about them were turned quivering into the air, there was no more emotion, no more pity, no more thought that two immortal souls had gone to judgement, no more restraint in any of the previous obscenities, than if the name of Christ had never been heard in this world, and there were no belief among men but that they perished like the beasts.

Some argued for the complete abolition of hanging. Many, like Dickens, wrote and spoke out against the spectacle of public executions and hanging was con-fined to behind closed doors in 1869.

William Calcraft carried out the last public execution in Britain, that of Michael Barrett, the Clerkenwell bomber, at Newgate on 26 May 1868. He retired in 1874 and died peacefully at his home in Hoxton in 1879. It is estimated Calcraft carried out about 450 executions, thirty-five of them women. Asked if he had nightmares or if his occupation preyed on his mind, Calcraft said, 'As soon as I have done it, it goes from me like a puff of tobacco smoke.' The hangmen who followed Calcraft all commented on how short his 'drops' were, the condemned taking up to ten or twenty minutes to slowly strangle to death at the end of a short rope. The executioners Marwood and Berry who followed Calcraft devel-oped the long drop and dislocation method of hanging and each one of them always said proudly, 'Calcraft hanged them – I execute them!'

William Marwood, a cobbler from Horncastle, Lincolnshire, took over from Calcraft and was duly appointed as official hangman by the Sheriffs of London and Middlesex in 1874. He received a retainer of £20 per annum plus £10 for

William Marwood, executioner; the man who developed the 'long drop'.

each execution plus travelling expenses, he was also able to keep the condemned person's clothes, however unlike Calcraft he did not receive a salary. Marwood had proved himself efficient a couple of years earlier after persuading the prison authorities at Lincoln to engage him to carry out the execution of William Frederick Horry on 1 April 1872 (Horry had been found guilty of and confessed to shooting his wife, Jane, in a fit of jealousy). It was to be not only his first execution but also the first in which he used the 'long drop' method. The execution, carried out in front of a large crowd on top of the castle's Cobb Hall tower, went without a hitch; prison authorities were impressed and considered this method highly efficient.

Marwood was the first British executioner to put his mind to the methods, especially the efficiency, of his craft. Carrying out experiments with sacks, he worked out the optimum points upon which an executed person's vertebrae can be dislocated taking into consideration their height and weight. He laid out the 'table' that helped an executioner to work out the suitable length of rope or 'drop' to break the condemned's neck, as opposed to too short a drop, which could strangle, or too long a drop, which could result in damage to the neck of the prisoner (or worse).

Marwood took advantage of Britain's magnificent railway system from the time of his appointment and carried out most of the executions in Britain and Ireland until he died 'in office' in 1883. Over his years as hangman he had executed 181 people, including nine women; his most infamous client was undoubtedly the notorious Charlie Peace, cat burglar and double murderer. Peace and Marwood were displayed beside one another in Madame Tussauds Chamber of Horrors for many years afterwards.

The final words on Marwood really should be made by the man himself. Shortly after the execution of Charles Peace, Marwood granted an interview with a reporter from the *Sheffield and Rotherham Independent*. The reportage is one of the most authentic and evocative of Marwood and paints such a picture the imagination of the reader can easily place themselves at the table; a silent and invisible witness present at the interview with the executioner:

'The Irish call me the Prince of Executioners!' A gentleman of medium height, with a ruddy face, puckered with human wrinkles and with bright eyes, shining with a merry light, utters these words to me in a voice sweet and low – almost as gentle as a woman's. It is Marwood, the executioner; he had just washed his hands of Peace's death and now sits opposite me in the cosy drawing room of a gentleman's villa, not far away from Armley Gaol. As he entered the room in his black suit of clerical cut, I had an idea that he dropped a carpet bag in the passage, a bag containing the rope and straps by the aid of which he had taken the life of a fellow-being an hour ago but he advanced towards me in such a pleasant way and bowed so politely that my dread soon vanished and in a few minutes we were in the midst of a quiet chat on the subject of Peace's execution.

Without snow fell thickly and a piercing wind swept round the house with an angry stormy sound but within the curtains were drawn; a bright fire sent its glow throughout the room and now and then gleamed on Marwood's face, making it look quite benevolent … He referred to the great skill he had attained in the science of hanging and told me how Peace met his death. 'A firmer step never walked to the scaffold,' he said. 'I admired his bravery; he met his fate like a man; he acknowledged his guilt and his hope in God with regard to his future was very good.'

'But,' I asked, 'don't you think he feared death?'

'No,' replied Marwood. 'During the seven years I have officiated as executioner I never met a man who faced death with greater calmness.'

'You mean to say, then, that he met his fate without a tremor?'

'Yes,' replied the executioner. 'It's true he shivered a bit, but not through fear. It was a bitter winter's morning and he complained of the cold.'

'It's not surprising,' I said 'that a man like Peace, who has been face to face with danger oft, should endeavour to die without betraying any weakness or timidity.'

'The bravery was the outcome of his nature,' replied Marwood. 'He was ignorant alike of weakness and timidity. I will prove it to you. He had been suffering from a cough for some days. The night before his execution he said to one of the warders, "I wonder whether Mr Marwood can cure this bad cough of mine?" The warder replied, "I have no doubt he could." And I can tell you that a man who jokes about getting hanged to cure a cough is no coward.'

'Do you think he suffered much?' I asked.

'Not in the least; he was dead instantly. But perhaps I had better tell you what occurred just before the execution. It is a most curious thing. He got hold of the idea that I should terribly punish him at the scaffold and he repeatedly asked the chief warder to be sure and tell me he wished for an interview about a quarter of an hour before he was led out to die. Accordingly at ten minutes to eight o'clock I went to the condemned cell which stands about in the centre of the gaol, some hundred yards from the place where the scaffold was erected. Peace was seated, he was in convict dress and there were several officials attending upon him. The bandage had been removed from his head and he did not wear spectacles. He was neither weak nor prostrate but sat upright on his chair, as if he had never known a moment's illness. When I appeared in the doorway, he seemed pleased and, holding out his hand, said, "I am glad to see you, Mr Marwood. I wish to have a word with you. I do hope you will not punish me. I hope you will do your work quickly."

"You shall not suffer from my hand," I replied and then Peace, gripping my arm, said, "God bless you. I hope I meet you in heaven. I am thankful to say my sins are all forgiven."

'It was now time to pinion him,' continued the executioner. 'He stood up at my request but did not really need the support of the two warders by his side. He was not at all nervous and quietly submitted to my operations. Pinioning is a very ingenious process. I run a main strap around the body and connected with it are two other straps, which take the small of the arm, so that the elbows are fastened close to the body, and the hands are free. Peace complained, saying, "The straps fit very tight." I replied, "It is better so; it will prevent you from suffering." He made no further objection and taking hold of the main strap so as to keep my hand on him, we started for the scaffold. The governor and the Under-Sheriff went first; then came the chaplain and I followed the condemned men, two warders attending him, one on each side. They grasped him by the arms but did not support him. He was bare headed. His face was pale but pinched by cold weather rather than fear. As he arrived near the scaffold he gave a very wistful look at my arrangements. They were all right and seemed to satisfy him, for he made no remark. He went up the steps leading to the drop with a firm tread, whilst the chaplain read the burial service. I brought him to a proper stand under the cross-bar and then strapped his legs. When that was done he wished to say something to the reporters and made a beautiful speech. Such a speech has never come from a condemned man I have executed. It was a really good speech. When he had finished it he asked for a drink but you know that was unreasonable and it could not be admitted, for the time for his execution had fully expired, so I placed the cap over his face and adjusted the rope, when he said, "I say, the rope fits very tight". I replied, "never mind; hold up your chin" and he did so immediately, so I could properly fix the rope. "Good bye all;

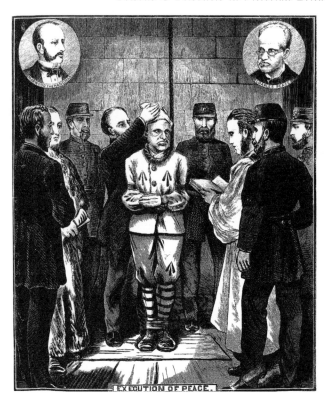

EXECUTION OF PEACE.

The execution of Charles Peace by William Marwood at Armley Gaol, Leeds on 25 February 1879.

God bless you," he kept repeating as I went for the lever. At this time he did not require anyone to support him but I told one of the warders to take hold of the back strap. Whilst he stood in this manner on the drop, with the noose around his neck, I pushed the lever forward; it withdrew the bolt from the swinging doors and Peace's body fell through the aperture beneath the platform. The drop was exactly nine feet four inches. Peace was dead in a moment; he never moved a finger or a muscle after he fell; so I carried out my promise to do it well and quickly.'

I must admit I was astonished at the matter of fact and yet complacent way in which Mr Marwood described the execution and modestly referred to his own dexterity but I was anxious to know by what method he had obtained such success as an executioner and endeavoured to glean from him the mysteries of his art. The explanation is explicit but rather embarrassing. The old system on which Calcraft rested his faith was, he tells me, the system of strangulation, which frequently resulted in great suffering, especially when the short drop did not kill the man and the executioner had to pull at his legs until the miserable being was lifeless. 'Note my process is humane,' said Marwood, 'for it entails no suffering whatever. My principles are rapidity and dislocation. When the neck is dislocated the man does not suffer at all – at least that is my opinion. I have no doubt if that if you examined Peace you would find his spinal cord severed. It is done in this way. I attach the rope to the cross-bar; the noose at the opposite end is formed by a brass ring woven in the rope and this is placed on the left side of the neck towards the chin.'

Anxious to give me a correct idea of his process, he places his finger on my own neck to signify the exact locality and I begin to grow nervous and to wonder whether I have committed some diabolical murder or other and am about to suffer for my sin. I suddenly become very wise to the adjustment of the noose … he says he has made this subject the study of his life and he continues to point out the merits of the long drop …

Still there is nothing terrible about Mr Marwood as he reclines in his easy chair and speaks in his soft, pleasant tones of the strange experiences he has gone through.

'I am doing God's work,' he says, 'according to the Divine command and the law of the British Crown. I do it simply as a matter of duty and as a Christian and I think no more of it than I do chatting to you now.'

Such is the affable man who executed Peace. Conscious that he is doing his duty, the character of the profession he follows has no influence upon him and he claims to be a benefactor of society.

I ask him what induced him to adopt such a mode of gaining his livelihood and he replied: 'Oh, when I heard the old gentleman, Calcraft, was breaking down and I saw the accounts of his bungling work, if I thought I could carry out the sentence of the law more mercifully it would be a service to the public. I always had a love of anatomy and even when a boy was greatly interested in executions but it is a most singular fact that I never saw an execution until I

Incidents from the life of Marwood, published by the *Illustrated Police News* shortly after his death in September 1883.

myself became an executioner. I do my duty with a kind hand and with a firm-ness and I believe I really render a benefit to society. I have been successful in every engagement and I am respected wherever I go. I have told you that in Ireland I am known as 'the Prince of Executioners'; in Scotland I have received the kindest treatment and if I were really a prince I could not be better served. In the past seven years more than one hundred persons have died by my hand but I cannot tell you the exact number as I do not now keep a record.'

'Are you haunted by the features of those you have executed?' I ask in des-peration, thinking that I may surprise him into some expression of feeling.

'Bless your life, no,' he says, smiling. 'I sleep as soundly as a child and am never disturbed by phantoms. Where there is guilt there is bad sleeping but I am not disturbed in the least for I am conscious that I try to live a blameless life. The other night I slept in the warder's apartments in Armley Gaol peacefully and undisturbed although I had superintended the erection of the scaffold and knew I had to execute Peace in the morning. It is a matter of duty with me entirely.'

'Have all the criminals who have received your attentions acted courageously on the scaffold?'

'Well,' Marwood replies, 'taking them altogether they are a brave lot. The worst job I ever had was with a Spaniard, a sailor, at Usk, Monmouth. He had murdered a man, his wife and three children and then set the house on fire. He was sentenced to death and when he saw me enter the cell with the straps, he fainted and was saved from falling by two warders. I put the straps upon him; and said in an authoritative tone, "Stand up, sir". It was only a sham faint. I told him I would not have such nonsense and he stood up immediately. With this lesson he walked out and was hanged quietly. Peace, however, gave me no trouble of this kind but met his fate like a man.'

I now ventured to ask the executioner if he was not looked upon with some degree of loathing when he became the successor of Calcraft and he freely admits this was the case. 'I was frequently jeered at,' he says, 'at first, but I put it down to people's ignorance and now I am received with the greatest kindness wherever my services are needed.'

'How does it affect you in your own town?' is the last question I put to Mr Marwood.

'Oh,' he replies, 'at Horncastle I am looked upon as one of the first men in the place. I am treated well by one and all. Detesting idleness I pass my vacant time in business and work in my shoe-shop near the church day after day, until such time as I am required elsewhere. It would have been better for those I have executed if they had preferred industry to idleness.'

I passed nearly two hours in the society of the hangman when our quiet chat was over. Then I rose and thanked him for his kindness and bade him adieu. As I left the room he shook me heartily by the hand, then said 'Good bye, God bless you,' and bowed me out of the villa with that polished courtesy which is always so becoming in a Crown official.

The next hangman of long service and note during the reign of Queen Victoria was James Berry, who was appointed Britain's chief executioner in 1884. Berry was a strongly built, no-nonsense Yorkshireman. Born at Heckmondwike and making his home at Bilton Place in Bradford, Berry had previously been employed in a variety of jobs including a railway porter, shoe salesman and even a police constable but had found his metier as public executioner. An efficient and methodical man in his work as executioner he was equally adept in his business practice and was the first executioner to use pre-printed invoices. These clearly laid out his terms of employment: £10 for carrying out the execution or £5 if the condemned was reprieved plus travelling expenses.

Unfortunately 1885, the year after his appointment, was not a good year for executioner Berry. On 23 February he had been engaged at Exeter to carry out the execution of John Lee (19) for the murder of his employer, Miss Emma Keyse, at 'The Glen' Babbacombe near Torquay, a house where he had been in service since he left school. Lee swore his innocence and had a dream the night before that he would not hang for the crime. In what has become arguably the most folklore-ridden of all British executions, Lee was made ready and placed on the gallows trap, the noose around his neck, the lever pushed but the trap refused to

James Berry, executioner.

THE DROP REFUSED TO WORK!

The scene on the gallows at Exeter Prison when the traps failed to drop and John Lee entered into legend as 'the man they could not hang'.

open. Lee was removed, the trap tested, it fell open easily. Set closed again Lee was put on the drop, lever pushed but still it would not open, despite Berry and the warders adding their weight by stamping on the trap doors. Lee was removed from the chamber, the trap tested again – it worked with no problems. For a third time Lee was brought back, made ready to meet his maker, but the trap doors failed again. The chaplain appealed to the governor to intercede, it was the medical officer who stepped forward and said to Berry, 'You may experiment as much as you like on a sack of flour, but you shall not experiment on this man any longer.' Lee was granted a reprieve from death but had to serve a life sentence and was released in December 1907.

Berry recovered his nerve to carry out the next couple of executions but then there was Moses Shrimpton, a 65-year-old poacher who had killed a police officer. Shrimpton's execution was set for 25 May 1885 at Worcester. Berry worked out the 'drop' from the prescribed table but had not considered the weakness of the old man's neck and almost tore Shrimpton's head from his body. There was no real criticism at the inquest. Berry regained his confidence again over the next six men he sent to their doom in the execution chambers of various prisons. Berry initially supplied his own ropes to his own design; made from Italian hemp three quarters of an inch thick, 13ft long, with the noose formed by the rope running through a brass ring spliced into one end (not the a-typical rope with 'hangman's knot' commonly used in America and so often depicted in films). Keen to stand-ardise and assure quality, modern Governments have always preferred to issue its operatives with their essential equipment, rather than allow them to use their own, this included hangman's ropes (this was also an attempt to stop the sale of grim relics such as lengths of hangman's rope). Although made to a similar specification to the ropes Berry had made himself, the rope he was to use for Goodale was one which had been supplied by the Government. Even so, Berry liked to use 'tried and tested' ropes at executions so he brought along the same one he had used the previous week on John Williams at Hereford.

Berry arrived at Norwich Castle Prison and took up his quarters on the afternoon of Saturday 28 November, leaving him time to attend divine service and have the rest of the day clear to ensure all the preparations were made for the execution on Monday morning. Goodale's conduct in prison had been exemplary. He was granted attendance by a Baptist minister, the Revd T.A. Wheeler. His sister and two sons bade him a final visit on Friday 27 and on the same evening Goodale requested to speak with the Prison governor, Mr A.E. Dent, who immediately went to the condemned cell with the Chief Warder. Goodale stated he wished to unburden his mind and confessed he had struck his wife as a result of her saying she liked other men better than him. He claimed he had 'struck her down with a piece of iron which laid on the ground near him.' He pleaded extreme provocation and further claimed his wife had fallen down the well after he hit her, he claimed he did not push her and that he had used the bloodstained ladder in an attempt to rescue her not to push her down. Despite the medical evidence and witness statements in court that confirmed the long history of arguments, threats and violence between Goodale and his wife that weighed against Goodale's claims, the governor forwarded the document to the Home Secretary and communicated these latest developments with Revd Wheeler. As a result, Wheeler and Mr W.H. Dakin, the ex-Sheriff of Norwich, proceeded to London and had an interview with the Under-Secretary of State. Neither application availed any reprieve for Goodale.

Norwich Castle Prison at the time of the 'Goodale Mess'.

Berry was informed that Goodale was a big man and that he weighed 15 stone and stood 5ft 11in in height. He was the second largest man Berry had executed. According to the 'table of drops' Goodale would require a drop of 7ft 8ins but Berry was not happy with this length. Berry had met Goodale in his cell but did not reveal who he was. It was plain to see that Goodale was a physical wreck and despite being a big-framed man, his neck was 'not very muscular' so Berry shortened the drop to 5ft 9in. The surgeon asked Berry if he thought this was enough of a drop to avoid strangulation, Berry assured him it would be enough. The governor was particularly nervous about the whole affair, he had erected the scaffold to Home Office specifications and one man had already been executed on it but he remained nervous. Apparently, he had already tested the drop on the Thursday morning and again on Saturday before Berry arrived in the presence of the prison engineer.

The officials for the execution: Under-Sheriff J.B.T. Hales, Mr Haynes S. Robinson the Gaol Surgeon, governor Dent and an invited number of local press men gathered at the prison from an early hour on 13 November 1885. At 7.30 a.m. on the morning of the execution Berry conducted his final tests on the gallows in the presence of the Under-Sheriff using a 16 stone weight, as per Home Office regulations. All preparations made, all seemed satisfied that everything had been done 'by the book' and with proper consideration to ensure the execution would run smoothly. Goodale had slept soundly over Sunday night, and waking at 5 a.m., he asked for something to eat almost as soon as his cell door was opened. Revd Wheeler also attended Goodale over much of his last time in the condemned cell.

At 7.55 a.m. the great bell of St Peter Mancroft church began to toll and the officials gathered by the condemned cell to make their dread procession to the prison bathroom, where Goodale would be pinioned. Berry recalled that the screams and cries of Goodale echoed around the prison. His fellow inmates shouted and beat on their doors in reply. Goodale had to be led down the passage to where he was to be pinioned. Berry continued; 'When I went forward to pinion him he was crying like a little child. Approaching him from behind I slipped the strap around his body. He wriggled to prevent me buckling it, and I had to tell him in a firm tone to be a man.' Eventually securing the pinions it was time to move off on the final walk to the gallows, Goodale refused to move and had to be dragged along, screaming and shouting. The gathered officials and, indeed, Berry had been somewhat unnerved by Goodale's display.

As Goodale got closer to the gallows he was seen to physically and mentally break down and seemed to pass between a state of collapse and terror in which he repeated, 'Oh, God, receive my soul,' a number of times on his short journey to the gallows trap. When in position, it appeared that Goodale's legs would not hold him any longer, so two warders were positioned beside him to hold him up while Berry pinioned his legs, put the white bag over his head and adjusted the noose around his neck. Berry, with fatal lever in hand, asked Goodale, 'Do you

A fanciful depiction of what happened at the execution of Robert Goodale on 30 November 1885.

wish to say anything?' Goodale replied in the negative and before the church bells of Norwich struck the final chime of eight Berry pulled the lever, the traps fell open and Goodale was shot to eternity. Berry recorded what happened next in his memoirs; 'We were horrified, however, to see the rope jerked upwards and for an instant I thought the noose had slipped from the culprit's head or that the rope had broken.'

As the black flag was hoisted on a flagstaff erected over the right-hand entrance to the gaol to let the crowd outside know that execution had been carried out, the governor, Surgeon and Berry looked into the pit below. Berry continues, having feared the noose had slipped off Goodale's head, '… it was worse than that for the jerk had severed the head entirely from the body and both had fallen into the bottom of the pit. Of course death was instantaneous so that the poor fellow had not suffered in any way; but it was terrible to think such a revolting thing should have occurred. We were all unnerved and shocked. The governor, whose efforts to prevent any accident had kept his nerves at full strain, fairly broke down and wept.'

When the onlookers had recovered their composure, as per Home Office regulations, an inquest was held on the body of Robert Goodale under the Coroner E.S. Bignold Esq. in the Magistrates Room at the castle. The witnesses all spoke favourably and fairly of the thoroughness of Berry, pointing out in particular when asked, that the executioner was sober. The head of Goodale had been severed from the body as cleanly as if done by a knife. The jury considered the evidence and their views were clear; 'Robert Goodale came to his death by hanging according to judgement of law, and in answer to the Coroner, the jury did not consider anyone was to blame for what had occurred.' Charles Mackie had been present at the execution as a press representative when he was a reporter on the *Norfolk Chronicle* and recalled the 'Goodale Mess' when he looked back on his career many years later. With quite some pride he declared he had been present at what could quite justifiably be called 'the last judicial beheading in England.'

Although acquitted of any blame, the 'Goodale Mess' haunted Berry for the rest of his career and probably for the rest of his life. Early in 1892 Berry resigned; during his career he had executed a total of 131 condemned criminals, both men and women. After a brief lecture tour he found religion and toured evangelical churches as a respectable preacher who declared he 'gave himself to Jesus.'

In the late nineteenth century, executions were dominated by one family of executioners – the Billingtons. James Billington was appointed executioner after the resignation of James Berry; he was joined in the craft of executioner over the next few years by his sons Thomas, William and John. Between them they were responsible for 235 executions in Britain between 1884 and 1905. But by far the most enduring family of executioners were the Pierrepoints. Henry Pierrepoint was appointed executioner in 1901, his brother Tom joined him in the craft in 1909 and he was followed by Henry's son – Albert. Albert Pierrepoint's name was

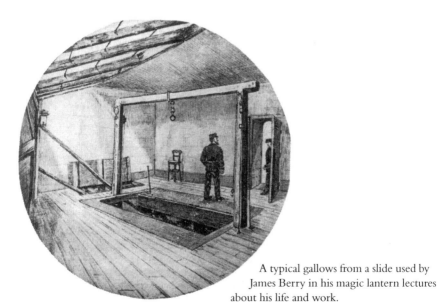

A typical gallows from a slide used by
James Berry in his magic lantern lectures
about his life and work.

added to the list of executioners in 1932; appointed Chief Executioner in 1940, he resigned in 1956 after officiating at over 400 executions.

At the turn of the nineteenth into the twentieth century few prisons still allowed reporters in to observe the executions and many prisons had established gallows within the prison or built onto the prison rather than the condemned being taken on that final long walk down echoing corridors and out into the yard where the execution shed awaited them. Most counties still had prisons with operative gallows within them. Crowds would still gather outside the prison gates but the only indication they would see that the execution had been carried out was the raising to the black flag and the official notices hung on the door. The execution protocol observed at this time was fine-tuned and explicitly described in the *Rules and Standing Orders for the Government of Local Prisons*.

The execution protocol begins with the receipt of the prisoner under sentence of death. The governor was duty bound to notify the High Sheriff – who was responsible for carrying out the sentence – and the Secretary of State on the day the sentence was pronounced with any special recommendation of the jury being fully set out in his correspondence. A detailed newspaper report of the trial from a reliable rather than sensational newspaper would be attached, along with a copy of the entry relating to the prisoner in the confidential before-trial calendar. Any observations relating to matters of importance which may have been suggested to the medical officer by the evidence given at the trial or by information obtained subsequently from the Director of Public Prosecutions would also be forwarded as soon as possible, as would be the notification of the date set for the execution.

The governor would also contact the Prison Commissioners asking to be furnished with the list of candidates reported as competent for the office of executioner, with information as to the conduct and efficiency of each of them and the regulations to be observed in carrying out the sentence. On receipt of these papers, the governor would transmit the list of candidates to the High Sheriff together with the memoranda issued by the Secretary of State in reference to executions, specifically the conditions to which any person acting as executioner or assistant executioner should conform.

When practicable, permanent warders would be assigned to watch the prisoner and, unless absolutely, necessary no one engaged temporarily would be permitted to come into contact with the condemned. The condemned would also be allowed private exercise and dietary requirements as the governor or medical officer may direct. A chaplain would have free access to visit and to be called for by the condemned. Any other visitor would only have access to the condemned having obtained an order from the governor or a prison commissioner.

The governor would then have to ensure the scaffold and all necessary appliances were in good order. He would have obtained the necessary equipment upon request from the stock held at Pentonville Prison. The items would be sent in two boxes, one small box containing the chains for adjusting the rope, the rest of the equipment in what looked like a long wooden toolbox painted grey and fastened with a sturdy retaining bar and padlock. Inside this larger box was:

1. The rope
2. The pinioning apparatus
3. The cap
4. A bag capable of containing sand to the same weight as the prisoner in clothes. The bag was made to an approved pattern with a very thick neck well padded on the outside with soft canvas to obviate any damage to the rope. The instructions sternly pointed out 'No unnecessary experiments should be carried out either with the rope or bag'
5. A piece of chalk (to mark the rope or floor with a 'T' to position the feet of the condemned as necessary)
6. A few feet of copper wire
7. A rule, or graduated pole, 6ft long
8. A piece of pack thread (just strong enough to support the excess coils of the rope without breaking)
9. A tackle to raise the bag of sand, or the body, out of the pit

A week before the execution the rope was tested by a competent officer in accordance with directions so that in case of any defect a new one may be obtained. The governor was authorised to pay each assistant executioner whom he may engage and who was actually present at the execution the sum of £2 2s to cover all charges for each attendance along with reasonable travelling expenses; normally a third-class railway fare and such cab fares shown to be absolutely necessary. The governor would also provide proper food and lodging for the executioner and assistants while they were required in the prison.

The governor would also ensure that the medical officer, sheriff, chaplain and coroner were provided with the correct papers to sign and confirm the judgement of death had been executed upon the offender and same papers displayed upon the prison door after the execution. He would also ensure the persons required or entitled to attend the execution were attended to.

On his arrival at the prison the day before the execution, the executioner was furnished by the governor and medical officer with all necessary information as to the height and weight of the culprit, his general condition, age and whether he was likely to offer any resistance. The executioner would observe the prisoner from an unseen location, often while he took some exercise, then, armed with all this information, the executioner would calculate the length of the drop required according to the 'Table of Drops' and his own experience. The governor and medical officer might recommend a departure from the table if, after careful examination, it appeared there were special reasons for such a departure. If the executioner disagreed with the other officials he would be entitled to ask that the amendment to his calculations be annotated and signed by the officials that demanded it. Because no official would wish to be held responsible for a botched execution, this was a very rare occurrence indeed.

Often the condemned cell was only divided from the execution chamber by a small lobby area that led to the door of the chamber. The night before the execution, the executioner, having worked out and agreed the drop, would set up the gallows using the test sack filled to correspond to the weight of the condemned and a test run performed in the presence of the prison governor. The bag would then be left hanging on the rope down the open pit all night to ensure the rope was stretched. Early on the morning of the execution the executioner and his assistant would return, pull the sand bag out of the pit and mark out the prescribed drop on the rope, allowing 13 inches for the neck. If the rope had stretched they would adjust the chains high in the chamber ceiling where the rope was fixed with a 'D' ring. They would also pull up the trap doors and set the release lever with the safety catch on. The rope was then coiled and the excess tied with pack thread so the noose would hang at a convenient height to be easily slipped over the head of the condemned.

All of the work in the execution chamber would be performed with as little noise as possible, keeping their conversation minimal, voices low and with the executioner and assistant wearing plimsolls.

As the appointed time for the execution approached, in some prisons about 30ft of coconut matting would be laid outside the condemned cell to avoid the sound of approaching booted feet over the iron grid floor. The executioner and

The landing and doorway (indicated by an arrow) of the condemned cell at Wakefield Prison, West Yorkshire in the early twentieth century.

his assistant with two warders in escort would gather in front of the condemned cell door. The prison governor, medical officer and sheriff would wait outside the door of the lobby area; the chaplain was usually inside the condemned cell with the prisoner. The governor would check his watch and as the chimes of the prison clock marked the hour so the life of the condemned would be tolled out also.

Upon a given signal at the appointed time all would enter their relevant doorways. The governor and officials would move through the lobby area and flatten themselves against the wall of the execution chamber. The executioner would lead in, the condemned normally sat with his back to the entrance door at this time. He would often stand up automatically and before he had a chance to turn around his hands would be pinioned by the executioner. Meanwhile, the other door in the condemned cell, which if the condemned had asked was told it led to a store room, opened into the lobby area and the prisoner was led through by the executioner, followed by the assistant and the warders. If the condemned offered resistance or was in a state of collapse he would be supported onto the gallows by the warders; two sturdy planks crossed the pit for them to stand on and ropes with hefty knots hung down for the warders to hang onto and steady themselves as the gallows traps opened. Many of those present were surprised at the size of the pit; in most prisons the gallows were large enough to take two or three condemned at a time, so when the traps did drop open it appeared 'as if the floor disappeared'.

Once inside the execution chamber the instructions for the executioner and his assistant were:

(i) Place the culprit exactly under the part of the beam to which the rope is attached. (This position would have been marked on the traps by the executioner with a 'T' shape in chalk.)
(ii) Put on the white linen cap.
(iii) Put on the rope around the neck quite tightly (with the cap between the rope and the neck), the metal eye being directed forwards and placed in front of the angle of the lower jaw, so that with the constriction of the neck it may come underneath the chin. The noose should be kept tight by means of a stiff leather washer or an Indian rubber washer or a wedge.

While the executioner is carrying out the above procedure the assistant executioner will:

(i) Strap the culprit's legs tightly.
(ii) Step back beyond the white safety line so as to be well clear of the trap doors.
(iii) Give a visual signal to the executioner to show that he is clear.

On receipt of the signal from his assistant the execution will:

(i) Withdraw the safety pin.

(ii) Pull the lever which lets down the trap doors.

In reality the lever was normally pushed to avoid slippage. Many executioners also took great pride and considered it most humane to carry out their duties as quickly as possible. It was quite common for them to leave only the merest tip of the safety pin in the lever socket to enable a rapid knock to release it and allow the lever to be pushed. In most cases the execution from the moment of entry to the condemned cell to the condemned dropped into the pit took less time than the steady chimes of the prison clock to mark the hour – about twenty seconds. In the 1940s and '50s, Albert Pierrepoint was noted for carrying out his executions in about ten seconds. But with such speed occasional accidents did occur, especially when the executioner was flustered by a condemned prisoner putting up a fight or if there was more than one condemned. Such was the case of William Seaman, Harry Fowler and Albert Milsom in 1896. Seaman had committed the 'Turner Street Murders', a nasty case where Seaman was disturbed by the elderly owner while burgling his house. Seaman ended up killing both the old man and his housekeeper. Milsom and Fowler were also burglars who killed when challenged by the occupant but when brought to court each one blamed the other and gave evidence against him. Fowler was so enraged by Milsom's testimony he violently attacked him in court.

All three were to hang together in what was to prove to be the last triple execution at Newgate. The date was set as 26 February 1896; James Billington was appointed executioner with William Warbrick as assistant. Tensions were high because there were very real fears that Fowler and Milsom would attempt to lash out at each other or cause trouble on the scaffold. Seaman was put between the two, to which he exclaimed, 'First time I've ever been a bloody peacemaker.' All were brought to the drop without incident and without doubt relieved to see the last strap passed around the ankles of the condemned, Billington pushed the lever, but he had not noticed that Warbrick had not cleared the pit and so was plummeted into it head first. Grabbing at whatever he could, Warbrick ended up catching hold of the condemned man he was nearest to and swung into the pit on Milsom's legs, only narrowly avoiding a nasty accident.

The body of the executed man or woman was left to hang for one hour, and then the executioner and his assistant would return and raise the body carefully from the pit using a block and tackle. The rope would then be removed from the neck and the straps removed from the body. In laying the body out for the inquest, the head was to be 'raised three inches by placing a small piece of wood under it.' The record of the execution was entered in the authorised book, with a copy sent to the Commissioners immediately after the inquest.

After the execution, the appliances would be carefully examined and any damage which may have occurred reported and repaired. The rope and pinioning apparatus was to be kept in a warm, dry place and all the leather lubricated with Vaseline or pure petroleum ointment before being returned in their transit box to Pentonville.

Regulations were keen to point out 'The governor will not allow casts to be taken of the heads of criminals who have been executed.' The burial of executed criminals was to be carried out by the authorities of the prison where the execution took place. There was an allowance of 5s each for the two prison officers who performed the special duties in connection with an execution: removing the body, placing it in a coffin then carrying it to and placing it in the grave then filling it in. And so would end the tale of the condemned; laid in a grave with a plain stone set in the wall above with their initials and date of execution carved thereon or perhaps with no marker at all, their place of burial only marked on a map and retained by the prison clerk or engineer. The last words really should go to Oscar Wilde who witnessed this final act and recoded it so eloquently when he recalled the tragic burial of Thomas Wooldridge after his execution at Reading Prison in 1896:

> The Warders strutted up and down,
> And kept their herd of brutes,
> Their uniforms were spick and span,
> And they wore their Sunday suits,
> But we knew the work they had been at
> By the quicklime on their boots.
> For where a grave had opened wide,
> There was no grave at all:
> Only a stretch of mud and sand
> By the hideous prison-wall,
> And a little heap of burning lime,
> That the man should have his pall.
>
> *The Ballad of Reading Gaol* (Smithers, 1898)

Select Bibliography

'A Ticket of Leave Man', *Convict Life* (Wyman & Sons, 1879)

Atholl, Justin *Prison on the Moor, The Story of Dartmoor Prison* (Long, 1953)

Atholl, Justin *Shadow of the Gallows* (Long, 1954)

Atholl, Justin *The Reluctant Hangman* (Long, 1956)

B.2., *Among the Broad-Arrow Men: A Plain Account of English Prison Life* (A & C Black, 1924)

Berry, James *My Experiences as an Executioner* (Originally published 1892, David & Charles reprint 1972)

Booth, Charles *Life and Labour of the People of London* (Macmillan, 1903)

Brodie, Allan, Croom, Jane and Davies, James O., *Behind Bars: The Hidden Architecture of England's Prisons* (English Heritage, 1999)

Chesney, Kellow *The Victorian Underworld* (Penguin, 1972)

Chesterton, George Laval *Revelations of Prison Life* (Hurst & Blackett, 1857)

Davitt, Michael *The Prison Life of Michael Davitt* (Lalor, 1882)

Davitt, Michael *Leaves from a Prison Diary* (2 vols) (Chapman & Hall, 1885)

DuCane, Sir Edmund *The Punishment and Prevention of Crime* (Macmillan, 1885)

Engel, Howard *Lord High Executioner* (Robson, 1997)

Evans, Stewart P. *Executioner: The Chronicles of James Berry, Victorian Hangman* (Sutton, 2004)

Fletcher, Mrs Susan Willis *Twelve Months in an English Prison* (Dillingham, 1884)

Forsythe, Bill (ed.) *The State of Prisons in Britain, 1775–1895* (Routledge, 2001)

Griffiths, Major Arthur *Mysteries of Police and Crime* (Cassell, 1898)

Holland, Merlin and Hart-Davis, Rupert (eds) *The Complete Letters of Oscar Wilde* (Henry Holt, 2000)

Hooper, E. Eden *History of Newgate and the Old Bailey and a Survey of The Fleet and other Old London Jails* (Underwood, 1935)

Hopkins, R. Thurston *Adventures with Phantoms* (Quality Press, 1946)

Hopkins, R. Hopkins *Ghosts over England* (Meridian, 1953)

Hopkins, R. Thurston *Life and Death at the Old Bailey* (1935)

Horsley, Revd J.W. *Jottings from Jail* (Unwin, 1887)

Horsely, Revd J.W. *Prisons and Prisoners* (1898)

Lambley, Terry *Nottingham: A Place of Execution* (Lambley, 1981)

May, Trevor *Victorian and Edwardian Prisons* (Shire, 2006)

Maybrick, Florence E. *Mrs Maybrick's Own Story: My Lost Fifteen Years* (Funk & Wagnalls, 1904)

Mayhew, Henry and Binny, John *The Criminal Prisons of London and Scenes of Prison Life* (Griffin & Co., 1862)

McConville, Sean *A History of English Prison Administration (vol. 1) 1750-1877* (Routledge, 1981)

McLaughlin, Stewart *Execution Suite: A History of the Gallows at Wandsworth Prison 1878–1993* (Wandsworth, 2004)

McLaughlin, Stewart *Wandsworth Prison: A History* (Wandsworth, 2001)

Morris, Norval and Rothman, David J. (eds) *The Oxford History of the Prison: The Practice of Punishment in Western Society* (Oxford University Press, 1998)

'One who has Endured It' *Five Years Penal Servitude* (Bentley & Son, 1878)

Pelham, Camden (ed.) *Chronicles of Crime* (Reeves & Turner, 1886)

Priestly, Philip *Victorian Prison Lives* (Pimlico, 1999)

Simon, Frances H. *Prisoner's Work and Vocational Training* (Routledge, 1999)

Sims, George R. *Living London* (Cassell, 1903)

Storey, Neil R. *A Grim Almanac of Cambridgeshire* (The History Press, 2009)

Storey, Neil R. *A Grim Almanac of Essex* (Sutton, 2005)

Storey, Neil R. *A Grim Almanac of Suffolk* (Sutton, 2004)

Storey, Neil R. *London: Crime, Death and Debauchery* (Sutton, 2007)

Storey, Neil R. *Norfolk Murders* (Sutton, 2006)

Wilde, Oscar *De Profundis* (Ross, 1905)

Wilde, Oscar *The Ballad of Reading Gaol* (Smithers, 1898)

Official Publications

Extracts from the Third Report of the Inspectory of Prisons for the Home District (HMSO 1838)

Nineteenth Report of the Inspectors of Prisons of Great Britain (HMSO, 1856)

Report from the Departmental Committee on Prisons (PP, 1895)

Report of the Committee of Inquiry as to the Rules Concerning the Wearing of Prison Dress (HMSO, 1889)

Rules and Standing Orders for the Government of Local Prisons (HMSO, 1902)

Select Committee of the House of Lords on the Present State of Discipline in Gaols and Houses of Correction in England and Wales (PP, 1863)

The warders of Wandsworth Prison, c. 1878. (Wandsworth Prison Museum)

Newspapers, Magazines & Periodicals

Annual Register
Birmingham Daily Post
Black & White Budget
Bristol Mercury
Cornhill Magazine
Family Tree Magazine
Famous Crimes
Fraser's Magazine
Gentleman's Magazine
Hampshire Telegraph and Sussex Chronicle
Harmsworth Magazine
Illuminated Magazine
Illustrated London News
Illustrated Police News
Leisure Hour
Lincolnshire Chronicle
Liverpool Weekly Mercury
Manchester Weekly Times & Examiner
Mirror
Northern Echo
Norfolk Chronicle
Norwich Mercury
Pall Mall Gazette
Penny Illustrated Paper
Police Gazette
Reynolds News
Sheffield and Rotherham Independent
Strand Magazine
The Graphic
The Observer
The Quiver
The Sphere
The Times
Thompson's Weekly News
Trewman's Exeter Flying Post or *Plymouth and Cornish Advertiser*

INDEX

Ahern, Thomas 32
Alderson, Mr Baron 125
Allen, Robert 130
American War of Independence 16
Amos, Alfred 124
Andrews, Revd W.W. 148, 149
Anthony, William 130, *131*
Armstrong, Eliza 157
Assizes 42, 43, 106, 109, 114, 121-142, 146, 169, 188
Auburn Prison (USA) 14

Babies (provision for in prison) 58, *59*
Baby Farming 180-7
Ballad of Reading Gaol, The 175-6, 214
Barker, George 121
Barnum, P.T. 157
Barrett, Michael 196
Baxter, Samuel 125
Beaumont, James 115-16
Beavis, Charles 126
Beer 67-8
Bellow, Lord 153
Bentham, Jeremy 10
Berry, James 196, 203-8
Bertillion, Alphonse 48
Billington, James 184, 185, 186, 208, 213
Billington, Thomas, William and John 208
Binny, John 76, 80
Birching 87-8, 89, 106-7, 112, 125, 129
'Black Maria' 35, 44, *45*
Blake, Revd C.J. 148
Bly, Inspector 132

Booth, Bramwell 157
Boots 36, 54, 58, 118, 120,
Borstal system 16-17
Bow Street 159
Brierley, Alfred 169
'Broad Arrow Men' 50, 54-5
Brown, Revd James 148
Brown, John 114
Brown, Joseph and Elijah 134
Brown, Constable William 133
Bryant, John 113
Buck, Revd W. 26-7
Burke, Rickard 32
Bundock, William 123
Butler, Josephene 157
Bysoath, Ellis 140

Calcraft, William 190-1, *191*, 193, 196-7, 200, 201, 202
Callaghan, Mary 43
Castro, Thomas (*see* Arthur Orton)
Cat-o'-nine tails 87, 89, 107-110
Caversham, Berkshire 182
Cells 8, 12, 13, 14, 15, 17, 19, 25, 26, 28, 29, 32, 34-5, 56, 60, 63, 64, *64*, 65-6, 83, 94, 97-8, 105, 157, 162, 165, 167, 183
Chamberlain, Fuller 138
Chaplain 7, 10, 14, *20*, 22-7, *27*, 33, 34-5, 62, 97, 148, 149, 151, 152, 165, 167-8, 172, 179, 184, 185, 186, 190, 193, 199, 204, 209, 210, 212
Chase, Thomas 136, *137*
Chastney, Eliza 145, 146

Classification of prisoners 17, 44, 55-7
Clothing, the prisoner's personal 49, 52
Cockburn, Sir Alexander 152-3
Cole, Thomas 135
Convicts and Prisoners – the difference
  between them 9
Corder, William 143
Coroner 146, 207-8, 210
Court of Common Pleas 152
Clay, William 139
Cooper, William 75
Coots, Edward 121
Copeland, Mr 123
Copsey, Faber 128
Cordrey, James 113
Cornwall, Harriet 130, *131*
Courvoisier, Francois Benjamin 191-5
Cramer, Dr Frederick 188
Crank 30, 76, 102-3, *103*, 163
'Crow's foot' 54
Cubitt, William 70-2, *72*
Currey, George 129

Dann, Elizabeth 132
'Dark Cell' 26, 32, 103-6, *105*
Davies, Isaac 126, *127*
Davis, Wardress Alice 43
Davitt, Michael 32, 84, 97, 101
Dawson, James 138
De Profundis 175, 180
Deaves, David 136
Debtors 9, 26-7, 69,
Deighton, John 141
Dent, Mr A.E. 205
Deputy Governor 26, 38, 66, 91, 105
Dickens, Charles 144, 194, 195, 196
Diets for prisoners 19, 28, 29, 42, 67-70, 209
Dilham, Norfolk 70
Divine Service 24, 26, 65, 66, 97, 205
Doughty, Sophia 136, *137*
Douglas, Lord Alfred 'Bosie' 174, 180
Du Cane, Sir Edmund 13, 17, 89
Dudley, Thomas 123
Duffy, Edward 32
Dyer, Mrs Amelia 'Annie' Elizabeth 180-7,
  182
Dyer, Maurice 136

Edwards, Ann 136, *137*
Edwards, Edward 113
Edwards, William Samuel 126, *127*
Eldred, PC John 138
Ellis, George Wilfred 132
Ellis, Sarah 181

Escapes 10, 55, 79, 88, 113-120, *114*, *118*, *119*
Execution protocol 209-214
Executions 23, 30-1, 87, 149-152, *150*, 181,
  184, 187, 188-214, *189*, *194*, *200*, *207*

'Fakers' 31
Farran, Caleb 135
Finch, Isaac 141-2
Finch, Martha 141
Firing stacks 128, 136, 194,
'First Fleet' 16
Fisher, Major Frank 126
'Flagellator' 39-41
Flogging 87, 106, 110-12, *111*
Flower, John 138
Ford, Clarissa 132
Fowler, Harry 184, 213
Fraser, Sir William 26
Freeman, William 122
Frost, Charles 130, *131*

Gaol Act (1823) 10
'Gaol Fever' 19, 28
'Garotters' 110
Garwood, Thomas 124
Gayfer, Frederick 139
Gaskin, William 135-6
Gill, William 128
Girkin, Elizabeth 129
Gladstone Committee 17
Godwin, Anne 114
Godwin, Thomas 114
Goodale, Robert 205-8
Goshawk, William 70
Governor 10, 12, 18-22, *20-1*, *22*
Great Baddow, Essex 190
Great Braxted, Essex 123
Greenacre, James 143
Greetham, Samuel 28
Griggs, Matilda 134
Grimwade, Robert 128
Grindell, John 124
Guiver, James 121, 123

Hales, James 123
Hales, William 123
Hall, Arthur 138
'Hanging Day' 188, 195
Hanly, Martin 32
Hansford, Warder William 42, *43*
Hard Labour 12, 13, 30, 34, 42, 46, 53, 68,
  69, 72, 75-7, 80, 87, 88, 100, 114, 115, 123,
  124, 126, 129, 130, 132, 133, 135, 136, 138,
  139, 153, 175, 181

'Hard Labour, Hard Fare, Hard Board' 13
Haslam, Annie 135
Hayward, Thomas 136
Heffer, David 123-4
Health of prisoners 12, 29, 30, 71, 92, 93, 100
Hindle, Henry 42-3, *43*
Home Secretary 10, 154, 155, 166, 172, 205
Horry, William Frederick 197
Horsley, Revd J.W. 35
Howard, John 67, 71
Humphrys, PC William 138

Ipswich 71, 121, 129, 132, 139, 140
'Incorrigibles' 70
Industrial School Act (1866) 16, 112
Inspectors of HM Prisons 10, 12, 30, 34, 109
Irish Republican Brotherhood 97
Isleham, Cambridgeshire 133

Jackson, John 120
Jager, Elizabeth 121
Jacques, Sampson 24, 25, 158, 159, 160, 163
Jarrett, Rebecca 157
Jermy, Isaac 144-5, *146*
Jermy, Jermy 145
Jonas, PC John 138
Jones, Thomas 104-6
'Junk' (*see* oakum)

Keeble, William 139
Kennedy, John 130, *131*
Key, Martha 136, *137*
King, Francis 132

Lang, William Cosmo Gordon 'C.G.' 25-6
Lee, John 203-4
Leech, John 195
Leonard, William 110-12
Letters 19, 25, 26, 27, 33, 39, 42, 57, 75, 102,
    125, 128, 129, 148, 152, 162, 166, 180,
    181, 184, 193, 195
Library, prison 26, 35, 57, 96, 164, 168
Lines, William 126, *127*
Lombroso, Cesare 48
Lovett, William 116-17
Lucas, Elias 188-190, *189*

McGorrery, Captain 22
Magistrates (see Visiting Justices)
Maiden Tribute of Modern Babylon 24, 157, 166
Mail bags 84
Malingering 31, 88, 93
Manning, Mr Frederick George and Mrs
    Marie 191, 195, 196

Manning, Cardinal 166
March, William 128
Marten, Maria 143
Martin, Warder 176-8
Marwood, William 196-203, *197, 200, 201*
Mason, Charles 126, *127*
Matron 19, 34, 172, 173
Maybrick, Florence 13-14, 55, 60, 66, 103-4,
    169-174, *170, 173*
Maybrick, James 169, *170*, 172
Mayhew, Henry 76, 80
Medical officer (*see* Surgeon)
Milsom, Albert 184, 213
Monk, James 113
Moreton Bay, Australia 16
Muller, Franz 191
Mullinger, James Bass 135
Murrels, Charles 135-6

Neavecy, John James 124-5
New Scotland Yard 49, 78
Newman, Leticia 139

O'Connor, Patrick 195
Oakley, John 121
Oakum 42, 60, 60, 70, 79-85, *81*, 102, 110,
    160, 163, 164, 165
Old Bailey 117, 192
'One Who has Endured It' 23, 44, 52, 61
Opium 12
Ordinary (see Chaplain)
Orridge, John 71
Orton, Arthur 152-7, *153, 156*
Oxley, John 117-18

Pall Mall Gazette 24, 34, 157, 158, 159
Palmer, Arthur 182-3
Palmer, Mary 'Polly' 182-4
Parke, Mr Baron 114
Parkinson, Thomas 139
Pay for warders 39, 41
Peace, Charles 10, 27, *47, 119*, 197, 198-202,
    200
Pearcey, Mrs Mary 183
Peel, Detective Inspector 119
Peeling, William Burton 74
Penal Colonies 10, 16-17, 141
Penal Servitude 17, 23, 43, 44, 48, 50, 52,
    61, 86, 87, 93, 97, 104, 110, 115, 116, 117,
    118, 123, 124, 126, 128, 129, 130, 132, 133,
    134, 138-140, 175
Peto, James 125
Photographing prisoners 45-51, *48, 49, 50*
Philadelphia Prison (USA) 14

Pierrepoint, Albert 208-9, 213
Pierrepoint, Henry 208
Pierrepoint, Tom 187, 208
Police 36, 39, 45, 48, 192, 196, 112, 117, 117,
    118-19, 120, 123, 126, 130, 133, 134, 138,
    145, 146, 181
Police Court 43, 124, 125, 126
Poole, William 138
Post Office, General 84, 129
Pot Fair, Cambridge 133
Prison Act (1877) 17
Prison Act (1898) 17
Prison Commission 17, 22, 28, 29, 35, 36,
    44, 176, 179, 209
Prison Porter 85
Prisons:
    Armley 27, 42, 43, 198, 200, 202
    Bedford 28, 67, 70, 71
    Bristol 17
    Brixton 71
    Bury St Edmunds 9
    Chatham 12, 40, 41, 78, 79
    Chester Castle 34, 97
    Coldbath Fields 24, 34, 71, 75, 75, 76, 80,
        81, 83, *107*, 157, 159, 161-5, *164*, 168
    Dartmoor 9, 78, 90-101, *92*, *95*, 102, 104,
        107, 114, 132, 154, *154*, 155
    Devon 33
    Dorset 109
    Ely 6, 34, 36, 67
    Exeter 203, *204*
    Fleet 9
    Gloucester 28, 109
    Grantham 34
    Holloway 43, 117, 119, 157, 161, 163, 165,
        166-9, *167*
    Horsemonger Lane 195
    Hull 34
    Huntingdon 19, 29, 114
    Ipswich 114
    King's Bench 9
    Leicester 35
    Lincoln Castle 45-6, 89, 197
    Liverpool 71
    Marshalsea 9
    Millbank 9, 10, *11*, 22, 32, 44, 46, 52, 54,
        61-2, 79, 84, 88, 97, 99, 100, *104*, *105*, 116,
        159, 160
    Newcastle-upon-Tyne 109
    Newgate 9, *16*, 23, 33, 87, 110-12, *111*, 154,
        158, 159, 183, 184, *185*, *186*, 187, 191-2,
        193, *194*, 196, 213
    Norman Cross 9
    Norwich 17

Norwich Castle 71, 125, 144, 146, 148,
    205, *205*
Norwich City 9, *11*, 71, 75
Nottingham 17
Pentonville 9, 14, 15, 18, 24, 38, 54, 63,
    64-6, 75, *103*, 117, 126, 157, 175, 209, 214
Perth 9
Portland 12, 31, 42, 78, *79*, 115-17
Portsea 25, 28
Portsmouth 12, 78, 100, 102, 154, 155,
    157
Reading 62, 175-9, *177*, 183, 214
Salford (New Bailey) 109
Shrewsbury 17
Spike Island (County Cork) 34
Springfield (Chelmsford, Essex) *20-1*, 22,
    71, 113, *115*
Strangeways (Manchester) 120
Swaffham 71, 74
Wisbech 12, 126, *127*, 130, *131*, 136, *137*
Woking 31, 55, 60, 66, 83, 103, 172, 174
Worcester 71, 109, 204
Pritchard, Dr Edwin 191
Pryke, Stephen 138
Public Works Prisons 9, 12-13, 30, 54, 78-9,
    93, 155,
Puddletown, Dorset 116
Punishments 102-112

Quaker reformers 14
Quarter Sessions 27, 29, 70, 109, 114, *122*

Read, Martha 146
Reader, Mary 188, *189*
Record keeping 8, 10, 19, 29, 30, 35, 45-9,
    51, 213
Red Barn Murder, Suffolk 143
Reddin, Daniel 32
Reformatory Schools 15-16, 25, 112, 125,
    126, 136, 214
Regulations 18, 19, 29, 44, 45-6, 48, 51, 61,
    73-5, 154, 155, 162, 163-4, 168, 169, 206,
    207
Religious Tract Society 96
Roberts, Revd H. 190
Roberts, John 129-130
Robinson, Haynes S. 206
Roden, Dr Luke 64
Rolfe, Baron 146, 148
Ropes, execution 31, 152, 196-7, 200-1,
    204-5, 207, 209, 210-13
Ross, Robert 180
Routine (daily) 13-14, 19, 31, 56, 63-84, 75,
    79, *81*

Rourke, John 117
Rush, James Blomfield 143-152 *146, 147, 150, 151*
Russell, Lord William 191
Rutterford, James 123-4

St Osyth (Essex) 128
Salvation Army 157
Sandford, Emily 148
Sanger's Circus 157
Schoolmaster 12, 26, 33-5
Scott, Chief Warder *186*, 187
'Screws' the 102, 155
Seaman, William 184, 213
Separate System 14-15, *15*, 23, 24, 54, *103*
Shaw, George 140-1
Shepherd, Maria 18
Shore, W. Teignmouth 144
Shot drill 76-8
Shrimpton, Moses 204
Silent System 13-14, 32
Silver, Henry 125
Simmonds, Arthur 75
Simms, Ann 140-1
Sing-Sing Prison (USA) 14
Smith, Mary 129
Solitary confinement 13-14, 26, 29, 83, 103-4, *105*, 162
Spence, John Douglas 125
Squirrell, Mary Anne 140
Staddon, Assistant Warder John 104
Stanfield Hall, Norfolk 141-6
'Star Class' 55-7, *57*
Stead, W.T. 157-169, *158, 161*
Stephens, Mr Justice 169
Stowmarket 70, 126
Surgeon 10, 27-32, 76, 85, 93, 110, 113, 206
Surveyor General of Prisons 10, 89

Taylor, John 139-140
Thackeray, William Makepeace 194
'The Man they could not Hang' (*see* John Lee)
Thurgood, George 124
Thurgood, James and William 121, 123
Thurston Hopkins, Robert
Tichbourne Claimant (see Arthur Orton)
Tichbourne, Dowager Lady 152-3
Tichbourne, Sir Roger Charles Doughty 152-3
Ticket of Leave 157
'Ticket of Leave Man' 18, 31, 102, 154
Transportation (Penal) 9, 10, 16-17, 90, 93, 114, 121, 125, 128, 134, 138, 141

Treadwheel 70-6, *72, 75*, 102, 163
Trendall, Albert 75
'Trusties' 67
Turnkey 18, 33, 34, 151, 159, 193
Tussauds 144, 153, 187, 197
Tyburn Tree 191

Uniforms (prisoners) 10, 52-5, *54*, 117, 161, 173, 214
Uniforms (warders) 36, *37*, 39
Uniforms (wardresses) 36, 38, *38*

Van Diemen's Land (Tasmania) 16, 17
Vicars, G. Rayleigh 85, 89
Visiting Justices (Magistrates) 10, 12, 18, 23, 26, 28, 29, 34, 43, 46, 58, 67, 70, 86, 104, 105, 106, 109, 110, 121, 126, 146, 149, 167, 178, 183, 184, 190, 207

Wall, Revd Charles 23
Waller, Thomas 129
Walsham, North 70
Walters, Margaret 181
Warbrick, William 184, 213
Warders 10, 18, 19, *20-1*, 34, 35, 35, 36-43, *37, 43*, 44, 45, 46, 47, 49, 52, 58, 59, 60, 61, 62, 63, 65-7, 74, 77-106, 92, 106, 110-17, 120, 155, 157, 159, 161-6, 168, 171-4, 176-9, 185-7, 198-200, 202, 204-6, 209, 212, 214, *216*
Wardresses 36, 38, *38*, 43, 183
Watkins, Frederick 134
Watson, Joseph 140
Webb, Warder 120
Wesby, James and John 123
Western, Sir Thomas 123
Wetheringsett, Suffolk 132
Wheeler, Revd T.A. 205, 206
Whiterod, Charles 134
Wilde, Oscar 62, 63, 174-180, *175*, 214
Williams, Mr Justice 133
Williams, John (arsonist) 128
Williams, John (murderer) 205
Williams, William 10
Willis, Rhoda 187
Wills, Justice Sir Alfred 175
Wilmot, Captain Eardley 89
Wilton, Elizabeth 124
Wooldridge, Charles Thomas 175

Young offenders 15-17, 107, 112
Youthful Offenders Act (1854) 15